THE DISCWORLD COMPANION

THE
DISCWORLD
COMPANION

Terry Pratchett
and
Stephen Briggs

VICTOR GOLLANCZ

LONDON

First published in Great Britain August 1994
by Victor Gollancz Ltd
A member of Cassell plc
Wellington House, 125–130 Strand, London WC2R 0BB
Second impression August 1994
Third impression December 1994

A catalogue record for this book is
available from the British Library.

ISBN 0 575 05764 5

Photoset by Rowland Phototypesetting Ltd,
Bury St Edmunds, Suffolk
Printed in Great Britain by
St Edmundsbury Press Ltd, Bury St Edmunds, Suffolk

CONTENTS

TURTLES ALL THE WAY

by Terry Pratchett

The Discworld is a place where stories happen.

I never thought that people would actually sit down and write the tune for the Lancre Stick and Bucket Dance, or form a Morris team called Mrs Widgery's Lodger, or design a scarf for Unseen University and actually sell lots of them. If I'd known that at the start I'd have had a headache. I never thought that it would be *real*.

I never thought people would ask me when Death's birthday is.

But reality is a bit untrustworthy at the best of times. There are plenty of people who believe that Elvis is alive, or that aliens occasionally land here to do highly personal things to people, or that the whole idea of evolution is a conspiracy of godless scientists. Almost all of these people can vote and some of them have got guns. When you look at it like that, the Discworld seems positively harmless.

Anyway, we seem to have a turtle-shaped hole in our consciousness. On every continent where turtles grow, early man looked at the things sunning themselves on a log (or disappearing with a 'plop' into the water at his shambling approach) and somehow formed the idea that a large version of one of those carries his world on its back.

Priests came along later and in order to justify their expenses added little extras, like world-circling snakes and huge elephants, and some time later the idea grew that the world was not round and flat but more like an upturned saucer. The basic idea, though, was turtles all the way. Why turtles is a mystery but turtles it was, in Africa, in Australia, in Asia, in North America.

Perhaps much modern malaise can be traced to a deep-seated ancestral fear that, at any moment, the whole thing will go 'plop'.

I came across the myth in some astronomy book when I was about nine. In those white-heat-of-technology days every astronomy book had an early chapter which was invisibly entitled 'Let's have a good laugh at the beliefs of those old farts in togas' (reality in those days being something called Zeta, a nuclear reactor that would soon be producing so much electricity we'd be paid to use it). And there was the Discworld, more or less. The image remained with me – possibly lodging in that turtle-shaped hole – and trotted forward for inspection much later when I needed it.

After eight million words, I still like the place. You can't help having a soft spot for something that stands between you and real work. And it has had a creeping reality, even to me. And this means that some things, regrettably, have to be right. The golden age of reckless invention has passed. Long ago I gave Nanny Ogg fifteen children, so fifteen children (given that she is at least in her seventies, and barring unexpected deaths) she must continue to have. It came as a big surprise to me to find that during the course of the books I had in fact named exactly fifteen.

It was a surprise because I've always been against too much chronicling. I've never felt that the author's job was to say what happened after the hero rode into the sunset, or to follow the fortunes of characters once they have strutted their way across the little stage.

But the Discworld is too big. And too many minor characters (such as Cut-Me-Own-Throat Dibbler) have wandered on to the page to sell someone a bun and then gradually insinuated themselves into the series. And sometimes even I forget who was who, and where things are. Readers don't like that sort of thing. They write me letters.

I found out by accident that Stephen Briggs knew a lot more about Discworld than I did. We discussed the psychology of this and decided that, since I had invented the places and characters, a little sanity pocket in my brain prevented me from thinking of them as facts. He, on the other hand, was seeing them in cold print and could treat them at least semi-seriously and he had – he admitted – put together a Discworld database in the course of writing his plays (of which, see later).

This was an amazing creation using small squares of compressed vegetable matter on which letters were made by means of small carbon particles from a stylus, giving an effect similar to the traditional word-processor screen. It seemed amazingly portable and I never once saw him have to change the batteries.

It was, he shyly suggested, something that other people might like to see. He expanded it, and I fleshed it out from my notes – I do keep *some* – and from the fragments and ideas and odds and ends of unused Discworld material that have accumulated over the years. And invented new stuff, too – that was the enjoyable bit.

Something strange happened. I'd always shied away from being too precise about the Discworld on the basis that too many solid facts would restrict the field of invention for future books. But while working on the Companion I found that the more clearly we focused, the more fresh story suggestions turned up. Stories turn on restrictions, after all: the door you must not open, the path you must not leave, the road you must follow . . . I thought that a Discworld encyclopaedia would be something that came towards the end of the series. Now I'm not so sure.

Last year we produced a map of Ankh-Morpork. The map of a fictional city entered the non-fiction bestseller lists. After all, it was a *real* map. And this is a real book about unreal places. I offer no apologies. I hope you'll find it enjoyable, if not informative.

Fantasy is like alcohol – too much is bad for you, a little bit makes the world a better place. Like an exercise bicycle it takes you nowhere, but it just might tone up the muscles that will. Daydreaming got us where we are today; early on in our evolution we learned to let our minds wander so well that they started coming back with souvenirs.

After all, if we didn't have the ability occasionally to unfocus reality, we'd still be sitting by the ancient river – fearful of the plop.

ABOUT THE COMPANION

by Stephen Briggs

Three years ago I was a civil servant who dabbled in amateur dramatics (er
. . . I still am). I had never heard of Terry Pratchett, Ankh-Morpork or the
Discworld. But I was always on the lookout for material that could be
adapted for my local drama club. Someone handed me *Wyrd Sisters*. I read
it. It has a lot of appeal for an actor. I wrote to the author, asking if we
could adapt it. To my surprise, he said yes – and he came and watched it,
and brought some champagne for the party afterwards.

I was, I now realize, passing gently into a different leg of the Trousers of
Time.

Wyrd Sisters went so well that we went on to stage *Mort* and *Guards!
Guards!* And, one day, I mentioned to Terry Pratchett that I was convinced
from my reading that Ankh-Morpork had a distinct shape. He doubted it –
he said he'd just put buildings and streets in wherever the plot required
them. I said that in this world they got put in wherever History demanded
them and I was sure the city was mappable. Fine, he said. Go ahead. And
that led to *The Streets of Ankh-Morpork*, published in 1993, possibly the
only map ever to get into the bestseller lists.

The arguments and constant reference-seeking involved in that project
led me to wonder out loud if it wasn't time for a *guide* to Discworld.

This is the result.

I have aimed to reference in the Companion every major location and
character of the Discworld canon, although a few people are left out whose
only role was to exist for a couple of lines in order, for example, to sell
Rincewind a drink or, more frequently, to die. I haven't got rid of *all* of
them. We all have a soft spot for the bit-part players on the great stage of

life. I also sought to distil from the pages certain major aspects of the Discworld – the nature of magic, wizardry, the layout of Death's House, the main City Guilds, and so on.

Additional material is drawn from the script of *Mort: the Big Comic*, and Terry's own notes; first drafts, false starts, character notes and miscellaneous Discworldiana are stored in a huge directory on his computer. It is called The Pit. Terry has expanded and extended most of the entries.

If you've bought this book, there is presumably a very good chance that you know something about the Discworld. It would be nice to think that the book will resolve doubts and end quarrels, but I am afraid I'll have to bring in here The Famous Note About Consistency.

Anyone reading, say, Tolkien will soon realize that they are reading about a world, something fully realized by its creator – capable of being mapped, chronicled, discussed, *pinned down*. Middle Earth, one feels, came first – the books were derived from that vision.

Whereas Terry Pratchett has gone on record many times as saying that he wanted to write books using a certain kind of world as a background. I would hate to say that he made it up as he went along, but Discworld was quite clearly bent around the stories and, over the years, things have . . . er . . . evolved.

Take, for example, Granny Weatherwax. While there has been no actual change in the character as such, the woman who defies the Queen of the Elves and more or less runs an entire kingdom from underneath in *Lords and Ladies* is a much more realized and complicated person – I feel – than the village witch of *Equal Rites*, the first book in which she appears. And trolls begin as little more than conventional monsters in *The Colour of Magic*, rapidly become quite talkative in *The Light Fantastic*, and by *Men At Arms* and *Soul Music* are, if a little slow of thinking, certainly capable of using a knife and fork even if not for the purposes originally envisaged.

That is, of course, natural development. And, perhaps, a bit of story-teller's licence – the author says that there are no inconsistencies in the Discworld books, merely alternative pasts.

I considered that certain things did need attention, though. Ankh-Morpork's calendar seemed a bit erratic and, as far as I could see, needed at least one huge re-organizational event to make various dates fit together. And there was a continuing discrepancy between the Discworld's astro-nomical year (the time taken for a point on the Rim to revolve back to its starting point, which is about 800 days long and contains two of each season) and the general usage of the word 'year' in the books, which is more or less identical to ours.

This was not, as it turned out, too much of a problem. Re-organizing the calendar is an ancient human sport, as are attempts by various people to pull it back into some kind of order (the leap year with its extra day is a bit of unremarked tinkering. And whatever did happen to the eleven days 'stolen' by Lord Chesterfield in 1752? Could we have them back now, with interest?). And as far as the year problem was concerned, it seemed eminently sensible that farmers everywhere on the Disc would quite rightly consider a year to be whatever fits the 'seedtime, quicken, harvest, plough' sequence – and that's what they'd call it, whatever a bunch of fancy wizards and astrologers up in Ankh-Morpork may say.

There are other little difficulties, in most cases readily overcome. The fact that names are sometimes spelled differently is a tribute to the Discworld's robust approach to spelling, for example.

And the Old language (Latatian) of Ankh-Morpork has been rendered into Latin – very bad, very doggy Latin. FABRICATI DIEM, PVNC belongs in the same dictionary as NIL ILLEGITIMI CARBORVNDVM.

What did surprise me was that the Discworld is mappable, and some maps – not of the entire Disc, at Terry Pratchett's express command – appear in this book. It became clear that Terry had a pretty good idea of the general location of places. As with Ankh-Morpork, which I also mapped, there is a sense that things were made up according to some unacknowledged pattern. Ankh-Morpork is a European city, more or less; draw a wiggly river and put a wall around it and everything else is a matter of fine tuning.

In the same way, the main continental mass of the Discworld works if you draw a circular sea opening at its 'western' end on to a larger ocean, and assemble the vaguely European people 'north' of it – shading towards a certain Scandinavian turn of mind the further you go – and put the more Arabic/African peoples to the 'south' of it. Does it sound familiar? In general terms Tolkien did something very similar except that Terry, in a more Glasnost-driven age, doesn't seem to have anything nasty threatening from the east.

It's not a lazy way of creating a world. It's the humorist's way of creating a world. We laughed at Djelibeybi in *Pyramids* not because it was a fantasy country but because it was Ancient Egypt turned up until the knob fell off. It is amazing that a world can so obviously be soldered together out of music hall jokes and *1066 And All That* humour and still have its own power.

All this is a way of leading up to The Excuse: that this is a chronicle of a world that exists on the very borders of reality, which is an enviable place from which to view our own; its existence is buffeted by the tides of history and the forces of narrative causality. It is astonishing that it is as coherent as it appears.

But of course you will know this, unless by some oversight you haven't read a Discworld book at all and are just reading this idly in the bookshop until the rain stops. In that case it's not too late! The whole collection is probably on a shelf over there. Go on . . . you can do without lunch for a month . . .

NOTE:

A name or word in SMALL CAPITALS indicates that it is the subject of a fuller, separate entry; regular references such as Ankh-Morpork and Unseen University are not flagged.

Where a character or reference occurs in only one or two books, this is indicated at the end of the entry.

The following abbreviations are used for the books:

The Colour of Magic COM
The Light Fantastic LF
Equal Rites ER
Mort M
Sourcery S
Wyrd Sisters WS
Pyramids P
Guards! Guards! GG
Eric E
Moving Pictures MP
Reaper Man RM
Witches Abroad WA
Small Gods SG
Lords and Ladies LL
Men At Arms MAA
Soul Music SM
Troll Bridge TB*
Theatre of Cruelty TOC†

* Short story published in *After the King* – it is, technically, not Discworld, but is so Discworld in 'feel' while also achieving a 'Middle Earth' feel as well, that I decided to include it.
† Short story published in WH Smith's *Bookcase*, now a collectors' item.

THE DISCWORLD A–Z

Abbys. Bishop. Prophet of the Omnian Church, to whom the Great God OM is said to have dictated the Codicils to the Book of OSSORY. Little is known of this great man except that he had a big beard, because this is essential wear for prophets. On the subject of beards, the famous Ephebian riddle about them – All men in this town do not shave themselves and are shaved by the barber. Who shaves the barber? – caused some head-scratching when it was printed in an almanac that got as far as LANCRE. People there couldn't see what was so philosophical about the statement because Lancre's barber is one Mrs Deacon, who is open for haircuts, warts and teeth two mornings a week. [SG]

Abraxas. Ephebian philosopher, also called Abraxas the Agnostic, and 'Charcoal' Abraxas (because he had been struck by lightning fifteen times – which suggests that being an agnostic requires an enviable strength of mind, not to say thickness of skull. His own comment, just before the fifteenth stroke, was 'They needn't think they can make me believe in them by smiting me the whole time'). He was the author of *On Religion*, and the man who found the Lost City of EE. And presumably lost it again. He was readily identified by the smell of burnt hair. [SG]

Abrim. Grand Vizier of AL KHALI. A tall, saturnine wizard, with a long thin moustache and wearing a turban with a pointy hat sticking out of it. He was once refused entry to Unseen University because they said he was mentally unstable. Given the apparent mental equilibrium of many of UU's faculty, one can only wonder at this exclusion. Driven by the ARCHCHANCELLOR'S HAT, Abrim was destroyed in a battle of magic. 'Never trust the Grand Vizier' is a popular Discworld saying which many oriental adventurers would have survived a whole lot longer by knowing. [S]

Achmed the Mad. Klatchian necromancer, who taught himself magic partly by trial, but mainly by error. Author of the NECROTELICOMNICON. It is said that he wrote it one day after he had drunk too much of the strange, thick Klatchian coffee (*see* FOOD AND DRINK), which sobers people up too much. Achmed preferred to be called 'Achmed the I Just

Get These Headaches'. He is also the author of *Achmed the I Just Get These Headaches's Book of Humorous Cat Stories*, the writing of which was said to have driven him mad in the first place. [MP]

Agantia. Queen of Skund. Just one of those people who turns up. CASANUNDA the dwarf claims to have received his title of 'Count' by performing a small service for the Queen; but since Skund is almost entirely forest and has next to no population, let alone a royal family, this is what is called, in historical terms, a lie. [LL]

Agatean Empire. Capital city: Hunghung. Principal and only port: BES PEL-ARGIC. Pop.: about 50,000,000. Old, cunning and very, very rich empire on the COUNTERWEIGHT CONTINENT. Ruled by the Sun Emperor, who is considered by his subjects to be a god (i.e. someone who can kill you instantly for no reason and not have to say sorry). Agatean architecture is inclined towards squat pyramids; there is a wall built round the entire Empire, patrolled by the Heavenly Guard in very heavy boots to jump on the fingers of the terminally inquisitive. Ladders and tall trees anywhere near the wall are emphatically discouraged.

There is only one port because the Empire does not encourage more contact with the outside world than is absolutely necessary. To be a citizen of the Agatean Empire is to be the most fortunate of mortals, and the government would like its citizens to remain steadfast in this belief; it is important, therefore, to encourage the suggestion that anywhere else is a mere barbaric wasteland.

Ajandurah's Wand of Utter Negativity.
Weapon used by MARCHESA to control

RINCEWIND and TWOFLOWER. Its use causes the victim not simply to cease to exist, but also never to have existed. An extremely dangerous device, discouraged at Unseen University. [COM]

Albert. DEATH's manservant. (*See* MAL-ICH, ALBERTO.)

Alchemists' Guild. Motto: OMNIS QVIS CORVSCAT EST OR.

Coat of arms: a shield quartered with, on the upper-right and lower-left quarters, guttées d'or on a field, azure. On the lower-right and upper-left quarters, a creuset, sable et enflammé on a field, gules.

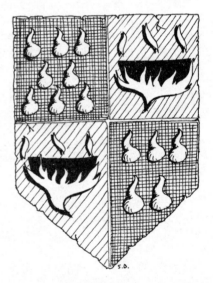

The Guildhall, located on the Street of Alchemists in Ankh-Morpork, is always new. It was explosively demolished and rebuilt four times over one two-year period – on the last occasion without a lecture and demonstration room, in the hope that this might prove helpful to its long-term prospects.

This tiny, despised Guild largely devotes itself to the aid of widows and orphans of those alchemists who had taken an overly relaxed attitude to po-tassium cyanide or who had distilled the juice of some interesting fungi and had drunk the result. There are in fact not very many widows and orphans, because alchemists find it difficult to relate to people long enough to form such relationships, and women often find it difficult to grow attached to people who have laminated themselves across the ceiling.

Alchemists are unco-operative in every other respect; every alchemist is a solitary individual, working in darkened rooms or hidden cellars and endlessly searching for the one longed-for breakthrough – the Philosopher's Stone, the Elixir of Life – or, failing that, enormous amounts of cash. This success has never been achieved, but they have succeeded in creating celluloid and popcorn (or, as they styled them, octo-cellulose and banged grains – the basis for the brief Discworld moving-picture industry centred around HOLY WOOD) and have managed to fail to dis-cover nuclear power, computers and elec-tricity. The only real skill that alchemists have developed is how to turn gold into less gold.

They tend to be thin, pink-eyed men, with that vague, unworldly expression that you get from spending too much time in the presence of boiling mercury.* They also tend to be nervous individuals – it comes from not knowing what the crucible they are experimenting with is going to do next.

The current head of the Guild is Thomas SILVERFISH, although in the nature of things there is a regular turn-over – and, indeed, rise and fall – of senior Guild members.

*Hence the phrase 'daft as an alchemist', for exactly the same reasons as those behind 'mad as a hatter', another profession that spent far too much time physically around mercury and mentally in orbit around Jupiter.

Alfonz. Sailor on the *Unnamed*, a trading boat belonging to CHIDDER's family. The boat's purpose is largely that of moving things from one place to another without disturbing people, particularly those people of a revenue frame of mind; its appearance is that of a slow merchant ship, which often leads pirates to engage in actions which they briefly regret. Alfonz himself is a mere walking canvas for so many instructive tattoos of a carnal nature that, strictly speaking, he should be dressed in a plain brown wrapper. [P]

Al Khali. City on the Hubward coast of KLATCH. It is rather like Ankh-Morpork, but with sand instead of mud. Popularly called the Gateway to the mysterious continent of Klatch. Al Khali's temple frescos are famous far and wide, at least among discerning connoisseurs (tours leave hourly from the Statue of OFFLER in the Square of 967 Delights* but are restricted to males over eighteen and married women).

The city is also known for its wind, blowing from the vastness of the deserts and continents nearer the Rim. A gentle but persistent breeze, it 'carries aromatic messages from the heart of the conti-nent, compounded of the chill of deserts, the stink of lions, the compost of jungles and the flatulence of wildebeest'.

The Seriph's palace, the RHOXIE, occu-pies most of the centre of the city that isn't covered by the artificial paradise constructed by Seriph CREOSOTE in his search for a more cerebral life. The patron deity of the city is Offler, the Crocodile God, a popular deity on the continent. [S, P]

*The Khalians are meticulous about things that interest them.

Alls Fallow. The one night of the year, according to legend, when witches and warlocks stay in bed. This is probably just a legend; the witches so far identified on the Discworld go to bed when they damn well feel like it. It is worth noting that no practising warlock has ever been found on the Disc and, indeed, no one even knows how many legs one should have.

Al-Ybi. Undistinguished Klatchian desert city, known in folklore as a place where criminals always claimed to be when accused of a crime. The Seriph of Al-Ybi was once cursed by a dyslexic deity, so that everything he touched turned to GLOD, a small dwarf. That was the most interesting thing that ever happened in Al-Ybi. In Al-Ybi, it is said, the Klatchians invented the concept of zero. That tells history everything it needs to know about what there was to do in Al-Ybi of an evening. [WA]

Amanita. *See* DEVICE, AMANITA.

Amonia. Queen of Lancre for about three hours. The guests played hide-and-seek at the wedding party; Amonia hid in a big, heavy chest in an attic and was not found for seven months. It seems she

is remembered in Discworld legend because the story is considered to be romantic. [LL]

Angua. Lance-constable of the Ankh-Morpork City WATCH. For most of the month she is a well-developed girl with ash-blonde hair. At full moon she is a werewolf, with a human intellect but with certain additional powers, such as the ability to smell colours and tear out a man's jugular vein. Angua forms a liaison with Corporal CARROT Ironfounders-son, also of the Watch. Well, a bit more than just a liaison. It appears that Carrot, whose main hobby is ambling the byways of Ankh-Morpork on foot, has been more than happy to forgo the slight monthly dampener on the relationship in exchange for a girlfriend who is always ready for a nice long walk. [MAA]

Animals of the Disc. The Discworld has a wide range of creatures that are peculiar (in both senses of the word) to it. Many remain decently shrouded in mystery, while others have been the subject of more detailed observation. Some of the more prominent of them include:

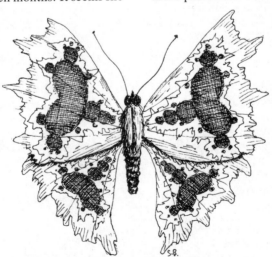

Papilio tempestae (Quantum Weather Butterfly)

Albatross, Pointless. It can fly from the Hub of the Discworld to the Rim without landing. When it does land, however, it seems to do nothing except wander around for a while taking a few photographs. [SG]

Basilisk. [S]

Blowfish, Deep Water. An extremely delicious but deadly fish, parts of whose body contain the poison which is distilled by the Assassins' Guild into 'bloat', the effect of which is to make the eater very briefly impersonate a Zeppelin. A very skilled cook indeed is needed to prepare the dish; his job is to make sure it contains no trace whatsoever of the fish. [P]

Bog Truffle, Klatchian Migratory. Pale, brown, warty and now extremely rare. Once whole bogs would appear to be on the move. Delicious on toast. [M]

BOOKWORM, .303.

Butterfly, Quantum Weather. The existence of this breed (identified, apart from its noticeable effects, by the interesting fractal patterns on its wings) probably owes a lot to the Discworld's precarious balance on the cusp of reality, where a good metaphor stands a fair chance of becoming real. In brief, the QWB can change the weather at a distance merely by flapping its wings. This probably originated as a survival mechanism – few predators would tolerate a very small but extremely localized thunderstorm. [MAA]

CHIMERA.

Coit, Three-banded. [WA]

Crowhawk, Lancre. [LL]

CUCKOO, CLOCK-BUILDING.

Elephant, Hermit. A very shy, thin-skinned species, which for preference wears abandoned huts for protection and concealment. It does not find these hard to obtain. Few people remain in a hut once an elephant has joined them. [MAA]

Fox, Lancre Reciprocating. Little is known of this creature except that, from context, it appears to act like a warrior about to go into battle, i.e., it probably drinks a lot and makes love as often as possible. [LL]

Lemma, Shadowing. A possibly invisible creature which stalks and eats mathematicians. [MAA]

Mongoose, Inflatable. In this creature evolution has found an efficient way of dealing with burrowing snakes. It is impervious to all snake venom, and its liver is highly prized as a result. [P]

Octarsier, Tree-dwelling. [COM]

Pig breeds: Lancre Stripe, Sto Saddleback. [LL]

Puff Eel, Deepwater. Caught only for its bladder and spleen, which contain a deadly yet tasty poison. [M]

PUZUMA, AMBIGUOUS.

RIMFISHER.

Ramtop sheep. Known for its wool, which can be knitted into vests of almost chain-mail quality. [GG]

SALAMANDERS.

SCALBIE.

Spikefish. [RM]

Stripefish, Red. [RM]

Tharga beasts. It is known that some creatures have a secondary brain. Tharga beasts, herded in some parts of the Ramtops for their meat and hair, have four – one for each leg. A tharga progresses by means of consensus, and therefore is frequently found stuck in crevasses, backed into thorn bushes, plunging over cliffs, etc., its only consolation being that it got there democratically. [M]

Thrush, Lancre Suicide. Many thrushes break open snails by banging them on a stone; this species attempts to dive-bomb them. [MAA]

VERMINE.

WORRIER, LAPPET-FACED.

Yok. Horned beast of burden and food, used by nomads in the Hub regions. Like a yak but heavier. [M]

Ankh, river. This mighty river flows from the RAMTOPS down to the CIRCLE SEA, passing through the great city of ANKH-MORPORK, by which time it is tidal, and very sluggish. Even before it enters Ankh-Morpork it is slow and heavy with the silt of the plains; by the time it gets to the seaward side of the city, even an agnostic could walk across it. The citizens of Ankh-Morpork are strangely proud of this fact. They say that it is hard to drown in the Ankh, but easy to suffocate.

Owing to the accretions of centuries, the bed of the river is in fact higher than some of the low-lying areas; when the winter snows swell the flow, some of the low-rent areas of Morpork flood – if you can use that word for a liquid you could pick up in a net. By the time it has passed

through the city, it can be called a liquid only because it moves faster than the land surrounding it.

There are said to be some mystic rivers, one drop of which can steal a man's life away. After its turbid passage through the twin cities, the Ankh could be one of them. Citizens of Ankh-Morpork, however, claim that the river's water is incredibly pure in any case: any water that has passed through so many kidneys, they reason, has to be very pure indeed. There are fish, of a sort, that have adapted to life in the Ankh, but their shape is not recorded because they explode when exposed to air or fresh water.

There are big river gates where the river flows out of the city. These, and the gates on some of the city's bridges, are used in time of fire to flood the city. It says a great deal for the stoicism of the citizens that being drenched in the waters of the river is considered preferable to being burned alive.

The Ankh is probably the only river in the universe on which murder investigators could chalk the outline of a corpse.

Ankh-Morpork. Mottoes: MERVS IN PECTVM ET IN AQVAM and QVANTI CANICVLA ILLE IN FENESTRA.

Coat of arms: a shield, supported by two Hippopotâmes Royales Bâillant – one enchainé, one couronné au cou – and surmounted by a Morpork Vautré Hululant, bearing an Ankh d'or, and ornée by a banner with the legend 'Merus In Pectum Et In Aquam'. The shield bisected by a tower en maçonnerie sans fenêtres and quartered by a fleuve, argent and azure, bend sinister. On the upper-right quarter a field, vert, of brassicae prasinae; on the lower-left quarter a field, sable. On the upper-left and lower-right quarters, bourses d'or on a field argent. Below the arms a ribbon with the legend '*Quanti Canicula Ille In Fenestra*'.

Pop: 1,000,000 (including the suburbs). Chief exports: manufactured goods, most of the processed animal and vegetable produce of the fertile STO PLAINS, trouble. Main 'invisible' exports: banking, assassination, wizardry, trouble.

Imports: raw materials, people, trouble.

In Fenestra (lit.: 'How much is that small dog in the window?'). Its origin is the subject of urban legend but can be traced, as can so many of the city's oddities, to the reign of King Ludwig the Tree.

Kings cannot become mad; this is self-evident. Peasants become insane, small traders and craftsmen go mad, nobles become eccentric, and King Ludwig was a little confused and so detached from reality that he couldn't make contact

The shield shows the TOWER OF ART, the oldest building in the city, and also celebrates both the river ANKH and the vast surrounding expanse of brassica fields which have combined to produce the city's prosperity and, to a great extent, its smell.

The younger of the two mottoes, *Merus In Pectum Et In Aquam* (lit.: 'Pure in mind and water') was devised by a rather high-minded committee in the early days of the First Republic, and is considered a jolly good laugh.

The older – and, strangely enough, the more popular – is *Quanti Canicula Ille*

with it even by shouting and prodding at it with a long stick.

King Ludwig's four-year reign was one of the happiest of the entire monarchical period, and people looked forward to his proclamations on subjects such as the need to develop a new kind of frog and the way invisible creatures spied on him when he went to the lavatory. It was less popular among the nobles. Since it would destroy the entire edifice of the monarchical system to admit that the man from whom all power derived actually did go around all day wearing his underpants on his head, an informal system was devised to suggest that, far from being confused, the King was airing an intellect both rarefied and subtle. Monographs were published, agreeing that the modern frog was indeed hopelessly outdated. There was even a brief vogue for wearing head lingerie.

Anything the King said was treated as an oracular utterance. On the day he was asked to choose from three suggested mottoes for the city, his comment, 'How much is that doggie in the window?', was agreed, by a small committee of courtiers, to be the most acceptable of the King's suggestions, the other two being 'Bduh bduh bduh bduh' and 'I think I want my potty now'.

It has subsequently been suggested that the motto is in fact marvellously devised for Ankh-Morpork, since it neatly encapsulates a) the city's intelligent questioning spirit, b) its concern for mercantile matters, and c) its love of animals. Readers who consider this strange should reflect that the motto on the Great Seal of the United States of America comes from a Latin poem about making salad dressing.*

Ankh-Morpork is the oldest existing city on the Discworld (and known to its citizens/denizens as the Big WAHOONIE). Bisected by the river Ankh, the city is really two cities: proud Ankh, Turnwise of the river, and pestilent Morpork on the Widdershins side, although the pestilence is quite democratic and in fact covers most of the city.

Nestling (or, more accurately, squatting) in the Sto Plains, close to the CIRCLE SEA, the city is theoretically built on loam, although in fact it is built on past incarnations of the city, rather like Troy but without the style.†

Ankh-Morpork has been burned down many times in its long history – out of revenge, carelessness, spite or even just for the insurance. Most of the stone buildings that actually make it a city have survived intact. Many people – that is, many people who live in stone houses – think that a good fire every hundred years or so is essential to the health of the city since it helps to keep down rats, roaches, fleas and, of course, people not rich enough to live in stone houses. Each time, it is rebuilt using the traditional local materials of tinder-dry wood and thatch waterproofed with tar.

It is generally accepted that the original building in the city was the Tower of Art, around which Unseen University grew up as a sort of keep, and some small parts of the first city wall are still visible. Over the centuries, however, the city's centre moved downstream as docks were built on the more navigable parts of the river; and fragments of city walls and the general layout of the roads give Ankh-Morpork the appearance, from the air, of a cut onion, although a cut onion smells rather different.*

Over the millennia the city has tried various forms of government; an ancient system of sewers – known only to the ASSASSINS' GUILD (until *Men At Arms*) – and a few other details testify to a glorious past (glorious being defined as a time when Thousands of People Could Be Persuaded by Men with Swords to Build Big Things out of Stone). There has been monarchy, oligarchy, anarchy and dictatorship. The current system appears to be a sort of highly specialized democracy; as they say in Ankh-Morpork, it's a case of One Man, One Vote – Lord VETINARI is the Man, he has the Vote.

In essence the city is governed as a result of the interplay of various pressure

Moretum, usually attributed to Virgil.

†A lot bigger, though. Troy covered only seven acres, but it did have Homer as director of tourism and publicity.

*i.e., better.

groups. Lord Vetinari positively encouraged the growth of the Guilds, of which there are now some 300 in the city. His reason for doing this may be discerned in his unpublished book *The Servant*, a compendium of advice and precepts to a young man setting out to govern a fictional city (in the book identified only as AM) in a passage which runs: 'Where there are clearly two sides to a question, make haste to see that these rapidly become two hundred.' In practice, the city's political structure consists entirely of a huge number of pressure groups plotting, fighting, conniving, forming alliances, shouting, scheming, intriguing and making plans, in the middle of which one man is quietly doing things his way.

Economically, the city is the profitable bottleneck between the Sto Plains and the rest of the Discworld. It is a service centre for the hinterland in several senses of the phrase, and carries out all the functions that citizens usually perform for their country cousins, such as selling them the Brass Bridge at a knockdown price. It is the big city you go to to seek your fortune. And other people also seek your fortune as soon as you arrive.

While it has many of the attributes of the classical fantasy city – Guilds, walls, wizards and so on – Ankh-Morpork is also a working city, with a very large number of small factories and workshops (generally in the Phedre Road and Cable Street areas, and more traditionally along the Street of Cunning Artificers). There is a flourishing cattle market and slaughterhouse district.

Fresh water used to be brought straight into the city centre by a viaduct now barely visible in Water Street, but it fell down centuries ago and, what with one thing and another, no one ever got around to rebuilding it. Water is now drawn from wells, which are very shallow indeed with Ankh-Morpork's high water table. This, along with the slaughterhouses and the cabbage fields and the spice houses and the breweries, is a major component of Ankh-Morpork's most famous civic attribute: its aforementioned Smell.

The citizens are proud of the smell; on a really good day, they carry chairs outside to enjoy it. They even put up a statue to it, to commemorate the time when troops of a rival state tried to invade by stealth one dark night; they managed to get only as far as the top of the walls when, to their horror, their nose plugs gave out.*

No enemies have ever entered Ankh-Morpork.

This is not entirely true. Technically they have, quite often; the city welcomes free-spending barbarian invaders, but somehow the puzzled raiders always find, after a few days, that they don't own their horses any more, and within a couple of months they're just another minority group with its own graffiti and food shops.

The city's inhabitants have brought the profession of interested bystander to a peak of perfection. These highly skilled gawpers will watch anything, especially if there's any possibility of anyone getting hurt in an amusing way.

The city's 'picturesque' SHADES, with its crowded docks, many bridges, its souks, its casbahs, its streets lined with nothing but temples, all point to its cosmopolitan style. It welcomes anyone – regardless of race, colour, class or creed – who has spending money in incredible amounts.

It has been said that the largest

---

*The statue, now sadly decayed, is located close to what is now the Haberdashers' Guild, in a formally unnamed area known locally as Fetter Lane, presumably a corruption of 'foetid' or 'fetor'.

View across the Ankh

26

dwarfish colony anywhere in the world is in Ankh-Morpork. This may be the case. Certainly the city is home to a large number of dwarfs, a growing number of trolls, and many undead and other special-interest groups. This has caused a number of problems but also some benefits – in jobs, for example. The silicon-based trolls gravitate towards messy jobs because, to them, nasty organic substances are of no more account than sand and gravel would be to a human; vampires tend to end up in the meat business, and often run shops catering for those of a kosher persuasion; undead often undertake dangerous tasks, such as working on high buildings, because nothing can happen to them that hasn't happened already.

The associated problems are more traditional. Trolls hate dwarfs, dwarfs hate trolls. It's a symmetrical arrangement that dates back thousands of years and has accumulated enough ill-feeling that the actual cause is now quite irrelevant. This mutual antagonism has been imported into the city.

Troll skin, which is as flexible as leather but much, much tougher and longer-lasting, is still occasionally used for clothing by the less socially sensitive, and there is a particularly disreputable tavern (and this is Ankh-Morpork we're talking about) which is not only called the Troll's Head but has a very old one on a pole over the door. On the other hand, trolls have been known to eat people (for their mineral content) and the troll game of aargrooha, in which a human head is kicked around by two teams wearing boots of obsidian until it either ends up in goal or bursts, is almost certainly still played in its classical form in remote mountain regions.

So, mingling in the streets of the city are people whose recent ancestors variously ate, skinned, beheaded or in some cases jumped up and down in heavy boots on one another. That there is not a permanent state of all-out war is a tribute to the unifying force of the Ankh-Morpork dollar.

There are two legends about the founding of Ankh-Morpork.

One relates that the two orphaned brothers who built the city were in fact found and suckled by a hippopotamus (lit. *orijeple*, although some historians hold that this is a mistranslation of *orejaple*, a type of glass-fronted drinks cabinet). Eight heraldic hippos line the city's Brass Bridge, facing out to sea. It is said that if danger ever threatens the city, they will run away. Nobody knows why the hippopotamus is the royal animal of Ankh-Morpork. The reasons are lost in the smogs of time. Rome had a she-wolf; on this basis, it is possible that the founders of Ankh-Morpork were suckled, or possibly trodden on, by a hippo. But a hippo seems at least as legitimate as a slug, the city animal of Seattle, Washington. It has been speculated that hippos once inhabited the Ankh. If so, they have long since dissolved.

The other legend, recounted less frequently by citizens, is that at an even earlier time a group of wise men survived a flood sent by the gods by building a huge boat, and on this boat they took two of every type of animal then existing on the Disc. After some weeks the combined manure was beginning to weigh the boat low in the water, so – the story runs – they tipped it over the side, and called it Ankh-Morpork. (*See also* CIVIL WAR, LAWS, MONARCHY, PATRICIAN.)

Ankhstones. Glittery jewels. Like Rhinestones, but a different river. [S]

Annaple, Nanny. A witch who lives over the mountain from BAD ASS (no further geographical location has ever been given; this is unfortunate, since from Bad Ass everywhere is behind some mountain or other). She owns a billy goat, which is absolutely traditional for a witch. She lost all her teeth by the age of twenty, and has a face so warty it looks like a sockful of marbles; this has led to some coolness between her and Granny WEATHERWAX, who has never succeeded in looking properly crone-like. [ER]

Anti-crimes. As you might expect on the Disc, even crime has its opposite. Merely giving someone something is not the opposite of robbery. To be an anti-crime, it has to be done in such a way as to cause outrage and/or humiliation to the victim. So there is breaking-and-decorating, proffering-with-embarrassment (as in most retirement presentations) and whitemailing (as in, for example, threatening to reveal to his enemies a mobster's secret donations to charity). Anti-crimes have never really caught on. [RM]

Antiphon. Ephebian writer. The greatest writer of comic plays in the world, at least according to Antiphon (in the plays, the actors hit one another with big sticks every time they make a joke and refuse to proceed until someone laughs). Looks as though he is built of pork. [P]

Apocralypse, the. The End of the World. The Triumph of the ICE GIANTS. The Teatime of the Gods. Believed to be the time when the Ice Giants, imprisoned by the gods, will break free and ride out on their dreadful glaciers to regain their ancient dominion, crushing out the flames of civilization until the world lies naked and frozen under the terrible cold stars and Time itself freezes over. Or so it is said. Discworld legend is as unreliable on this as it is on so many other things, hence the name.

Heralding the event – should it ever happen and not just be an interesting tale someone wrote down after too many mushrooms – a dreadful ruler has to arise, there must be a terrible war and the four dread Horsemen (DEATH, WAR, FAMINE and PESTILENCE) have to ride. Then the creatures from the DUNGEON DIMENSIONS will break into the world . . . again.

This has all nearly happened once, but it was delayed and then postponed, partly because three of the four Horsemen had their horses stolen while they were enjoying a pub lunch.

Arch-astronomer. Ruler of KRULL. Responsible for the building of the POTENT VOYAGER and for the death of Goldeneyes Silverhand DACTYLOS, its designer. [COM]

Archchancellor. Master of Unseen University in Ankh-Morpork and the official leader of all the wizards on the Disc (a polite fiction on a par with the Queen of England also being Queen of Australia). Once upon a time this would have meant that he was the most powerful in the handling of magic, but in more quiet times senior wizards tend to look upon actual magic as a bit beneath them. They prefer administration, which is safer and nearly as much fun, and also big dinners.

The Archchancellor is elected on the Eve of Small Gods. Well, not exactly elected, because wizards don't have any truck with the undignified business of voting, and it is well known that Archchancellors are selected by the gods (which wizards don't believe in). The double doors to the Great Hall are locked and triple-barred. An incoming Archchancellor has to request entry three times before they will be unlocked, signifying that he is appointed with the consent of wizardry in general.

In more recent times, the lifespan of Archchancellors has been seen to be a bit on the short side, as wizardry's natural ambition took its toll. Unseen University has been in existence for thousands of years, and the average Archchancellor remains in office for about eleven months.

Unseen University has had many different kinds of Archchancellor over the years: big ones, small ones, cunning ones, slightly insane ones, extremely insane ones – they've come, they've served (in some cases not long enough for anyone to be able to complete the official painting to be hung in the Great Hall) and they've died. The senior wizard in a world of magic has the same prospects of long-term employment as a pogo-stick tester in a minefield.

It should be noted that Mustrum RID-CULLY, at the time of writing, seems to have had a very successful and, above all, injury-free career as AC.

Other Archchancellors thus far encountered include:

Badger, William
Bewdley
Buckleby
CHURN, Ezrolith
CUTANGLE
Hopkins, 'Trouter'
RIDCULLY, Mustrum (the current
  incumbent)
Scrawn
SPOLD, Greyhald 'Tudgy'
TRYMON, Ymper (305th)
Wayzygoose, Virrid (didn't actually
  make it) [S]
WEATHERWAX, Galder (304th)

Archchancellor's Hat. The old hat, now replaced (*see* RIDCULLY, Mustrum), was worn by the head of all wizards, on the head of all wizards. (This is to say, *metaphorically* it was worn by all wizards – it is similar to the idea that 'every soldier

has a field marshal's baton in his knapsack'.*)

It was what every wizard aspired to, the symbol of organized magic, the pointy tip of the profession. Through the old hat spoke all the Archchancellors who had ever lived. So it was always believed.

In fact, it was rather battered, with its gold thread tattered and unravelling. It was pointy, of course, with a wide, floppy brim. It was covered with gold lace, pearls, bands of purest VERMINE, sparkling ANKHSTONES, some incredibly tasteless sequins and – a real giveaway – a circle of OCTARINES round its crown, blazing in all eight colours of the spectrum. It was kept on a velvet cushion in a tall, round and battered leather box. When it spoke, which it did when fighting the Sourcerer, it had a clothy voice, with a choral effect, like a lot of voices talking at the same time, in almost perfect unison. [S]

*In the case of Corporal NOBBS, his knapsack was found to contain three field marshal's batons, a general's helmet, a colonel's dress dagger, fifteen pairs of boots, some still occupied, and three gold teeth.

Archmandrite of B'Ituni. A previous owner of the black sword KRING. B'Ituni is little more than a fortified oasis near the Klatch–Hershebian border. [COM]

Argavisti. General of the Ephebian army, involved in the brief war against OMNIA. [SG]

Aristocrates. Secretary to the Tyrant of EPHEBE. The author of *Platitudes*. [SG]

Artela. Wife of TEPPICYMON XXVII and mother of TEPPIC. She used to be a concubine. A vague woman who was fond of cats, she died in a swimming accident (insofar as a crocodile was involved). [P]

Arthur, Barking Mad. Member of the DOG GUILD. One-eyed, bad-tempered Rottweiler, killed by Big FIDO. [MAA]

Artorollo. Past king of Ankh-Morpork. Little fat man, squeaky voice. This seems to be all that anyone can remember about him. [M]

AshkEnte, Rite of. Spell performed to summon and bind DEATH. It is generally done with reluctance, because senior wizards are usually very old and would prefer not to do anything to draw Death's attention to themselves. On the other hand, it is also very effective, since Death knows almost everything that is going on because he is usually closely involved.

The Rite has evolved over the years. It used to be thought that eight wizards were required, each at his station on the point of a great ceremonial octogram, swaying and chanting, arms held out sideways so their fingertips just touched; there was also a requirement for dribbly candles, thuribles, green smoke and all the other tedious paraphernalia of traditional High magic. In fact, it can be performed by a couple of people with three small bits of wood and 4cc of mouse blood; it can even be performed with two bits of wood and a fresh egg.

There are in fact ten ways of performing the Rite; nine of them kill you instantly and the other one is very hard to remember.

Ashk-ur-men-tep. Past king of DJELIBEYBI (Third Empire). Virtually identical to all the other kings. Djelibeybi has never encouraged originality. [P]

Asphalt. Very short, broad, troll with showbusiness experience, mostly to do with mucking out circus elephants. Employed as a roadie by the BAND WITH ROCKS IN. Although shorter than a dwarf, Asphalt makes up for it in breadth. [SM]

Assassins' Guild. Motto: NIL MORTIFI, SINE LVCRE.

Coat of arms: a shield, bisected by a bend sinister, purpure. In the upper-right half a poignard d'or, draped with a masque en sable, lined gris on a field, gules. In the bottom-left half two croix d'or on a sable field.

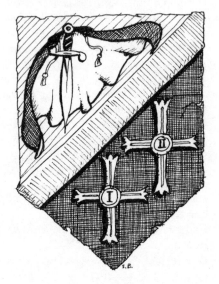

There have always been assassins, and even organized bands of assassins, in Ankh-Morpork. The Guild of Assassins in its modern form is quite recent, however, and it is another result of Lord VETINARI's distinctive civic policy.

The light and airy Guild building, which looks more like the premises of a gentlemen's club, is located in Filigree Street, Ankh-Morpork. The gates on the sole entrance to the Guild are said never to shut because DEATH is open for business all the time, but it is really because the hinges rusted centuries ago (although by the time of *Men At Arms* clearly someone had done something about this). A prominent feature of the building is its weathervane, in the shape of a creeping man with a big cloak; his outstretched dagger is always turned to stab the wind. Like most of the Guilds, the Assassins' building also has a clock tower and chiming clock. This is purposely kept slightly behind all the other clocks in the city (a reminder that, however important you are, you may one day find the Assassins behind you).

The Guild library is one of the largest in the city. In certain specialized areas it is *the* largest (these cover such fields as anatomy, poisons, weaponry, and philosophical works on the regrettable brevity of human life and the best means of bringing this about).

The Assassins' Guild offers the best all-round education in the world. A qualified assassin should be at home in any company, and be able to play at least one musical instrument. Anyone inhumed by a graduate of the Guild school can go to his rest satisfied that he has been annulled by someone of taste and discretion, and probably also a social equal. The entrance exam is not strenuous: the school is easy to get into and easy to get out of (the trick is to get out upright). Sons of dead assassins always get a free scholarship. Only one student in fifteen actually becomes an assassin; many boys are sent to the school simply for the education.

Promotion in the Guild proper is by competitive examination – the Practical being the most important and indeed the only part.

Assassins are always well dressed in stylish black (the senior assassins also wear a purple teaching sash). His appearance* is very important to an assassin. All assassins have a full-length

*The school does not take female pupils, but it is accepted that some of the best assassins in the world are female, often entirely self-taught, and female tutors are sometimes found in the Guild.

mirror in their rooms; it would be a terrible insult to anyone to kill them when you were badly dressed, they say.

Apart from their stylish clothing they can also be recognized by their Guild salute – the thumb pressed against the first two fingers of the right hand and rubbed gently, the ancient sign of a man expecting to be paid. Of course, another way of recognizing them is when, at dead of night, someone stabs you. That was them. Presumably someone cared enough about you to pay.

The monetary aspect is vital. The Assassins profess a great regard for the sanctity of human life, and therefore charge enormous amounts for taking it away. As they say: 'We do not kill merely for a handful of silver. It's a lapful of gold or nothing.' Killing for any other reason is an absolute and unforgivable violation of Guild rules, and any Assassin discovered in breach of this rule would find himself at the very pointed end of his Guild's displeasure. By law, they must always leave a receipt.

Incidentally, they do not kill in bulk; they offer a personal service. Even the most famous assassins never killed more than thirty people in all their lives. They would consider guns and bombs as reducing the whole thing to the level of a farce.

Astfgl. Supreme Life President of HELL. One-time King of the Demons, Lord of Hell and Master of the Pit. *A* Pit, in any case. Despite his undoubted power, he is, like most demons, unimaginative, single-minded and irredeemably stupid in a bureaucratic, industrious sort of way. He favours a moustache, red silk coat, crimson tights and a cowl with two rather sophisticated horns on it, plus a trident (with a loose end). Nevertheless, when he loses control of his appearance, his talons show through his red silk gloves, he sprouts bat-like wings and his skull is framed by great coiled ram horns. Demons have no specific shape and it is assumed that he chose these two forms, which show a certain amount of flair, after seeing an illustration somewhere. [E]

Astrolabe. One of the Disc's finest astrolabes is kept in a large, star-filled room in KRULL. It includes the entire Great A'TUIN-Elephant-Disc system wrought in brass and picked out with tiny jewels. Around it the stars and planets wheel on fine silver wires. On the walls the constellations have been made of tiny phosphorescent seed pearls set out on vast tapestries of jet-black velvet. These were, of course, the constellations current at the time of the room's decoration – several would be unrecognizable now owing to the turtle's movement through space. The planets are minor bodies of rock picked up and sometimes discarded by the system as it moves through space, and seem to have no other role in Discworld astronomy or astrology than to be considered a bloody nuisance. [COM]

Astrozoologists. Krullian scientists interested in studying the nature of the Great A'TUIN. Specifically, its sex. [COM]

Atavarr's Personal Gravitational Upset. Little-used and hard-to-master spell used by GARHARTRA against RINCEWIND. It makes the body believe that gravity is acting at right angles to the norm. [COM]

A'Tuin, the Great. The star turtle who carries the Discworld on its back. Tenthousand-mile-long member of the species *Chelys galactica*, and the only turtle ever to feature on the Hertzsprung-Russell Diagram. Almost as big as the Disc it carries. Sex unknown.

Shell-frosted with frozen methane, pitted with meteor craters and scoured with asteroidal dust, its eyes are like ancient seas, crusted with rheum. Its brain is the size of a continent, through which thoughts move like glittering glaciers.

It is as large as worlds. As patient as a brick. Great A'Tuin is the only creature in the entire universe that knows exactly where it is going.

Upon its back stand Berilia, Tubul, Great T'Phon and Jerakeen, the four giant elephants upon whose shoulders the disc of the world rests. A tiny sun and moon spin around them on a complicated orbit to induce seasons, although probably nowhere else in the multiverse is it sometimes necessary for an elephant to cock its leg to allow the sun to go past.

After the events of *The Light Fantastic*, the Great A'Tuin was orbited by eight baby turtles, each with four small world-elephant calves and tiny discworlds, covered in smoke and volcanoes. They have subsequently begun their own cosmic journeys.

Wizards have tried to tune into Great A'Tuin's mind. They trained up on tortoises and giant sea turtles to get the hang of the Chelonian mind. But although they knew that the Great A'Tuin's mind would be big, they rather foolishly hadn't realized it would be slow. After thirty years all they found out was that the Great A'Tuin was looking forward to something.

People have asked: how does the Disc move on the shoulders of the elephants? What does the Turtle eat? One may as well ask: what kind of smell has yellow got? It is how things *are*.

Auditors of Reality. It has to be understood that the universe of the Discworld is almost entirely animistic. Everything is conscious at some level. The level of reality in the vicinity of the Disc is so low that the distance between the real and the imagined is very small and, frequently, non-existent (hence the *de facto* existence of such beings as the HOG-FATHER, OLD MAN TROUBLE, the TOOTH FAIRIES and the SOUL CAKE TUESDAY DUCK). On the Discworld, even thunderstorms can think.

It follows – at least, it follows on Discworld – that this inherent consciousness should turn up even at the most basic of levels, such as those involving the very nature of reality itself. They are therefore policed by the Auditors of Reality, a race of non-individualized beings whose job it is to make sure the universe functions properly and doesn't just do what it likes. If you travelled faster than light, it is quite possible that it is they who would fine you for speeding.

In appearance they look like small grey empty robes, with a cowl. They act entirely on consensus; they hate and distrust individuality, which for them is instantly fatal. It is clear that they regard life itself as being unnecessary, untidy, and contrary to good order. One of their greatest enemies is DEATH, partly because as immortals they fear death far more than humans do (they are like high-stakes gamblers with everything to lose) and partly because of his tendency to tip the scales of history very slightly in favour of humanity. [RM]

Aurora corialis. (also Aurora coriolis). The Hublights. Great curtains of cold fire whose frosty tints illuminate and colour the midnight snows with silent streamers of OCTARINE, blue and green from the roof of the world. Caused by the vast discharge of magic from the Disc's standing field earthing itself in the green ice mountains of the Hub.

Autocondimentor. Someone who will put certainly salt and probably pepper on any meal you put in front of them whatever it is and regardless of how much it's got on it already and regardless of how it tastes. These people really exist (even on Earth) and fast-food empires have saved millions by recognizing their existence. Mustrum RIDCULLY is such a one; in fact he is one of the extreme variety, who regards any meal as no more than a foundation for salt, pepper, mustard, pickles, ketchup and sauce. [RM]

Azrael. The Great Attractor, the Death of Universes, the Beginning and End of Time.

He is DEATH's master – although it is uncertain whether Death is a truly separate entity or merely one aspect of the whole. He is a creature so large that in real space his length can be measured only in terms of the speed of light. On his dark, sad face his eyes are so big a supernova would be a mere suggestion of a gleam on the iris. He is also keeper of the ultimate clock, from which all TIME originates. Other clocks tell what time it is – but the ultimate clock tells Time what it is. [RM]

Bad Ass. Village in the kingdom of LAN-
CRE in the RAMTOPS. Not a large village,
and it wouldn't show up on a map of the
mountains. It barely shows up on a map
of the village. This is a small community,
close-knit to the point of a trawlerman's
sock, where front doors are used only by
brides and corpses and back doors are
always left unlocked.

The valley occupied by Bad Ass over-
looks a panorama of lesser mountains
and foothills. From there, you can see to
the edge of the world. In the long winter
snows, the roads out of the village are
lined with boards to reduce drifting and
to stop travellers from straying. Markers
are also carved into the bark of every
tenth tree, out to a distance of nearly
two miles. Many a life has been saved by
the pattern of notches found by probing
fingers under the clinging snow.

A narrow bridge over a stream leads to
the village smithy, birthplace of Eskarina
Smith (ESK).

Baker. A weaver in LANCRE, and a
member of the Lancre Morris Men. [LL]

Band With Rocks In, The. A musical
group formed by IMP Y 'BUDDY' CELYN,
Glod GLODSSON, Lias 'Cliff' BLUESTONE
and, for a brief period when they needed
a keyboard player, the LIBRARIAN. [SM]

Bands, Musical (names of).
&U ('And You')
BAND WITH ROCKS IN, THE
Bertie the Balladeer & His
    Troubadour Rascals
Big Troll & Some Other Trolls, a
Blots, the
Boyz From the Wood
Dwarfs with Altitude
Grisham Frord Close Harmony
    Singers
Insanity
Lead Balloon
Snori Snoriscousin & His Brass Idiots
Suck
Surreptitious Fabric, the
We're Certainly Dwarfs
Whom, the

Quite a large number of these are various names briefly assumed and quickly
discarded by the band that eventually
performed in the famous Free Festival
as 'Ande Supporting Bands'.

Barbarian Invaders Machine, the. A device apparently invented by LEONARD OF QUIRM. Weight: 2 tons. Construction: big blocks of wood, and lots of cogwheels. Motive power: weights on a pulley and twisted rubber bands. Purpose: on the insertion of one penny in the slot, the player has the opportunity to fire little spears at the ranks of wooden barbarian invaders as they wobble across the proscenium. Occasionally a badly carved horseman jerks past and extra points are scored if he is hit. A device ahead of its time. [SM]

Beano. A clown, murdered by Edward D'EATH. His only crime – apart, it could be argued, from being a clown – was that he was about the right height and had a room in the right place. [MAA]

Bearhugger, Jimkin. Owner of a distillery in Ankh-Morpork. Manufacturer of Bearhugger's Very Fine Whiskey, Bearhugger's Old Persnickety and Jimkin Bearhugger's Old Selected Dragon's Blood Whiskey – on the bottle of which it says: 'Every bottle matured for up to seven minutes' and 'Ha' a drop afore ye go'. It is cheap and powerful; you could also light fires or clean spoons with it. And probably fuel aircraft.

A recent but short-lived line, which never caught on despite the best scientific recommendation, was Bearhugger's Homeopathic Sipping Whiskey. It is a founding fact of homeopathy that the effectiveness of a remedy increases with dilution. Jimkin decided, therefore, that this idea could profitably be applied to his own product. Strangely enough, the slogan 'Every drop diluted 1 Million Times!' failed to attract custom even though, in theory, merely being in the same room as an uncorked bottle of the stuff should make the purchaser riotously drunk.

Beggars' Guild. Motto: MONETA SVPER-VACANEA, MAGISTER?

Coat of arms: a shield, quartered. In the top-right quarter, three dragons, courant et or, on a field, gules. In the bottom-left quarter a dragon, gardant et or on a field, gules. In the top-left and bottom-right quarters a pattern of caltraps, argent, on a field, azure.

The question asked most frequently by visitors to Ankh-Morpork is 'Why haven't I got any money left?' The next most frequently asked question, at least by those who already know their way to the areas of the SHADES generally associated with female companionship of the professional kind, is 'What has that coat of arms got to do with begging? Dragons on a field of gools? Doesn't sound like beggary to me.' These people have failed, of course, to understand the very essence of beggary. This is a worn-out, much-patched *second-hand* coat of arms.

This is the oldest Guild in Ankh-Morpork. And also the richest, since the beggars never buy anything they can beg.

The Beggars' Guild predates the formalized Guild system of Ankh-Morpork by hundreds if not thousands of years, and it has a strict class structure and hierarchy all of its own. While all the Guilds are to some extent separate societies within society, this is particularly true of the Beggars.

The first mention of the Guild's classes of membership is some six hundred years before the present and says that the Guild includes: 'Rufflers, Uprightmen, Rogues, Wild rogues, Priggers or pransers, People calling you Jimmy, Palliards, Fraters, Mutterers, Mumblers, Freshwater mariners or whipjacks, Drummerers, Drunken tinkers, Swaddlers or Peddlers, Jarkemen or patricoes, Demanders for glimmer or fire, Bawdy baskets, Mortes Autem-mortem, Walking mortes, Doxies, Dells, Kinching mortes and Kinchin cooes.' (This list has a certain coincidence with the beggars found in Elizabethan England.)

In fact, however, most of these classes were more correctly various low grades of thief or conman and their descendants have long since decamped to the newer Guilds. Classes of beggars in the city now include: Twitchers, Droolers, Dribblers, Mumblers, Mutterers, Walking-Along-Shouters, Demanders of a Chip, People who call other people Jimmy, People who need Tuppence for a Cup of Tea, People who need Eightpence for a Meal,

ready enough to do so. Equally, he would be within his rights to report a mere Dribbler he saw attempting to sneak a Mumble. Especially a mumble in the wrong place; one of the important functions of the Guild is to arrange patrols and shifts so that beggary is properly distributed among the streets.

Pavement artists, people with harmonicas and people who make money by standing still in interesting ways are not beggars. No beggar would dream of providing any kind of service or reward, except to the extent that the donor may

People with placards saying 'Why lie? I need a beer' and Foul Ole RON, agreed by his fellow beggars to be in a class by himself if only because no one will share it with him.

While the classes may appear interchangeable to the unpractised eye, their duties are carefully compartmentalized and the demarcation lines enforced. While a Mumbler in good standing might risk an occasional Mutter, he'd be very unwise to try Walking-Along-Shouting until the Guild judged him senior and

feel themselves to be a better person for donating. Doing anything for the money except asking for it is against the tenets of true beggary. Such money as the beggars do make, it must be stressed, is entirely obtained by (1) begging and (2) not begging.

(1) is self-explanatory. (2) owes a lot to what might be called the Ankh-Morpork view of social economics. You clearly don't want a lot of beggars hanging around at your wedding or other salubrious occasions, so the accepted thing

to do is send the Guild a small sum of money and a kind of anti-invitation, which sees to it that men with interesting running sores and a body odour you could split wood with do not turn up. You'd be amazed at how many will turn up should this small precaution not be taken. This is very similar to the scheme run by the Thieves' Guild, whereby a small payment every year ensures the safety of person and property.

The Guild offers a highly specialized schooling and other social benefits for its members. It is ruled by a council under the chairmanship of the current King or Queen of the Beggars (current incumbent: Queen MOLLY of the Beggars).

Beginning, the. There are various theories about the beginning of the universe. These include the Egg, a theory based upon the Great Egg of the Universe, and the Clearing of the Throat, followed by the Word. Others have also propounded the 'Drawing of the Breath' and the 'Scratching of the Head and Trying to Remember It, It Was On the Tip of My Tongue'. One of the objects of The LISTENERS – or Listening Monks – is to determine, by careful analysis of the very faint echoes, what the Word was. By definition, all theories about the beginning of the universe are true. [LF]

Bel-Shamharoth. The Soul-Eater, the Soul-Render, the Sender of Eight. Not Evil, for even Evil has a certain vitality. Bel-Shamharoth is the flip side of the coin of which Good and Evil are one side. One of the old, dark gods of the NECROTELICOMNICON. Although it has never been explicitly said, it is likely that he is one of the creatures of the DUNGEON DIMENSIONS who has managed to survive in this world.

The inner dimensions of his eight-sided temple disobey a fairly basic rule of architecture by being bigger than the outside. It is full of corridors, of tunnels full of unpleasant carvings and occasional disjointed skeletons, hell-lit by a light so violet that it is almost black. The eight-sided crystals set at intervals in the walls and ceiling shed a rather unpleasant glow that doesn't so much illuminate as outline the darkness. The floor is a continuous mosaic of eight-sided tiles, and the corridor walls and ceilings are angled to give the corridors eight sides. In those places where part of the masonry has fallen in, even the stones have eight sides. All routes lead to the centre, where there is an intense violet light, illuminating a wide room with eight walls and eight passages radiating off it. There is a low, eight-sided altar but in the centre of the room is a huge stone slab, eight-sided (of course) and slightly tilted. Under that is a black tentacled creature with an enormous eye – Bel-Shamharoth – all suckers and tentacles and mandibles. [COM, ER]

Belafon. A young druid who delivers rocks for stone circles. When RINCEWIND and TWOFLOWER landed on the $30' \times 10'$ bluish rock on which Belafon was flying, he was carrying a sickle and wearing a long, wet night-shirt and a square of oil-skin tied across his head and knotted under his chin. [LF]

Bentzen. Captain of Duke FELMET's personal bodyguard. [WS]

Berilia. One of four giant elephants upon whose broad and star-tanned shoulders the Disc of the world rests. [COM]

Bertie. Leader of Bertie the Balladeer and His Troubadour Rascals, a traditional musical group. Wears a gold lamé doublet. [SM]

Beryl. Wife of MICA the Bridge Troll. [TB] There's also a Beryl married to Kwartz in LF. It is a common enough name for female trolls, who are generally named after precious or semi-precious stones.

Bes Pelargic. Major seaport of the AGATEAN EMPIRE. The city includes a Red Triangle District. Little more is known, owing to the Empire's emphatic lack of interest in the outside world.

Bethan. Seventeen-year-old virgin rescued from druidical sacrifice by COHEN the Barbarian. An attractive but pale young lady, she was first encountered wearing a long white robe, with a gold torc around her neck. She subsequently married Cohen. Well, we say married . . . it is clear that Cohen has 'married' many women during the course of a long and adventurous life, but none of them seems to be any the worse for the experience and they often end up richer, since he has never mastered the art of spending money. [LF]

Billet, Drum. A wizard who, in long cloak and with his carven staff, visited BAD ASS to hand his staff over to ESK, the blacksmith's daughter – in the mistaken belief that she was in fact a son. He died after passing over the staff and was initially reincarnated as an apple tree, so covered in mistletoe that it looked green even in midwinter. The tree produced very small fruit which passed from stomach-twisting sourness to wasp-filled rottenness overnight. 'Green Billets' are now prized in LANCRE as a very good apple for the making of SCUMBLE. [ER]

Billias, Skarmer. A whiskery, red-faced wizard. Head of the Order of the Silver Star. Resembled a small captive balloon that had been draped in blue velvet and VERMINE. Killed by COIN. [S]

Binky. The flying horse of DEATH. A real, flesh-and-blood horse. Wears a silver and black harness, with an ornate silver saddle. Behind the saddle is a scabbard for Death's folding scythe, and the saddle bag contains his riding cloak. Binky is extremely intelligent and undoubtedly better treated than most beasts of burden on the Disc.

He leaves no hoofprints in normal circumstances, but when travelling in whatever is Death's equivalent of hyperspace he does sometimes leave glowing prints in the air.

Bird, Gaffer. When we encounter him in the chronicles, Gaffer is head handleman in HOLY WOOD. His hands are stained with chemicals and he has no eyebrows (a sure sign of someone who has been around octo-cellulose for any length of time). Wears a back-to-front cap. Assorted tools hang from his belt. He believes everything can be repaired with a piece of string, unlike most people in his position in the modern film industry, who believe everything can be repaired with sticky tape. [MP]

Birdwhistle. Author of *The Legendes and Antiquities of the Ramtops*. [LL]

Black Celestial Dragon of Fire. Manner in which Agateans expect DEATH to appear to them. They are wrong. [M]

Black Roger. Huge, jet-black dog, looking like a pit bull terrier crossed with a mincing machine. A member of the Ankh-Morpork DOG GUILD. [MAA]

Bleakey. A vampire who works in the slaughterhouse in Ankh-Morpork. [MAA]

Blenkin. Manservant to Edward D'EATH. [MAA]

Blind Hugh. A beggar at the Pearl Dock, Ankh-Morpork. The nerves in his body tend to vibrate at fifty paces from even a small amount of impure gold. [COM]

Blind Io. Chief of the GODS, by virtue of his constant vigilance. He has blank skin where his eyes should be. The eyes themselves, of which he has an impressively large number, lead a semi-independent life, orbiting around him. It is said that they can see everything that happens everywhere. This taciturn god is all the Disc's thunder gods, using false noses, different voices and seventy different hammers when he needs to appear to the various different believers. It is also said that he arrived on the Discworld after some terrible and mysterious incident in another Eventuality – a sort of cosmic ticket-of-leave man.

Bloat. A poison, extracted from the deep sea blowfish, *Singularis minutia gigantica*, which protects itself from its enemies by inflating itself to many times its normal size. If the poison is taken by humans, the effect is to make every cell in the body instantaneously swell some 2,000 times. This is invariably fatal, and very loud. You don't need to bury the victims, just redecorate over the top. [P]

Bloody Stupid. Camel living in TSORT. [P]

Bluestone, Lias. A troll. When first seen, he was wearing two large squares of darkish glass in front of his eyes (a troll development to minimize the effects of sunlight). He plays large round rocks, a traditional troll instrument, under his stage name of Cliff – considered by all to be exactly the wrong kind of name for anyone who wants to last any time at all in the field of popular music. Since he is both a troll and a drummer, he could be said to have thrown a 'one' in the great dice game of intellect. [SM]

Bobby, St. The Most Holy St Bobby. Made a bishop of the Omnian church because he was in the desert with the Prophet OSSORY. St Bobby was a donkey and, in the words of Mustrum RIDCULLY, the somewhat irreverent Archchancellor of Unseen University, a righteous ass. [SG]

Boffo. A clown. Doorkeeper at the FOOLS' GUILD. A very small man, with huge boots. His face is plastered with flesh-coloured make-up, on which is painted a big frown; his hair is a couple of old mops dyed red. He has a hoop in his trousers to make him look amusingly overweight, and a pair of rubber braces to allow his trousers to bounce up and down as he walks. Like most clowns, he was brought up to believe that a custard pie in the face represents the acme of humour. There can be few souls more miserable. [MAA]

Boggi's. Dress shop in Kings Way, Ankh-Morpork. High-class modes for the affluent. [LL]

Boggis, Bengy. Bengy 'Lightfoot' Boggis. The real name of Brother FINGERS. [GG]

Boggis, J. H. J. H. 'Flannelfoot' Boggis. A thief in Ankh-Morpork [WS]. The large Boggis family includes some of Ankh-Morpork's most respected thieves.

Bonsai Mountains. The most testing form of bonsai, practised only by History Monks and other very long-lived persons who don't mind waiting a thousand years to see what happens next. The mountains are selected while they are small, and their growth is artificially restricted; careful positioning of mirrors and wind screens encourages the formation of the miniature glaciers, forests and lakes that are part of the mountain's original morphic field.

Just any old piece of rock won't do. The trick is to spot the mountains while they are young. In a sense the expert is selecting that piece of rock which, after the normal processes of continental collision and crustal upheaval, will be at the very peak – i.e., from one point of view, the rock with the correct morphic field which will cause the rest of the mountain to form underneath it. A wrong choice here will be bound to lead to disappointment after a hundred years or so.

Books. The Disc is a veritable treasure-house of books. These include:
Achmed the I Just Get These Headaches's Book of Humorous Cat Stories [MP]
Adventures with Crossbow and Rod [MP]
Anima Unnaturale (Broomfog) [S]
Ankh-Morpork Almanack and Booke of Dayes (A.J. Loop) [LL]
Ankh-Morporke, Citie of One Thousand Surprises, Wellcome to [S, MP, RM]
Ankh-Morpork Succesfion, The (Thighbiter) [MAA]
Bestiary (Philo) [SG]
Boke of the Film, The (Deccan Ribobe and others) [MP]
Book of Alberto Malich the Mage, The [LF]
Book of Creation [SG]
Book of Going Forth Around Elevenish [LF]
Book of Staying in the Pit [P]
Bumper Fun Grimoire [LF]
Casplock's Compleet Lexicon of Majik with Precepts for the Wise [S]
Ceremonies and Protocols of the Kingdom of Lancre [LL]
Civics (Ibid) [SG]
Cordat, The [P]
De Chelonian Mobile [SG]
Demonologie [E]
Demonologie Malyfycorum of Hanchanse thee Unsatysfactory [ER]
Dictionary of City Biography [GG]
Dictionary of Eye-Watering Words [GG]
Discourse on Historical Inevitability (Ibid) [P]
Discourses (Ibid) [SG]
Diseases of the Dragon (Sybil Deirdre Olgivanna Ramkin) [GG]
Ectopia (Gnomon) [SG]
Ego-Video Liber Deorum (Koomi of Smale) [SG]
Etiquette, Lady Deirdre Waggon's Book of [MAA]
Farmer's Almanac & Seed Catalogue [RM]
FULLOMYTH
Gardening In Difficult Conditions [SM]
Ge Fordge's Compendyum of Sex Majick [S]
Geometries (Legibus) [SG]
Guitar Primer, Blert Wheedown's [SM]
Inne Juste 7 Dayes I wille make You a Barbearian Hero! (Cohen) [S]
Insects, Howe to Kille (Humptulip) [LL]
Iyt Gryet Teymple hyte Tsort, Y Hiystory Myistical [LF]
Jane's All the World's Siege Weapons [LL]

Joy of Tantric Sex, with Illustrations for the Advanced Student, The (A Lady) [E]

Lacemaking Through the Ages [GG]

Laws & Ordinances of The Cities of Ankh & Morpork [GG]

Legendes and Antiquities of the Ramtops, The (Birdwhistle) [LL]

Little Folks' Book of Flower Fairies, The [LF]

Little Pieces for Tiny Fingers [P]

Logic & Paradox (Wold) [SM]

Maleficio's Discouverie of Demonologie [S]

Mallificarum Sumpta Diabolicite Occularis Singularum [E]

Man of the Woods, The (General Sir Roderick Purdeigh)

Martial Arts [LL]

Mechanics (Grido) [SG]

Meditations (Didactylos) [SG]

Monster Fun Book [WS]

Monster Fun Grimoire [M]

My Life Among the Sponge-Eating Coral-House-Dwelling Pygmies (General Sir Roderick Purdeigh)

Names of the Ants (Humptemper) [E]

NECROTELICOMNICON

Necrotelicomnicon Discussed for Students, With Practical Experiments [MP]

Nosehinger on the Laws of Contract [LF]

Occult Primer (Woddeley) [S]

Octarine Fairy Book [COM]

OCTAVO, The

Plants, On the Nature of (Orinjcrates) [SG]

Platitudes (Aristocrates) [SG]

Principles of Ideal Government (Ibid) [P]

Principles of Navigation (Dykeri) [SG]

Pseudopolis, 130 Days of [P]

Reflections (Xeno) [SG]

Religion, On (Abraxas) [SG]

Septateuch [SG]

Servant, The (unpublished work by Havelock, Lord Vetinari)

Shuttered Palace, The (translated from the Klatchian by A Gentleman, with Hand-Coloured Plates for the Connoisseur in A Strictly Limited Edition) [P]

Stripfettle's Believe-It-Or-Not Grimoire [RM]

Summoning of Dragons, The (Tubul de Malachite) [GG]

Thaumic Imponderability, Theory of, The (Marrowleaf)

Theologies (Hierarch) [SG]

True Arte of Levitatione [P]

Twurp's Peerage [LL, MA]

Way of the Scorpion, The [WA]

(*See also* PLAYS)

HISTORY BOOKS

The books from which history is derived. Guarded by the History Monks, in their monastery in a hidden valley in the high RAMTOPS. There are over 20,000 of them, each 10 feet high, bound in lead, and the letters are so small that they have to be read with a magnifying glass. When people say 'It is written', it is written *here*. [SG]

MAGICAL BOOKS

Magical books are more than just pulp and paper; their curly magical writing moves around the page, twisting and writhing in an attempt not to be read by a non-wizard.

All books of magic have a life of their own. In the LIBRARY of Unseen University some of the really energetic ones can't simply be chained to the bookshelves; they have to be nailed shut or kept between steel plates. Or – in the case of the volumes on tantric sex magic for the serious connoisseur – kept under very cold water to stop them bursting into flames and scorching their severely plain covers.

42

Things can happen to browsers in magical libraries that make having your face pulled off by tentacled monstrosities from the DUNGEON DIMENSIONS seem a mere light massage by comparison. No one in possession of a complete set of marbles would like to settle down with a book of magic, because even the individual words have a private and vindictive life of their own and reading them, in short, is a kind of mental Indian wrestling. Many a young wizard has tried to read a grimoire that is too strong for him, and people who hear the screams find only his pointy shoes with a wisp of smoke coming out of them.

After the first Age of Magic the disposal of grimoires became a severe problem on the Discworld. A spell is still a spell even when imprisoned temporarily in parchment and ink. It has potency. This is not a problem while the book's owner still lives, but on his death the spell book becomes a source of uncontrolled power that cannot easily be defused. In short, spell books leak magic. Various solutions have been tried. Countries near the Rim simply took the books and threw them over the Edge. Near the Hub less satisfactory alternatives were available. Inserting the offending books in canisters of negatively polarized OCTIRON and sinking them in the fathomless depths of the sea was one (burial in deep caves on land was earlier ruled out after some districts complained of walking trees and five-headed cats), but before long the magic seeped out and eventually fishermen complained of shoals of invisible fish and psychic clams.

A temporary solution was the construction, in various centres of magical lore, of large rooms made of denatured octiron, which is impervious to most forms of magic. Here the more critical grimoires can be stored until their potency has attenuated. That was how there came to be, at the Library of Unseen University, the OCTAVO, greatest of all grimoires. At least one legend suggests that it has always been there and that the university grew up around it.

Bookworm, .303. The fastest insect on the Discworld. It evolved in magical libraries, where it is necessary to eat

extremely quickly to avoid being affected by the thaumic radiations. An adult .303 bookworm can eat through a shelf of books so fast that it ricochets off the wall. [P, GG]

Borgle, Nodar. A Klatchian who ran a large canteen in HOLY WOOD, with a cuisine very nearly on a par with that of C. M. O. T. DIBBLER himself. [MP]

Borrowing. Magical technique employed by some witches to enter the mind of other living creatures. The witch reaches out to share a mind with a forest creature, while her body remains behind in a sleep so deep that it can be mistaken for death (which is why when Granny WEATHERWAX, a very skilled exponent of the craft, goes borrowing, her apparently lifeless hands hold a piece of card on which is written I ATE'NT DEAD). The witch rides on the animal's mind, steering it gently; it is important not to upset the owner, who would undoubtedly panic if it realized that the witch's mind was there as well. There is a price for this skill: no one asks you to pay it, but the very absence of a demand is a moral obligation to a witch. The borrower's motto is: Leave nothing but memories, take nothing but experience.

The more apparently complex a mind is, the harder it is to borrow. For the purposes of most witches the 'best' minds are those of small uncomplicated creatures, like rabbits and most birds. Humans, with their interweaving parallel streams of thought, are very hard. Hardest of all, though, is a hive mind; borrowing the mind of a swarm of bees, for example, when all its components might be travelling in various directions and at varying speeds, is the Everest of borrowing. It is known to have been achieved once.

A built-in danger is that a witch, by accident or design, will become so immersed in the mind of the 'borrowed' creature that she will not return. Indeed, it has sometimes been suggested that witches never die – they merely don't come back.

Borvorius. Imperiator of the Tsortean army. [SG]

Bottomley, Duke. Leather-skinned farm worker who also helps out with the harvest at Miss FLITWORTH's. Duke's parents have upwardly mobile if rather simplistic ideas about class structure – his brothers are called Squire, Earl and King. [RM]

Brass Neck. Village in the RAMTOPS, under Leaping Mountain and in the next valley to BAD ASS. [ER]

Bravd (the Hublander). Big, strong barbarian. Thick as two short planks, if the planks are extremely thick (*see* STANDARDS). [COM]

Breccia. Troll actor in the clicks. Also the name of an oft-alluded-to secret society of trolls, similar to the popular images of the Mafia or the Chinese Tongs or the Rotary Club. [MP, SM]

Broadman. Former landlord of the Broken DRUM, Ankh-Morpork. A fat little man with small black beady eyes. He was killed while setting fire to his own pub shortly after learning the strange new concept of 'insurance'. [COM]

Broken Drum. (*See* DRUM).

Bronze Psepha. One of the dragons of the WYRMBERG. This dragon, with its long, equine head and bronze-gold wings, is ridden by K!SDRA. Like all the dragons of the Wyrmberg, he was imaginary and given solid existence by the very high level of ambient magic (*see* MAGIC) in the area. [COM]

Brooks, Mr. Royal Beekeeper in LANCRE. Although most of the Castle staff are known by their surname, Mr Brooks, like the cook and the butler, has the privilege of an honorific. He treats everyone as an equal – not *his* equal, but equal to everyone else and slightly inferior to him. This is perhaps because he deals with royalty in his hives every day. A truly skilled man, and probably as near to being a witch as you can be while wearing trousers. Hates wasps. [LL]

Brown Islands. Land of big waves and men who surf, rumoured to be the place where bread grows on trees and young women find little white balls in oysters. Located somewhere between the CIRCLE SEA and the COUNTERWEIGHT CONTINENT.

Insofar as there is any trading between the two continents, it takes place here. [COM, SG]

Brutha. First seen as a loyal and devout novice in the Omnian church, wearing huge sandals and a grubby robe, tending the Temple garden. He was then about seventeen years old, with a big, round, red, honest face and ham-sized hands, a body like a barrel, and tree-trunk legs ending in splay-feet and knock-ankles.

Brutha didn't leave his small village until he was twelve. He was by nature kind, generous and therefore marked down by FATE as a natural target. The other novices called him the Big Dumb Ox. Brutha mastered neither reading nor writing, but he had an absolutely perfect memory, which more or less compensated; all he needed to do was glance at a text in order to be able to write it – or, from his point of view, draw it – in its entirety. When the Great God OM was trapped in the form of a tortoise, Brutha – whose quiet and unquestioning belief meant he was the only person left in the entire country who could hear the god speak – carried him round in a wickerwork box slung over his shoulder.

Although Brutha was made a bishop by VORBIS, he was later personally appointed CENOBIARCH by the Great God Om. He died after having reached a great age. [SG]

Butch. A dog in Ankh-Morpork. His top and bottom set of fangs have grown so large that he appears to be looking at the world through bars, and he is bow-legged; this is what calling a dog 'Butch' does to it. A member of the DOG GUILD. [MAA]

Butts, Eulalie. Miss Butts co-founded and runs the QUIRM COLLEGE FOR YOUNG LADIES, a large boarding school which is single-sex although she would probably prefer it to be no sex whatsoever. She is short, but with a bearing and manner that make people think she is tall even while they're looking down at her. She is not unkind, despite a lifetime of being gently dried out on the stove of education. She is conscientious and a stickler for propriety, and did not deserve to have SUSAN Sto Helit as a pupil. [SM]

B'zugda-Hiara. Dwarfish insult. Means 'Lawn Ornament'. [WA]

Cake, Mrs Evadne. A small medium, living in Elm Street, Ankh-Morpork. Squat and short-sighted, she is almost perfectly circular; in spite of this she looms tremendously, largely because of her hat, which she wears at all times. It is huge and black and covered with stuffed birds, wax fruit and other assorted decorative items, all painted black. Carrying an enormous handbag, she travels under her hat like a basket travels under a balloon, grumbling away to herself – her mouth is constantly moving.

Mrs Cake is a very religious woman: there isn't a temple, church, mosque or small group of standing stones anywhere in the city that she hasn't attended at one time or another. Strait-laced and intolerant in most respects she is, in fact, exactly the kind of person who disapproves of people like her. Apart from church work, her main hobby is dressmaking.

She is not a bead curtain and incense medium. She is actually very good at her profession, with a lifetime of involvement in the spirit world, an involvement which – it must be said – the spirits feel they could well have done without. With her precognition switched on, she has a disconcerting tendency to respond to questions before they're asked.

Mrs Cake has a daughter, Ludmilla, who is a werewolf. It is because of this that she has a surprisingly understanding attitude to the undead and morphically challenged, and by the time of *Men At Arms* (when Ludmilla had left home) she had opened her home as a lodging house for those of a nocturnal and fur-growing persuasion.

It is very clear that Mrs Cake is, at least in practical terms, a witch.

Cake, Ludmilla. Daughter of Mrs Evadne CAKE. A werewolf. When in human form, Ludmilla is still built to a scale slightly larger than normal: she is the sort of person who goes through life crouching slightly and looking apologetic in case she inadvertently looms. She has magnificent hair, which crowns her head and flows out behind her like a cloak. She also has slightly pointed ears and teeth which, while white and beautiful, catch the light in a disturbing way. Like all werewolves, her habit of staring at people's throats while she talks to them tends to put a damper on conversation. [RM]

Cakebread. Person once cursed by Nanny OGG for kicking her cat. Since her cat is GREEBO, it is amazing that Cakebread survived long enough to be cursed. [WS]

Calendars (The Discworld Year). The calendar of a planet that is flat and revolves on the back of four giant elephants is always difficult to establish.

It can be derived, though, by starting with the fact that the spin year – defined by the time taken for a point on the Rim to turn one full circle – is about 800 days long. The tiny sun orbits in a fairly flat ellipse, being rather closer to the surface of the disc at the Rim than at the Hub (thus making the Hub rather cooler than the Rim). This ellipse is stable and stationary with respect to the turtle – the sun passes between two of the elephants.

The effect of all this is that the 'spin year' contains two of each season – two summers, two winters, and so on. The winters occur when our theoretical point is at 90 degrees to the orbit of the sun, and the summers when it is directly under the orbit.

In theory this should mean that the point on the Rim should be extremely cold during the 'winters', whereas it has been established that the climate on the Rim is quite mild all year round. It has been suggested by wizards at Unseen University that this is caused by the scatter effect of the very high magical flux around the edge of the Disc, which tends to equalize temperatures all around the circumference.

In the days of the Ankh-Morpork Empire this was fully understood and the Great Year was divided into eight seasons – Winter Prime, Spring Prime, Summer Prime, Autumn Prime, Winter Secundus, Spring Secundus, and so on. But this was always a purist's view of the calendar, of interest only to wizards and astrologers. Most people – and certainly most in rural areas – really dealt quite sensibly in what were technically half-years, a little longer than a terrestrial year, but noted that in some years the sun rose on your left as you faced the Hub, and in others it rose on your right. Apart from that, they followed the natural year. You plough, you sow, it grows, you harvest – that's a year, no matter what some daft old man in Ankh-Morpork says.

This has caused some confusion over the naming of various festivals. HOGSWATCHNIGHT and Crueltide are, from the farmer's point of view, the 'same' festival, although in fact they are the middle and end of the year. Midsummer Eve and Small Gods Eve are also 'the same' for practical purposes. In rural areas Hogswatchnight and Midsummer Eve tend to be used to refer to both festivals, since they refer to natural, homely things (the beginning of summer and the killing of animals).

There are thirteen months in the year – Offle, February, March, April, May, June, Grune, August, Spune, Sektober, Ember, December and Ick. There are eight days in a week, Octeday being the eighth.

Centuries and years are given names, usually chosen by astrologers. The time we are mostly concerned with is in the final years of the Century of the Fruitbat, which follows the Century of the Three Lice.

Ankh-Morpork also numbers its years for governmental purposes, although the numbering system has been tinkered with as the fortunes of the city have changed. Initially they dated from the founding of the city, but Ankh-Morpork has been burned, razed, rebuilt – lost and founded, as it were – many times, and various rulers with more pride than sense have started the numbering from one all over again, usually from some vitally important event such as their accession to power. But the recent calendar can be deduced as follows:

Unseen University is known to be two thousand years old in its present form (although in one form or another there has been some kind of magical presence on the site since the creation of Discworld). It was founded in what was then known as AM 1282 by Alberto MAL-ICH, during the closing days of the Ankh-Morpork Empire. (This lasted from AM 1, the building of one of the first cities in what is now the SHADES area, until shortly after the founding of UU.)

The wizards began numbering their years from that date, since it didn't matter much to them what the year was called on the other side of the walls. And, as the civil calendar was tinkered with, and revised when people lost count, or found nineteen days that shouldn't have been there, or mislaid the whole of Grune, the city eventually took to using the University's Ankh-Morpork Years, which at least were reliable and happened one after the other, apart from 1456, which for some reason happened twice.

The fact that there are therefore at least two 'counts' has not really caused confusion – historians know their history and don't get confused, and most other people don't need to think much outside the present century.

The Century of the Fruitbat is therefore the twentieth century. The Ankh-Morpork CIVIL WAR, which took place in 432 by the city count at the time, took place in AM 1688 by the more reliable University calendar. Students should in any case be wary of references to the 'civil war'; there have been at least seven in the city's recorded history, as well as a large number of uncivil or even downright impolite ones. That was, however,

the last one, and marked the end of the lengthy monarchical period in the city's history. Since then the city has been ruled by a succession of oligarchies and self-elected dictators of varying degrees of sanity. (*See also* KINGS, MONARCHY, PATRICIAN.)

Carbonaceous. A troll in LANCRE who climbed the COPPERHEAD mountain with the young RIDCULLY. [LL]

Carding, Marmaric. An eighth-level wizard. Head of the Hoodwinkers. This 17-stone wizard, with his beringed fingers and vein-crazed jowls, was killed by COIN's staff. [S]

Caroc cards. Distilled wisdom of the Ancients. Deck of cards used on the Discworld for fortune telling and for card games (see CRIPPLE MR ONION). Cards *named* in the Discworld canon include The Star, The Importance of Washing the Hands (Temperance), The Moon, The Dome of the Sky, The Pool of Night (the Moon), Death, the Eight of Octograms, the Four of Elephants, the Ace of Turtles. [LF, M, LL]

Carpenter, Obidiah. Tailor in LANCRE. Also a general poacher, cess-pit cleaner and approximate carpenter (as in 'with a couple of nails it'll stay up all right'). A member of the Lancre Morris Men. [LL]

Carrot (Carrot Ironfoundersson). A dwarf (by adoption). His adoptive dwarf parents found him in the woods as a toddler, wandering near the bodies of his real parents, who had been victims of a bandit attack. Also in the wreckage of the cart was a sword, and a ring that was very similar to one recorded as having once been a part of the royal jewellery of Ankh.

When first encountered in the chronicles he was 6'6" tall and nearly sixteen years old with a big, honest forehead, mighty neck and impressively pink skin, due to scrubbing. He became known as Carrot not because of his red hair, kept short for reasons of hygiene, but because of his shape – the kind of tapering shape a boy gets through clean living, healthy eating and good mountain air in huge lungfuls. When Carrot flexes his muscles, other muscles have to move out of the way first. He has a punch that even trolls have learned to respect. He walks with a habitual stoop, which comes from being 6 feet tall while living with dwarfs. Like all dwarfs, when he's away he writes home at least once a week.

His adoptive parents, embarrassed at his size and by the fact that he reached puberty at what in dwarf terms is about playgroup age, realized that he needed

to be among his own kind. They arranged for him to join the Night WATCH in Ankh-Morpork because, they had been told, it would make a man of him.

Being very literal-minded is a dwarfish trait. It is one which Carrot shares. In the whole of his life (prior to his arrival in Ankh-Morpork) no one ever really lied to him or gave him an instruction that he wasn't meant to take literally.

He is direct, honest, good-natured and honourable in all his dealings. Despite a full year in the Watch he still thinks everyone is decent underneath and would get along just fine if only they made the effort. He is genuinely, almost supernaturally likeable. And he is astonishingly simple – which is not at all the same as 'stupid'. It is just that he sees the world shorn of all the little lies and prevarications that other people erect in order to sleep at night.

After a few initial setbacks, Carrot has had an exemplary career as a policeman, often helped by the fact that people confuse his simplicity with idiocy.

He has a crown-shaped birthmark at the top of his left arm. Coupled with his sword, his charisma, his natural leadership, and his deep and almost embarrassing love of Ankh-Morpork, this rather suggests that he is the long-lost rightful heir to the throne of the city. It is a subject that he avoids, to the point – it has been hinted – of destroying any written evidence to the fact. He seriously believes that to be a policeman is to be the guardian of civilization. He is, in fact, very happy in his job.

This is just as well for Ankh-Morpork. Few civilizations can survive long under an honest, just and strong leader, which is why they generally take care never to elect them. [GG, TOC, MAA]

Carter, Bestiality. LANCRE's only baker. Married to Eva. A member of the Lancre Morris Men. His parents, though of a logical turn of mind, got the wrong end of the stick when it came to naming their children. Their first four children (all girls) were called Hope, Chastity, Prudence and Charity; then the boys were, with a sort of misplaced recognition of the need for balance, called Anger, Jealousy, Bestiality and Covetousness. [LL]

Casanunda, Count Giamo. A dwarf. The most enthusiastic lover in the history of the Disc. He also claims to be the Disc's greatest liar – his card says 'World's 2nd Greatest Lover. Finest Swordsman. Outrageous Liar. Soldier of Fortune. Stepladders Repaired.' However, all this may be a lie.

Casanunda is 3'9" tall, with a typically dwarfish bullet head. But he eschews dwarfish clothing and goes in for periwigs, satins and lace, being aware that big iron boots and great prickly beards attract only ladies of a specialized taste.

Everything his fellow dwarfs do very occasionally as nature demands he does all the time, sometimes in the back of a sedan chair and once upside down in a tree – but with care and attention to detail that is typically dwarfish. He received his title after performing a small service for Queen AGANTIA of Skund (details unknown). He has a natural attraction for Nanny OGG, who is probably his female equivalent. [RM, WA, LL]

Catroaster. Disc philosopher. Found floating face down in the Ankh within hours of uttering the famous line 'When a man is tired of Ankh-Morpork, he is tired of ankle-deep slurry.' [M]

Cena. Prophet of the Omnian religion. A tall fellow with a full beard, whose eyes wobbled when he talked. His sandals remain as a religious artefact. [SG]

Cenobiarch. Head of the Omnian religion. The Superior Iam. After him come six archpriests, thirty lesser iams, hundreds of bishops, deacons, subdeacons and priests, plus the inquisitors and exquisitors (*see* QUISITION). Then novices, bull breeders, torturers and Vestigial Virgins. [SG]

Cern. One of the sons of Gordo SMITH, and brother of Eskarina. [ER]

Chalky. Troll who runs a wholesale building supplies firm in Ankh-Morpork. He also does jobbing printing, cheap pottery and, in short, all those little jobs that need to be done to a budget, badly and quick. [RM, MAA]

Champot. Past king of LANCRE, who built LANCRE CASTLE. As a ghost, he carries his head under his arm. Since he died of gout, this may take some explaining. [WS]

Chance. Broadly, the greater the odds against anything happening the more likely it is to happen on the Discworld. It's summed up by the saying – amounting to a scientific law – that million-to-one chances crop up nine times out of ten.

Changebasket, Skrelt. Wizard, and refounder of the Ancient and Truly Original Sages of the Unbroken Circle. By dint of close study Skrelt learned that although a wizard's spells will say themselves when he dies, a Great Spell will simply take refuge in the nearest mind open and ready to receive it. [ER]

Charnel, Brother. A priest who stole the altar gold from the Temple of OFFLER and had it made into a horn, and played magical music until the gods caught up with him and . . . The story always ends with those terrible three dots, as if legend itself is too scared to continue. [SM]

Cheese, Mr. Owner of the Bucket in Gleam Street, Ankh-Morpork. The Bucket, which lacks charm, ambience or even many customers, is now the bar of choice for the City WATCH. Watchmen don't like to see things that'd put them back on duty when they just want a quiet drink. [MAA]

Cheesewaller, C. V. A very elderly wizard (D.M. (Unseen), B.Thau, B.F.) who lives in QUIRM. He has a talking brass plate outside his premises, a piece of stage magickery that is typical of jobbing wizards in small towns where the natives need to be impressed from the word go.

The same thinking applies to his props, which happen to include a raven and a talking skull. [SM]

Cheesewright, G. Fellow student of TEPPIC at the ASSASSINS' GUILD in Ankh-Morpork. A skinny young man with red hair and a face that is one large freckle. [P]

Chelonauts. Men who journey – or at least intend to journey – below the Rim to explore the mysteries of the Great A'TUIN. Their suits are of fine white leather, hung about with straps and brass nozzles and other unfamiliar and suspicious contrivances. The leggings end in high, thick-soled boots, and the arms are shoved into big supple gauntlets. Topping it all is a big copper helmet designed to fit on the heavy collars around the neck of the suits. The helmet has a crest of white feathers on top and a little glass window in front. [COM]

Chert. Troll who runs a sawmill near Cut-

shade Forest in the RAMTOPS. He also sells coffins. [WA, TB]

Chidder. Classmate of TEPPIC at the ASSASSINS' GUILD in Ankh-Morpork. When first encountered he was wearing a plain black suit which looked as though it had been nailed on to him in bits. He ambles through life as though he's already worked it all out. Teppic calls him 'Chiddy'. His family are merchant venturers. They provide things that people want. [P]

Weathervane atop the Assassins' Guild Building

Chillum, Millie. Servant at LANCRE CASTLE. A small, dark girl with a tendency to call her female superiors (i.e., everyone else) 'm'm'. [LL]

Chimera. A desert creature, with the legs of a mermaid, the hair of a tortoise, the teeth of a fowl, the wings of a snake, the breath of a furnace and the temperament of a rubber balloon in a hurricane. Clearly a magical remnant. It is not known whether chimera breed and, if so, with what. [S]

Chimeria. Desert country, now invisible on any map. Original home of a hero called Codice (hero: very strong, beats people up, can't read if his index finger is removed, wears a leather loincloth whatever the weather).

Chimeria is possibly a *brigadoon*, of which there are a number on the Disc. These are areas which, owing to a localized instability in reality, do not have a continuous existence in one place and may turn up for only one day every hundred years before once again being squeezed out of the local universe. They reappear either randomly or at lengthy fixed intervals, a common denominator being that no time passes inside the brigadoon between appearances. The lost city of EE is probably one of these, as is the village of Turnover in the RAMTOPS (a special case). In all likelihood there are also a large number of rural areas, or stretches of ocean, where the phenomenon passes unnoticed owing to the absence of anyone to notice it. For anyone interested in further research, a good place to begin looking is any area where sea-going vessels disappear or strange and theoretically extinct animals stroll out of the undergrowth.

Although most brigadoons do have a generalized geographical location to which they are anchored, occasionally one loses this point of contact and floats randomly across the worlds, coming to earth again in any time or place. Evidence suggests that the Wandering SHOPS use some kind of controlled version of this phenomenon on their travels.

Ching Aling. Method of divining used by the Hublandish. It involves the throwing of yarrow sticks into the air, observing the ensuing pattern, interpreting the results using a reference book and pretending you have the faintest idea what it's talking about. (Example: the Octo-

gram 8,887: Illegality, the Unatoning Goose.) [M]

Chrysoprase. (also Krysoprase [LF], and Chrystophrase [WS]). Well . . . trolls were never good at spelling. A troll gang leader and extortionist; when he demands an arm and a leg in payment, he means it. Owns the Cavern, a troll night-club, and wears jewellery made from the diamond teeth of other troll gangsters who have come second in their business dealings with him. He is said to be big in the BRECCIA, a rather inefficiently organized troll crime syndicate. [MAA]

Chubby. A swamp dragon. Rescued by Lady RAMKIN from a blacksmith in Easy Street. Exploded by Edward D'EATH. His blue collar was an important clue in one of the Night WATCH's few real homicide cases. [MAA]

Chume. The Notorious Herring Thrower. [RM]

Churn, Ezrolith. Very old wizard and a former ARCHCHANCELLOR of Unseen University. He had been writing a treatise on 'Some Little Known Aspects of Kuian Rain-Making Rituals'. [E]

Circle Sea. A sizeable but almost landlocked sea approximately halfway between the Hub and the Rim, opening at its Turnwise side into the Rim Ocean. Its principal trading ports are Ankh-Morpork, on the STO PLAINS coast, and AL KHALI and EPHEBE on the Rimwards side. Discworld civilization, which can broadly be defined as those countries that have invented the fork as well as the knife, is found around its historic coasts.

Circumfence. A barrier built by the Kingdom of KRULL around almost a third of

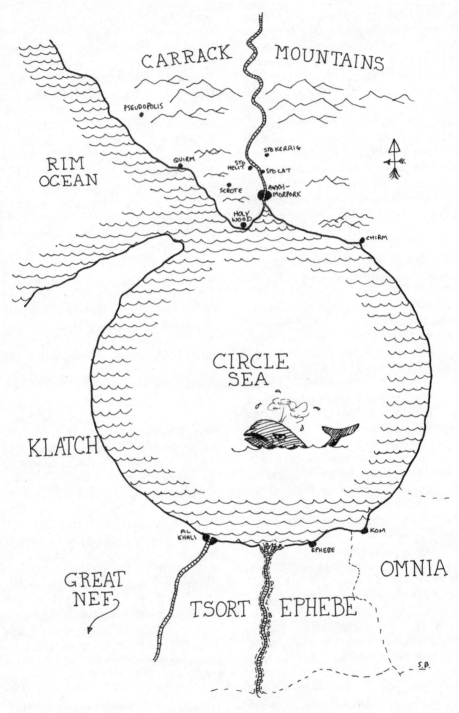

Map of the Circle Sea area

the Disc, to catch salvage. Seven navies patrol it constantly to keep it in repair and bring its salvage back to Krull. [COM]

Civil War. The Ankh-Morpork Civil War ran from 8.32 p.m., Grune 3, 432 to 10.45 a.m., Grune 4, 432 (but see the Discworld CALENDAR – by the calendar now commonly used, this would have been 1688). The origins of the war have always been the subject of heated debate among historians. There are two theories:

1. The common people, having been heavily taxed by a particularly stupid and unpleasant king, decided that enough was enough and that it was time to do away with the outmoded concept of monarchy and replace it with, as it turned out, a series of despotic overlords who still taxed heavily but at least had the decency not to pretend the gods had given them the right to do it, which made everyone feel a bit better, *or*

2. One of the players in a game of CRIPPLE MR ONION in a tavern accused another of palming more than the usual number of aces, and knives were drawn, and then someone hit someone with a bench, and then someone else stabbed someone, and arrows started to fly, and someone swung on a chandelier, and a carelessly hurled axe hit someone in the street, and then the WATCH was called in, and someone set fire to the place, and someone hit a lot of people with a table, and then everyone lost their tempers and commenced fighting.

According to the history books, the decisive battle that ended the Ankh-Morpork Civil War was fought between two handfuls of bone-weary men in a swamp early one misty morning and, although one side claimed victory, it ended with a practical score of Humans 0, Ravens 1,000, which is the case with most battles.

The famous fire during the Civil War is noteworthy simply because it was started by both sides at the same time in order to stop the city falling into enemy hands. It was not otherwise impressive; the ANKH had been particularly high that summer, and most of the city was too damp to burn. [MP]

Cleph-ptah-re. Past queen of DJELIBEYBI. TEPPIC's aunt. [P]

Clete, Mr. Secretary of the MUSICIANS' GUILD. Had a pointed nose and a strange, mirthless laugh ('Hat. Hat. Hat.'). He looked like something you might get if you extracted fossilized genetic material from something in amber and then gave it a suit.

For some years he was very active in Ankh-Morpork's Guild system, into which he fitted like a moray eel fits into a reef.

Many people have sought power by great feats of arms or complex diplomatic negotiations, but Clete followed what we might call the Grand Vizier road to power. He did things. Trivial and thankless but essential things. Keeping Minutes, for example (after all, no one remembers what they decided until they read the Minutes). Making sure the membership roll is quite up to date. Filing. Organizing. He worked hard on behalf of the THIEVES' GUILD, although he wasn't a thief (at least in the normal sense). Then there was a rather more senior vacancy in the FOOLS' GUILD, and Mr Clete was no fool and took it immediately. And finally there was the Secretaryship of the MUSICIANS' GUILD. Since technically he should have been a musician, he bought a comb and paper. Mr Clete believed in organization rather more than he believed in the people and things that needed organizing. [SM]

Clubs and societies. Ankh-Morpork has a wide range of clubs catering for its vast population. These include:

BRECCIA [SM]

Cavern Club – a sort of Kennel Club for the breeders of pedigree swamp dragons. Not to be confused with the Cavern, in Quarry Lane, which is a club for the cooler sort of human and the nastier sort of troll. [GG, SM]

Country Landowners' Association [MAA]

ELUCIDATED BRETHREN OF THE EBON NIGHT

Fine Art Appreciation Society (A-M) – believed by Sergeant Colon to be an excuse for men to 'paint pictures of women in the nudd' [GG]

Folk-Dance & Song Club (M) – not much is known except that one of its keenest members is Corporal 'Nobby' Nobbs of the City WATCH. This is like finding King Herod attending meetings of the Bethlehem Playgroup Association. [GG]

FRESH START CLUB

Friendly Flamethrowers' League – another dragon organization. Whereas the Cavern Club judges, however, would award points for pointiness of ear and healthiness of scale, the Flamethrowers are a much jollier bunch whose dragon shows include categories like The Dragon Who the Judges Would Most Like To Cook On. [GG, MAA]

Illuminated & Ancient Brethren of Ee – one of Ankh-Morpork's many well-known secret societies [GG]

Silicon Anti-Defamation League (often considered, without any real evidence, to be a front organization for the Breccia). This is a troll organization, formed originally by working trolls in Ankh-Morpork who were fed up with the way trolls in general were stereotyped as big, slow, violent and stupid. Initially their response was to knuckle around to an offender's house and pull off his arms. Things have since settled down a bit, and the SADL is now just another one of Ankh-Morpork's numerous pressure groups. [MAA, MP]

Skunk Club, Brewer Street, SoSo. You can buy drinks and watch females of various species take their clothes off (in the case of trolls, put their clothes *on*; trolls are normally stone naked, in their natural surroundings, and the males find the idea of the females wearing fifteen overcoats strangely exciting. They've never understood why humans seem to see things the other way – after all, they say, it's not as if you don't know what to expect. Most troll *robers* get embarrassed and rush off after putting on no more than fourteen layers of clothing).

Young Men's Pagan Association [LF]

Young Men's Reformed Cultists of the Ichor God Bel-Shamharoth Association [P]

Coalface. A troll privy cleaner in Ankh-Morpork. Sometime right-hand troll for CHRYSOPRASE, but not a henchman on account of failing to understand how to hench; subsequently enlisted into the militia by Corporal CARROT. Considered stupid by other trolls. This is like being considered flat by other carpets. [MAA]

Cohen the Barbarian. The greatest hero the Disc has ever produced, with an uncanny ability to get close to money. His father drove him out of the tribe when he was eleven. When first encountered, he was a skinny, little 87-year-old;

totally bald, with a beard almost down to his knees and a pair of matchstick legs on which varicose veins have traced the street map of quite a large city.

Cohen has only one working eye – the other is covered by a black patch. His thin body is a network of scars and twanging white-hot tendonitis. He has so many scars that you could play noughts and crosses on him, although your hand would be chopped off if you dared. His teeth quit long ago but, inspired by TWOFLOWER, he now has a set of dentures made of troll's teeth, which are diamond. He also suffers from lumbago, arthritis, backache, piles and bad digestion, and smells strongly of peppermints.

Although he can read, after a fashion, he has never really mastered the pen and he still signs his name with an 'x', which he usually spells wrong. He is, nevertheless, claimed as the author of *Inne Juste 7 Dayes I wille make You a Barbearian Hero!* There is some evidence that C. M. O. T. DIBBLER was involved in this publication.

He rolls his own cigarettes, and rides around on a horse which looks like a shrink-wrapped toast rack and has a haemorrhoid ring tied to the saddle. He carries a sword whose grip has been polished smooth by the passage of decades and whose blade has an edge like a badly maintained saw.

Cohen, in fact, just goes on doing what he has always done. He probably would like to retire but barbarian heroing is what he does best. Many a younger opponent has challenged him in the belief that he can't be any good because he is so old, whereas a moment's thought would suggest that since he's managed to become old he must be very good indeed. His answer, when asked what are the greatest things in life, is: 'hot water, good dentishtry and shoft lavatory paper'. [LF, S, TB]

Coin. The eighth son of the wizard IPSLORE THE RED and a SOURCERER. When we encounter him, he looks about ten years old, with a slender, young face framed by a mass of blond hair, a thin mouth and two golden eyes that seem to glow from within. He wears a simple white robe. He inherited his staff from his father; it is of black OCTIRON, so dark that it looks like a slit in the world, with a meshwork of silver and gold carvings that give it a rich and sinister tastelessness. Most wizards have no taste, of course, but this staff has a very stylish kind of tastelessness.

While acting under the influence of the staff, Coin causes wholesale devastation in Ankh-Morpork and puts at risk the continued existence of the Discworld itself. After his technical defeat by the wizard RINCEWIND, he retires to a better plane. [S]

Collar, Mrs. Bedder at the ASSASSINS' GUILD. TEPPIC's bedder in the sixth form (for those readers who have escaped the clutches of higher education, a bedder . . . well, makes beds, cleans the rooms, and so on. And nothing more.). [P]

Colon, Frederick. Sergeant in the Ankh-Morpork City WATCH. Age believed to be about sixty. A fat man with a huge red face like a harvest moon, he is married with three grown-up children, and some grandchildren. He likes the peace and quiet of the night and owes thirty years of happy marriage to the fact that Mrs Colon works all day gutting fish and he works all night.

Fred Colon used to be in an army (city unknown) but has been in the City Watch for thirty years, and has known Captain VIMES for over twenty years. He smokes a pipe, and wears sandals with his Watch uniform, along with a breast-plate with impressive pectoral muscles embossed on it, which his chest and stomach fit into in the same way that jelly fits into a mould.

He is the sort of man who, in a military career, will automatically gravitate to the post of sergeant. As a civilian, his natural role would be something like a sausage butcher – some job where a big red face and a tendency to sweat even in frosty weather are practically part of the specification.

Computers. The Disc's main known computer is the great computer of the skies on the Vortex Plains. It is an immense construction of grey and black slabs of stone, arranged in concentric circles and mystic avenues; a triumph of the silicon chunk, a miracle of modern masonic technology. Designed and built by druids.

However, the original computer has long been discarded and new circles are constantly being built, only to be replaced by even bigger circles before the first ones have been made to function properly.

Younger wizards in Unseen University are also known to be experimenting with computer-like devices; the only one so far chronicled is a vast assemblage of glass tubes full of busy ants. It may work if they can get all the bugs in it. (*See also* RIKTOR.) [LF, SM]

Confectionery School of Architecture. A style responsible for the house encountered by RINCEWIND and TWOFLOWER in *The Light Fantastic*; the style in which gingerbread houses are built. [LF]

Conina. One of the daughters of COHEN the Barbarian, and therefore genetically a barbarian heroine who, unfortunately, wants to be a hairdresser. A superb fighter, she carries a large number of concealed weapons, although absolutely

anything she can get hold of – a hairgrip, a piece of paper, a hamster – is used as a deadly weapon.

Her hair is long and almost pure white, her skin tanned. She is a demure and surprisingly small figure. Although she inherits her looks from her mother, a temple dancer, she inherits from her father sinews you could moor a boat with, reflexes like a snake on hot tin, a terrible urge to steal things and a sensation that she should be throwing a knife at everyone she meets. [S]

Conjurers' Guild.   Motto: NVNC ILLE EST MAGICVS.

Coat of arms: a shield, decorated with a vierge, dévêtée on a field, azure et etoilé. The whole bisected by a bend, sinister et indented.

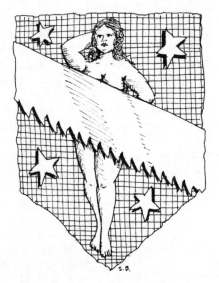

The Conjurers have a very small Guildhouse annoyingly close to Unseen University in Ankh-Morpork, but it's really more of a club house – there is no such thing as a professional conjurer, it being more of an evenings-and-weekends hobby for respectable men who do other jobs during the day. They tend to be jolly and fat and well balanced and inclined to drop their aitches and drink beer and, besides the usual cries of 'hey presto!', pepper their normal conversation with terms like 'many moons ago' and 'for my sins'. They go around with sad thin women in spangly tights and unsuitable feathers in their hair; it's impossible to imagine a conjurer without one (as in the Amazing Bonko and Doris). And they infuriate wizards by not realizing how lowly they are in the magical pecking order and by telling them jokes and slapping them on the back. They are very popular in Ankh-Morpork – knowing something is done by trickery and sleight-of-hand is somehow much more intriguing than boring old magic. (*See also* THAUMATUR-GISTS.) [ER]

Cool, Monks of. Tiny and exclusive monastery, hidden in a really cool and laid-back valley in the lower RAMTOPS. They're so cool they sometimes never get out of bed. [LL]

Coplei, Bosun. Bosun of the Omnian ship, the *Fin of God*. [SG]

Copolymer. The greatest storyteller in the history of the world. It is only unfortunate that this basic skill is confounded by a very poor memory and a lack of any practical narrative ability so that, for example, his actual stories tend to proceed on the lines of: 'It was a Thursday . . . no, I tell a lie, it was a Wednesday . . . when . . . what's his name, tip of my tongue, forget my own head next . . . set out . . . ' [P]

Copperhead (Mountain). One of the more impressive mountains in the RAM-TOP chain, on the edge of the Kingdom of LANCRE; the mountain and its lesser mountains and foothills are home to both dwarfs (in whose mines CARROT Ironfoun-dersson grew to a slightly concussed manhood) and trolls.

Cori Celesti. A spire of grey stone and green ice ten miles high at the Disc's hub. It rises through the clouds and supports at its peak the realm of DUNMANI-FESTIN, home of the Disc gods. As the AURORA CORIALIS discharges over it, it becomes a column of cold, coruscating fire. Other mountains cluster around it, and although these are no more mountains than termite mounds by comparison, in reality each one is a majestic assortment of cols, ridges, faces, cliffs, screes and glaciers that any normal mountain range would be happy to associate with.

Corksock. Proprietor of Corksock's Natty Clothing in Ankh-Morpork. [MAA]

Cornice Overlooking Broadway. A GARGOYLE on the Opera House, Ankh-Morpork. [MAA]

Cosmopilite, Mrs Marietta. Seamstress who lives at 3 Quirm Street, Ankh-Morpork. A little old lady. During the HOLY WOOD times she became a wardrobe mistress, becoming Vice President in Charge of Wardrobe.

She is known occasionally to run a haberdashery shop and is also a religious icon. This is because people always assume that wisdom is, well, more wise if it comes from a long way away. So while impressionable people in Ankh-Morpork follow the path of distant religious teachers with names like LOB-SANG and Gompa, the orange-robed, bald young men from the high mountains follow the Way of Mrs Cosmopilite (down to the shops, dropping in on her sister for a cup of tea, an appointment with the chiropodist, and then back home). She finds this very embarrassing.

Cotton, Corporal. Or is it Medium? or Handwash Only? Anyway, a Corporal in the . . . er . . . KLATCHIAN FOREIGN LEGION whose soldiers are so successful at joining to forget that they have to rely on the labels in their uniforms to remind themselves who they are. [SM]

Counterweight Continent. Almost a legend. A small continent, but equal in weight to all the mighty land masses on its opposite hemicircle. It is said to be made of gold – the area is also known as the Aurient, or 'place where the gold comes from'. But sailors searching for it return empty-handed or not at all. In fact, although gold is very common there, most of the mass is made up of vast deposits of OCTIRON deep within the crust. There is a very small amount of surreptitious trading. (*See also* AGATEAN EMPIRE.)

Counterwise wine.
(*See* RE-ANNUAL PLANTS.)

Counting pines. These grow right on the permanent snowline of the high RAMTOPS. They are one of the few known examples of borrowed evolution. The counting pines let other vegetables do their evolving for them, to save all the millions of years of trial and error. A pine seed coming to rest anywhere on the Disc immediately picks up the most effective local genetic code via morphic resonance and grows into whatever best suits the soil and climate, usually doing much better than the native trees themselves, which it usually usurps.

What makes them particularly noteworthy is the way they count. Being dimly aware that human beings learned to tell the age of a tree by counting the

rings, the original counting pines decided that this was *why humans cut trees down*. Overnight every counting pine readjusted its genetic code to produce, at about eye-level on its trunk, in pale letters, its precise age. Within a year they were felled almost to extinction by the ornamental house number-plate industry, and only a very few survive in hard-to-reach areas. [RM]

Crash. Son of a rich dealer in hay and feedstuffs. Also the leader of a would-be Music With Rocks In group, originally called Insanity. [SM]

Creator, the. A little rat-faced man, with a slightly put-upon voice made for complaining with. He created the Discworld while the main universe was being built, and it was obviously on a budget. It is clear that World Creation is a purely mechanical function and doesn't call for any godlike attributes. [E]

Creosote. Seriph of AL KHALI. A rather fat, middle-aged man whose chief pleasure is in writing very bad poetry and indulging in the kind of simple life only the very rich can afford. His grandfather built up the family fortune by somewhat mysterious means, which left the family in possession of a magic carpet, lamp and ring and a deep distrust of caves. Creosote, however, bears out the old Klatchian saying 'Going from very rich to quite poor in three generations' (Klatchian sayings lose something in the translation) and the money he did not squander on building an artificial Paradise around his palace was stolen from him by his evil Grand Vizier. Creosote is very fond of stories, and somehow manages to confuse the practice of narration with that of sex, and is given to accosting decent young women and asking them for a swift anecdote. The many trite comments that could be addended here will, out of decency, not be made. [S]

Cripple Mr Onion. Very complex card game played with great intensity on the Disc. Winning combinations include: Two Card Onion, Broken Flush, Three Card Onion, Double Bagel, a Five Card Onion, a Double Onion, a Triple Onion (three kings and three aces) and a Great Onion, which is unbeatable except with a perfect nine-card run. If you are unable to tell 1 from 11 you may lose money playing Cripple Mr Onion.

Cruces, Dr. Head tutor at the ASSASSINS' GUILD in Ankh-Morpork in TEPPIC's day. Later became Master of Assassins. A lean figure, with a soft voice. Came to a bad end in complex circumstances. [P, MAA]

Cuckoo, Clock-building. Lives in the RAMTOPS. It builds clocks to nest in, as a part of its courtship ritual. There is nothing very wonderful about this and it does not, emphatically, suggest that the universe was created according to any kind of Divine plan. The clocks are not very good and some of them lose as many as five minutes a day. [RM]

Cuddy, Acting-constable. First (genetic) dwarf member of the Ankh-Morpork City WATCH. One glass eye, the usual dwarfish steel-capped boots, and a tendency to use his battle axe rather than the official truncheon. [MAA]

The Assassins' Guild

Cumber, Miss. Teaches Language at the QUIRM COLLEGE FOR YOUNG LADIES. [SM]

Cumberbatch, Silas. Used to be a town crier in Ankh-Morpork. Now a member of the WATCH. Has a voice that can be heard three streets away, and no neighbours. [MAA]

Cupidor, Mme. Mistress of Mad King SOUP II of LANCRE. Owner of one of the world's most complex wigs, which housed a small take-away linguini shop. [LL]

Currency. The 'hardest' currency on Discworld (outside the AGATEAN EMPIRE) is the Ankh-Morpork dollar (one hundred pennies equals one dollar; in addition, ancient tradition says that ten pence is one shilling, twenty-five pence is half a ton, fifty pence is a nob/a ton/half a bar/a knocker).

The sequin-sized dollars are theoretically made of gold but the metal has been adulterated so often over recent years that, technically, there is more gold in an equivalent weight of sea water. In a sense, then, Ankh-Morpork is on the gold standard in all respects except the one of actually having any gold to speak of.

But Ankh-Morpork is, despite superficialities, a stable city. It is also, despite more superficialities, a rich one. Its dollar is therefore the currency of choice throughout the lands washed by the CIRCLE SEA. Other city states have their own currencies but it is wise to ensure that these are firmly linked to the dollar, because Ankh-Morpork is the only place with anything worth buying.

These trailing currencies include the Ephebian *derechmi* (fifty cercs = one derechmi), the Djelibeybian *talent* (worth one Ankh-Morpork penny) and the Omnian *obol*. The smallest denomination coin is the Zchloty leaden quarter *iotum*, which is worth less than the lead it is made of.

In the Agatean Empire, where gold is as plentiful as copper, the basic unit of currency is the *rhinu*. The rate of exchange with the dollar has never been officially established, other than to say that a handful of *rhinu* would significantly increase the amount of gold in circulation in the whole of the STO PLAINS.

The unit of currency in LANCRE is the Lancre penny, which weighs more than an ounce. Money is not much used in that country; currency is, in any case, only a universally accepted IOU, and Lancre is small enough for everyone to remember what they owe and are owed. The fact that they choose not to, and spend much of their time in highly enjoyable rows, is just part of civic life and whiles away the long winter evenings.

Curry, Annabel. Nine-year-old orphan of Corporal Curry of the City WATCH, whose upbringing is secretly paid for by Captain VIMES. [MAA]

Curry Gardens. Klatchian eating house in Ankh-Morpork. On the corner of God Street and Blood Alley. The sign on the back door reads: 'Curry Gardens. Kitchren Entlance. Keep Out. Ris Means You.' [M]

Cutangle. Past ARCHCHANCELLOR of Unseen University and Archmage of the Silver Star. An eighth-level wizard. He is very fat, with waggly jowls and extensive stomach regions. In his youth, he knew Esme Weatherwax, who lived in a neighbouring village. He was the first Archchancellor to admit a woman to Unseen University. [ER]

Cutangle, Acktur. Father of CUTANGLE, the Archchancellor. Used to live in a big house under Leaping Mountain. [ER]

Cutwell, Igneous. A young wizard in Wall Street, STO LAT. Cutwell is twenty years old, with curly hair and no beard. He is basically good-humoured, with a round, rather plump face – pink and white like a pork pie.

When we first meet him he is wearing a grubby hooded robe with frayed edges and a pointy hat which had seen better days. He lodges in a very untidy house with peeling plaster, and a blackened brass plaque by the door – 'Igneous Cutwell, D.M. (Unseen), Marster of the Infinit, Illuminartus, Wyzard to Princes, Gardian of the Sacred Portalls, If Out leave Maile with Mrs Nugent Next Door'. On the door is a heavy knocker that talks – a common bit of flammery used by a wizard to impress the customers.

The room inside combines the usual get-it-in-a-kit wizard's workroom, down to the stuffed alligator and things in jars, with the typical room of a student (that is to say, with no recognizable flat surfaces and a carpet that parts company with the sole of the foot only with reluctance).

Cutwell enjoys food, although not to the point of actually cooking any; he grazes, more or less on whatever seems to be available when the cupboards are rummaged at 3 a.m. When he is made Royal Recognizer, with a salary and a much better wardrobe, this tendency towards indiscriminate eating of anything vaguely organic and stationary means his highly decorated clothing achieves even greater degrees of decoration.

He is later promoted, by Queen KELI, to Wizard First Grade of STO LAT, and Ipississimuss. This is an important wizarding distinction that is only ever written down and never said aloud owing to the trouble this can cause among non-swimmers. [M]

Cyril. Myopic cockerel with a poor memory and dyslexia. Lives on Miss FLITWORTH's farm. [RM]

Dactylos, Goldeneyes Silverhand. The world is divided into those who can, and those who can afford to employ those who can. Unfortunately, the latter category often gets very jealous of its employees. History is full of the tragic stories of craftsmen who are killed or disabled or imprisoned by their masters to stop them running off and making something even better for someone else – people like Daedalus, Wayland Smith, and Hephaistos. Their Discworld cousin never knew when to give up. He made the Metal Warriors that guard the tomb of Pitchiu (for which he was given much gold and had his eyes put out and replaced with golden ones). He designed the Light Dams of the Great NEF (for which he was loaded with fine silks, and was then hamstrung so that he could not escape – but in fact he did escape, in a silk and bamboo flying machine). He built the Palace of the Seven Deserts (for which he was showered with silver and had his right hand cut off and replaced with a mechanical silver hand). He finally built the POTENT VOYAGER, the vessel intended for lowering over the Rim from KRULL (for which he was killed by the ARCH-ASTRONOMER). It would seem that his ingenuity lacked some vital facets in the area of self-preservation. [COM]

Dancers, the. Eight stones in a circle in the RAMTOPS. Each stone is about man-height and barely thicker than a fat man. They are not shaped or positioned in any significant way; someone has just dragged eight rocks into a rough circle, wide enough to throw a stone across. Made of thunderbolt iron, they look as if long ago they were melted and formed into their current shapes. Three of the stones have names: the first two are the Piper and the Drummer; the third is the Leaper, and no one in Lancre has yet been unfortunate enough to find out why.

To find them you must follow an over-grown path up to the moor land, a few miles from the town of LANCRE. People say that when it starts to rain, the rain always falls inside the circle a few seconds after it falls outside, as if the rain were coming from further away. Also, when clouds cross the sun, the light inside the circle fades a moment or two after the light outside. It is apparent that the meteoric iron of the stones contains magnetism, a very minor and little-understood form of energy on the Discworld. Because of this, the stones form a barrier between the human world and the world of the . . . lords and ladies. (*See* ELVES.) [LL]

Dances. Four dances are referred to in specific terms:

'*Gathering Peasecods*' and '*Gathering Sweet Lilacs*'. Both folk dances, but they are somewhat emasculated versions, since they are danced by the members of the Ankh-Morpork Folk Dance Society. Anything with 'folk' in it will refer, sooner or later, to sex.

Serpent Dance. A quaint Morporkian folkway which consists of getting rather drunk, holding the waist of the person in front, and then wobbling and giggling uproariously in a long crocodile that winds through as many rooms as possible, preferably one with breakables, while kicking one leg vaguely in time with the beat, or at least in time with some beat.

The Lancre Stick and Bucket Dance. A folk dance, shrouded in ancient mystery. Shouldn't be done when there are women present (in case of sexual morrisment); it is danced to the folk tune 'Mrs Widgery's Lodger'.

D'Arrangement, Lady Volentia. A thin, quite useless but good-natured high-born lady, who was fated to be a guest at a ball in GENUA when Granny WEATHERWAX needed to borrow a dress and a wig in a hurry. [WA]

Dblah, Cut-Me-Own-Hand-Off. Purveyor in OMNIA of suspiciously new holy relics, suspiciously old rancid sweetmeats on a stick, gritty figs and long-past-the-sell-by dates. Sidling everywhere and wearing the *djellaba* of the desert tribes, Dblah's nickname comes from his catch phrase: 'And at that price, I'm cutting me own hand off'. It is clear that he is a distant cousin, alter ego, psychic double or somatype of the even more famous Cut-Me-Own-Throat DIBBLER. [SG]

Death. The Defeater of Empires, the Swallower of Oceans, the Thief of Years, the Ultimate Reality, the Harvester of Mankind, the Assassin against Whom No Lock Will Hold, the only friend of the poor and the best doctor for the mortally wounded. An anthropomorphic personification. Almost the oldest creature in the universe (obviously something had to die first . . .)

He is a 7-foot-tall skeleton of polished bone, in whose eye sockets there are tiny points of light (usually blue). He normally wears a robe apparently woven of absolute darkness – and sometimes also a riding cloak fastened with a silver brooch bearing his own personal monogram, the Infinite Omega. He smells, not unpleasantly, of the air in old, forgotten rooms.

Death's scythe looks normal enough, except for the blade, which is so thin you can see through it – a pale blue shimmer that could slice flame and chop sound. His sword has the same ice-blue, shadow-thin blade, of the extreme thinness necessary to separate body from soul.

His face, of necessity, is frozen into a calcareous grin. His voice is felt rather than heard. He is seen only by cats, professional practitioners of magic, and those who are about to die or are already dead – although there is some evidence that he can be glimpsed by those in a heightened state of awareness, a not uncommon state given the Discworld's normal alarums. When he needs to communicate with the living (i.e. those who are going to continue living) he is perceived very vaguely by them in some form that does not disturb them. There was a period when he made an effort to appear in whatever form the client expected (scarab beetles, black dragons, and so on). This foundered because it was usually impossible to know what the client was expecting until after they were dead. He decided that, since no one ever really expected to die anyway, he might as well please himself and he henceforth stuck to the familiar black-cowled robe.

His horse, though pale as per traditional specification, is entirely alive and called BINKY. Death once tried a skeleton horse after seeing a woodcut of himself on one – Death is easily influenced by that sort of thing – but he had to keep stopping to wire bits back on. The fiery steed that he tried next used to set fire to the stables.

Despite rumour, he is not cruel. He is just terribly, terribly good at his job. It is said that he doesn't get angry, because anger is an emotion, and for emotion you need glands; however, he does seem to be capable of a piece of intellectual disapproval which has a very similar effect. He is a traditionalist who prides himself on his personal service, and, despite the absence of glands, can become depressed when this is not appreciated.

Humanity intrigues Death. He is particularly fascinated by mankind's ability to complicate an existence which, from Death's point of view, is momentary. He appears to spend a lot of time trying to learn, by logical deduction, the things that humanity takes for granted. In the process, he seems to have developed what can only be called preferences and likings – for cats, for example, and curry. He has tried to take up the banjo, but lacks any skill with such a living thing as music.

Death has a property not locatable on any normal atlas, on which he has called into being a house and garden. There are no colours there except black, white and shades of grey; Death could use others but fails to see their significance. And, because he almost by definition lacks true creative ability – he can only copy what he has seen – no real time passes in his domain. Nor do things live or grow in the normal sense, unless they are brought in from outside, but they exist in an apparently unchanging, healthy state.

He appears to derive his opinion of how he should live by observing people, but the nuances consistently escape him. He has a bedroom, for example, because although Death never sleeps, it's right that houses have bedrooms. He also has a bathroom, although the ablutionary fixtures were supplied by a plumber from Ankh-Morpork because plumbing is among those activities where Death's constructive abilities find themselves cramped; he was not aware that pipes were hollow inside, for example. On his dressing table he has a pair of silver-backed hairbrushes and a little glass tray for cufflinks, despite having neither hair nor cuffs. He thinks that's what he ought to have.

As with all creatures that have existence, Death has an hourglass/lifetimer that measures the length of his days. His is several times the size of normal people's glasses, and is black, thin and decorated with a complicated skull-and-bones motif. It has no sand in it.

There is a strong suggestion in the books that Death is somehow *on our side*.

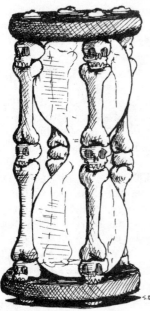

Death and being dead. From the point of view of the recently dead, the world suddenly looks at one and the same time very complicated and very simple.

It is complicated because, while death frees the mind from the strait-jacket of three dimensions, it also cuts it away from TIME, which is only another dimension. So a cat can be seen as a tiny kitten and a fat, half-blind old moggy and every stage in between. All at once. Since it will have started off small it will look like a white, cat-shaped carrot – a description that will have to do until people invent proper four-dimensional adjectives (generally, however, the dead stick to normal temporal perception by force of habit, one of the strongest forces in the universe).

It is simple, on the other hand, because the self-delusion that attends the living is immediately stripped away. The dead see the world as real for the first time.

There appears on Discworld, as everywhere else, to be no general consensus about the afterlife. Some religions believe that the dead must journey across a vast empty desert, or sea, or range of metaphorical mountains, in order to receive some kind of judgement at the end. There are various heavens and hells, and it appears that the soul's ultimate destination is that place where its owner, shorn by death of all self-deception, believes he or she ought to go. Which suggests that they won't go to any kind of hell if they don't know about it, a depressing thought that should call for the instant cessation of all missionary activity.

Basically, everyone gets what they think is coming to them. This does not seem fair, but then no one ever said it would be.

d'Eath, Edward. The thirty-seventh Lord d'Eath. A trained and qualified assassin who was also the first person ever to pass the post-graduate course with full marks. Although the family were at one time very rich, the money was frittered away and Edward, dreaming of better days, was forced into cramped lodgings in Kingsway in Ankh-Morpork. As sometimes happens with people who don't mix with other humans often enough to have their mental clocks reset to 'sanity', he developed strange notions and became obsessed with Ankh-Morpork's royal heritage and its noble past, i.e. the time when the d'Eaths had money and power. He very foolishly set in motion the events of *Men At Arms* and shortly afterwards met his death (no relation). [MAA]

Death, House of. The Farewell Tour.

The land on which DEATH's house rests floats in space. It can only be described as raw surface. Seen edge on, it has no apparent thickness. When walked on it appears quite solid. To get to the house we walk across the black moors, through a gate and up a little path leading to a small black house, backed by an extensive garden. Deep in the garden is an apparently bottomless pit, through which souls travel to their next destination. There are extensive areas of topiary and an ornamental fish pond. In keeping with Death's erratic approach to matters of taste, there are also cheery little skeletal garden gnomes.

There is a bird table. One may speculate upon the nature of the birds.

There is an orchard, where black apple trees grow black fruit. Among the trees are Death's beehives; the bees are big, black and slow in their movements, storing glistening black honey in pure white combs. It's anyone's guess what it tastes like, or what would happen to any living person who ate it.

On the front lawn is a sundial. It has no gnomon, because no time passes here (see below) and in any case there is no sun. The sky is night-black, with visible stars, although the landscape is quite brilliantly illuminated.

The back garden contains a large vegetable patch. Real plants grow here, from real seeds brought from the World and fed with compost derived from the stables. There is a tendency, however, for all the plants to be black. It may be that at some genetic level they enter into the spirit of the thing. Surrounding the garden are rolling fields of corn, making a strange golden splash of colour in the otherwise sombre landscape. Elsewhere, within the house as well as in the garden, there is no colour other than that which has been imported from the World by the human occupants.

To one side of the house, as we enter, is the courtyard leading to the stable block, from which a stone-flagged passageway leads into the main hall of the house. We, however, are going to use the front door.

Notice the mat with 'Welcome' on it. The hall beyond is obviously much bigger than the whole house appears to be from the outside. This is Death's domain; dimensions are entirely arbitrary and the size of rooms depends entirely upon the degree of perception of the observer.

For example, this is Death's observation of his servant ALBERT bringing him a cup of tea:

Albert approached very carefully.

It had continually puzzled Death in his more introspective moments, and this was one of them, why his servant always walked the same path across the floor.

I MEAN, he thought, CONSIDER THE SIZE OF THE ROOM . . .

. . . which went on to infinity, or as near infinity as makes no difference. In fact it was about a mile. That's big for a room, whereas infinity you can hardly see.

Death had got rather flustered when he'd created the house. Time and space were things to be manipulated, not obeyed. The internal dimensions had been a little too generous. He'd forgotten to make the outside bigger than the inside. It was the same with the garden. When he'd begun to take a little more interest in these things he'd realized the role people seemed to think that colour played in concepts like, for example, roses. But he'd made them black. He liked black. It went with anything. It went with everything, sooner or later.

The humans he'd known – and there had been a few – had responded to the impossible size of the rooms in a strange way, by simply ignoring them.

Take Albert, now. The big door had opened, Albert had stepped through, carefully balancing a cup and saucer . . .

. . . and a moment later had been well inside the room, on the edge of the relatively small square of carpet that surrounded Death's desk. Death gave up wondering how Albert covered the intervening space when it dawned on him that, to his servant, there was no intervening space . . .

At this point it should be added that, since all dimensions here have a certain subjective element, so also does the dimension of TIME. No time passes in the real sense. But *something* passes; a dropped cup will hit the floor and break, so there must be some 'time' in which this can happen and some framework in which the cup is *now* broken but was *once* whole. What there appears to be, in fact, is a sort of subjective recirculating time, very similar to that experienced in DJELIBEYBI owing to the temporal braking power of its many pyramids. It is as though, instead of proceeding in a straight line like a train, time spins gently in a circle like a carousel; people can talk and move about and even appear to travel, while in fact never actually going anywhere.

The hall is illuminated by tall, narrow windows, is full of doors and is decorated with a lot of funeral drapes. The arched doorways are decorated with a skull-and-bones motif. To one side is an umbrella stand with a scythe in it. The floor is covered with black and white tiles.

Ahead of us are two curved wooden staircases, leading to a bare wooden corridor lined with yellow candles set in holders in the walls. This leads to the private area of the house – the bedrooms and other facilities. The staircases are covered with strange and disturbing carvings, which do not bear close examination, possibly because they are hor-

rible but more probably because of general tastelessness. (No one on the Disc has yet sold paintings on black velvet, or pictures of jolly dogs sitting at the table having dinner, but if they did, and if by chance they sold them at Death's door, he would certainly buy several copies. Death, as has been intimated elsewhere, has no artistic taste. It is not simply that he cannot see the difference between, say, the *Mona Ogg* and a set of three plaster flying ducks – for him there is no difference. In fact, he would probably prefer the ducks, which are more cheerful. He likes a bit of life around the place.)

Occupying the space between the staircases is a large grandfather clock. Two things about the clock are worthy of notice: first, it has a very long pendulum, with a knife-edged and very sharp weight. Second, the clock has no hands because there is, strictly speaking, nothing for it to measure.

Then there is the passageway leading to the stables. Another one leads eventually to Death's study. In real terms his study is probably more than a mile across, with shadows of what might be wheels and strange machinery in its distant recesses. The rest of the furniture, out of deference to the house's human occupants, is grouped on a square of carpet in what has to be called the 'conceptual' room.

Large hourglasses cover every flat surface – work in progress, as it were. There are also a lot of fat, yellow and runny candles. Apart from the imposing and ornate desk and large, leather swivel-chair, the room also contains bookcases, more shelves of hourglasses, a large lectern with a map on it and a black baize card table. In one corner and dominating the room, however, is a large disc of the world. This magnificent feature is complete down to solid silver elephants standing on the back of a Great A'TUIN cast in bronze and more than a metre long. The rivers are picked out in veins of jade, the deserts are powdered diamonds and the most notable cities are picked out in precious stones.

On the scarred woodwork of the desk is a large ledger, an abacus, an inkwell and pen and a scythe-shaped paper knife. There is also what can only be called an executive toy (you swing one ball against a small lead slab, where it stops). As we turn to leave the room we note the sword, Death's other working tool, in the rack by the door.

We turn left into the corridor and unlock the door into the long Lifetimer room.

This tiled room is vast by any or all standards. In here are serried rows of hourglasses of all manner of designs, stretching away into the distance on row after row of shelves. Here and there the shelves are divided by stone pillars inscribed with angular markings. The sound in this room, of hissing sand, is deafening (but the discerning may hear the 'pop' and 'ping' as empty hourglasses vanish and new, full ones reappear elsewhere).

Leaving the roaring sand behind us we return to the main hallway and find, through another door, the extensive library of the house. As we open the door with its protesting creak (there is no rust; Death knows that some doors *should* creak) a gust of warm air drifts out. Entering the book-lined room, one is struck immediately by the sound of subdued scratching, as of a room full of clerks all writing away with quill pens. This is the library of the autobiographies – each book writing itself as its subject drifts through their life.

Lighting a candle to supplement the light from the high windows and moving aside the rickety library ladder, we come to a little alcove and pass through another door which leads us down stone steps into the velvet gloom of the stack. In this vast space are stored biographies more than five hundred years old. The room is as dark and silent as a cave deep underground. The shelves are barely far enough apart for one person to walk between them and they tower up well beyond the dome of our candlelight. The dusty floor records our footprints.

Everyone who ever lived and died is recorded here. Go far enough through the book-lined darkness and the books become scrolls, the scrolls become wax tablets, the tablets become mere scratchy stones . . .

And now our tour takes us back, through the entrance hall and down a few steps into the kitchen. Again, this is a smaller room within a great black cavern, but the little square of light suggests a low, warm room, with copper pans hanging from the non-existent ceiling and a vast black iron stove – a Little Moloch, almost certainly imported from Ankh-Morpork – along the whole of one wall (or edge). In the centre of the floor is a white scrubbed table and some chairs. On another wall is a set of bells connecting with the rest of the house.

One of them jangles.

That's the back door over there. I should use it quickly, if I were you . . .

Death, New. A hooded figure, carrying a scythe and riding a burning skeletal steed. Taller even than DEATH himself, he had no face . . . smoke curled formlessly between the top of his robe and a golden crown. Called into existence as a result of Death's temporary retirement, and lacking any of the empathy resulting from thousands of years of close personal contact with humanity. [RM]

Death of Rats. About six inches high, the

Death of Rats wears a black robe and holds a small scythe in one skeletal paw or, when he needs to hurry and wants to use all four legs, his mouth. He has a bone-white nose with brittle grey whiskers protruding from its shadowy hood. As his name suggests, he specializes in rats but also does gerbils, mice and hamsters if it is DEATH's busy time.

Death's Glory. Dry fly invented by DEATH when he was looking for ways of having Fun. He'd heard that fishing was fun. In fact fishing is like being dead, but with the additional disadvantage of being alive to experience it. [M]

Dehydrated Ocean. Sited at the heart of the Great NEF. Water on the Disc has an uncommon fourth state, caused by intense heat combined with the strange desiccating effects of OCTARINE light; it dehydrates, leaving a silvery residue like free-flowing sand through which a well-designed hull can glide with ease. Said to have very strange fish. Dehydrated water can easily be reconstituted by adding water. [COM]

Deities and supernatural beings. There are 3,000 known major gods on the Disc, and more are discovered by research theologians every week.

It is quite probable that some deities feature under many different names. In fact many gods, by means of false noses and other props, can appear in religious chronicles under anything up to a hundred different names and descriptions.

Since belief is the true life-force of the gods, this is a good way of getting as much of it as they can – rather like working in a fast-food joint or running a minicab in your spare time, although it is more on the level of fraudulently claiming a thousand different Social Security Giros by means of forged IDs.

It seems likely that this is particularly prevalent in DJELIBEYBI, where the plethora of gods with short explosive names, like Nat, Wat and Zak, suggests a particularly profitable scam by someone with a dictionary and little imagination.

Known gods – and 'god-like entities'* include:

Alohura, Goddess of Lightning (beTrobi) [COM]
Astoria, Goddess of Love (Ephebe) [SG]
AZRAEL
Bast, Cat-Headed God (Djeli) [P]
BEL-SHAMHAROTH
Bin (Djeli) [P]
BLIND IO

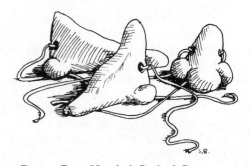

Bunu, Goat-Headed God of Goats (Djeli) [P]
Cephnet (Djeli) [P]
Cephut, God of Cutlery (Djeli) [P]
Chance [COM]
Chefet, Dog-Headed God of Metalwork (Djeli) [P]
Chondrodite, God of Love (Troll) [MP]
Cubal, Fire God (Ephebe) [SG]
DEATH
Destiny [COM, M]
Dhek (Djeli) [P]
F'rum [S]
Famine [LF]

*i.e., not human, but immensely powerful, capricious, self-centred and generally amoral; unfortunately, this definition includes most monsters and demons as well, but there you are.

FATE

Fedecks, Messenger of the Gods (Ephebe) [SG]

Fhez, Crocodile-Headed God of the Lower Djel (Djeli) [P]

Flatulus, God of the Winds (Ephebe) [SG]

Fon (Djeli) [P]

Foorgol, God of Avalanches [SG]

Gigalith, God of Wisdom (Troll) [MP]

Grune, God of Unseasonal Fruit [RM]

Hast (Djeli) [P]

Hat, Vulture-Headed God of Unexpected Guests (Djeli) [P]

HERNE THE HUNTED

Herpentine Triskeles (Djeli) [P]

Hinki [RM]

HOKI of the Woods, Hoki the Jokester

Hotologa Andrews (Genua) [WA]

Hyperopia, Goddess of Shoes [RM]

Io (Djeli) [P]

Jeht, Boatman of the Solar Orb (Djeli) [P]

Jimi, God of Beggars [MAA]

Juf, Cobra-Headed God of Papyrus (Djeli) [P]

Ket, Ibis-Headed God of Justice (Djeli) [P]

Khefin, Two-Faced God of Gateways (Djeli) [P]

Lady Bon Anna (Genua) [WA]

LUCK (the Lady)

Mister Safeway (Genua) [WA]

Moon Goddess (Druidic) [LF]

Nept (Djeli) [P]

Nesh (Djeli) [P]

Net (Djeli) [P]

Night [COM]

OFFLER, Crocodile God

OM

Ordpor the Tasteless [RM]

Orexis-Nupt (Djeli) [P]

Orm, Great [P]

P'tang P'tang, Newt God [SG]

Patina, Goddess of Wisdom (Ephebe) [SG]

Pestilence [LF]

Petulia, Goddess of Negotiable Affection (Ephebe) [SG]

Ptooie (Djeli) [P]

Put, Lion-Headed God of Justice (Djeli) [P]

QUEZOVERCOATL, the Feathered Boa (Tezuman)

Reg, God of Club Musicians [SM]

Sandelfon, God of Corridors [RM]

Sarduk, Goddess of Caves (Djeli) [P]

Scrab, Pusher of the Ball of the Sun (Djeli) [P]

Sea Queen, the [SG]

Sessifet, Goddess of the Afternoon (Djeli) [P]

Set (Djeli) [P]

Seven-Handed Sek [M]

Silicarous, God of Good Fortune (Troll) [MP]

Silur, Catfish-Headed God (Djeli) [P]

Skelde, Spirit of the Smoke [LF]

Sky God [LF]

Smimto, God of Wine (Tsort) [SG]

Sot (Djeli) [P]

Steikhegel, God of Isolated Cow Byres [M]

Stride Wide Man (Genua) [WA]

Syncope (Djeli) [P]

Teg, Horse-Headed God of Agriculture (Djeli) [P]

Thrrp, Charioteer of the Sun (Djeli) [P]

Thrume [RM]

Topaxci, God of the Red Mushroom [LF]

Tuvelpit, God of Wine (Ephebe) [SG]

Tzut, Snake-Headed God of the Upper Djel (Djeli) [P]

Umcherrel, Soul of the Forest [LF]

Ur Gilash [SG]

Vut, Dog-Headed God of the Evening (Djeli) [P]

War [LF]

What, Sky Goddess (Djeli) [P]

Yay (Djeli) [P]

Zephyrus, God of Slight Breezes [COM]

Delcross, Miss. Co-founder, with Miss BUTTS, of the QUIRM COLLEGE FOR YOUNG LADIES. She teaches Biology and Hygiene, and is keen on eurythmics. [SM]

Demonologists, nature of. Surreptitious, pale men who get up to complicated things in darkened rooms and have damp, weak handshakes. Technically they are wizards, although Unseen University frowns on the practice. [E]

Demons. Demons have existed on the Disc for at least as long as the gods, who in many ways they closely resemble. Indeed, some – such as QUEZOVERCOATL – can be both at the same time. The difference is basically the same as that between terrorists and freedom fighters.

Demons don't breathe. They belong to the same space–time continuum, more or less, as humans, and have a deep and abiding interest in humanity's day-to-day affairs. Their home is a spacious dimension close to reality, traditionally decorated in shades of flame and maintained at roasting point. This isn't actually necessary, but if there is one thing that your average demon is, it is a traditionalist (in fact it's hard to think of many other things that it is; a demon is generally as capable of original thought as a parrot is capable of original swearwords).

In the centre of the inferno, rising majestically from a lake of lava substitute and with unparalleled views of the Eight Circles, lies the city of Pandemonium.

As has been indicated, demons are not great innovative thinkers and really need the spice of human ingenuity. They are strong believers in precedence and hierarchy. Numb and mindless stupidity is part of what being a demon is all about.

Smaller and more controllable varieties of demon may be employed in picture boxes, watches, doorknockers and hinges. After a few years, however, they invariably escape or simply evaporate.

Demons we have met include:
ASTFGL
Azaremoth [E]
Beezlemoth, Earl [E]
Drazometh the Putrid, Duke [E]
QUEZOVERCOATL
Riinjswin [E]
URGLEFLOGGAH
Vizzimuth [E]
Winswin [E]
WXRTHLTL-JWLPKLZ

Demurrage, Aliss. Black Aliss. A very powerful witch, who lived near the forest of Skund (itself an area of strong residual magic). Some of her best-known exploits involved turning a pumpkin into a royal coach and sending a whole palace to sleep for a hundred years.

She was not called Black Aliss because of her exploits, which were the result of bad temper rather than actual malice. She was called Black Aliss because of her fingernails. And her teeth. She had a sweet tooth and as a result used to live in a real gingerbread cottage (similar to the one still standing when discovered by RINCEWIND and TWOFLOWER in *The Light Fantastic*); this followed early experiments with broccoli and bran cottages, which didn't seem to have the same frisson and smelled a lot worse. All the same, modern witches declare that she never really ate anyone. Well, perhaps a *few* people, but only rarely, and more or less by accident and short-sightedness, and that hardly made her a *cannibal*. A couple of kids shoved her into her own oven in the end.

She is generally spoken of by modern witches, who live in more democratic times when such ungoverned excesses of power are frowned upon, with a sort of wistful disapproval.

Detritus. A troll. In many ways, *the* troll. He is the troll many people in Ankh-Morpork, particularly University students, think of when they hear the word, bringing back as it does vague memories of sudden concussion and extreme pain.

He is rangy rather than huge (for a troll) and is widely believed to have an IQ the size of a walnut. His knuckles drag on the ground, but that is not unusual among trolls, although his ability to touch the ground with his lower lip when moving fast is the envy of many. Like most of his fellows, when not employed in some office that requires a uniform he wears a ragged loincloth to cover whatever it is that trolls feel it is necessary to conceal.

Lacking any other skill and finding even unskilled labour mentally taxing, Detritus finds work anywhere a hired fist is required. When first encountered, he was working as a splatter at the Mended DRUM in Ankh-Morpork (like a bouncer, but trolls use more force) but he has since become upwardly mobile, or at least horizontally portable. His career began to move when he found employment hitting people in the HOLY WOOD moving picture industry, where he met RUBY, a singer.

It is obvious that her influence caused him to rethink his life goals, because he later became an Acting-constable in the Ankh-Morpork City WATCH, a profession in which his unquestioning obedience to orders and a loud voice proved a major, or at least sergeant, advantage.

Detritus is by no means particularly evil, although he has appeared on evil's payroll. Rather, he represents your basic unreconstructed troll. Most trolls, when they've settled down in Ankh-Morpork, tend to adopt some human ways, not

always to the benefit of society. But Detritus is fundamentally, and very nearly literally, the salt of the earth, a throwback (or, given the trollish view of TIME, a throw-forward) to the days when all a troll needed was a punch that could smash trees.

Devant-Molei, Rosie. Runs the SUNSHINE SANCTUARY FOR SICK DRAGONS in Ankh-Morpork. Described as having the build of someone who could pick up carthorses in one hand and shoe them with the other. One of a particular type of high-born lady who is seldom seen not wearing rubber boots. [GG]

Devereaux. Innkeeper in GENUA. Not fat or red-faced, and this was practically a hanging offence under Genua's strange laws. [WA]

DeVice, Amanita. One of DIAMANDA's coven in LANCRE. She has a dagger and skull tattoo on her arm (drawn in ink). [LL]

Diamanda. Her real name is Lucy Tockley, but she felt that Diamanda was more witchy, and the mere fact that someone could think a phrase like that should tell us everything about them that we need to know. And, indeed, she does paint her nails black, and wears black lace and a floppy black velvet hat with a veil and does all the other necro-nerdy things that people do when they are young and therefore immortal. This naturally skinny seventeen-year-old was the leader of the self-taught coven of young girls in LANCRE, up until Granny WEATHERWAX found out about it. [LL]

Dibbler, Cut-Me-Own-Throat. Wheresoever two or three are gathered together, someone else will turn up and try to sell them something hot in a bun. This person will probably be C. M. O. T. Dibbler.

Dibbler is the purveyor of absolutely anything that can be sold hurriedly from an open suitcase in a busy street. He likes to describe himself as a merchant adventurer; everyone else likes to describe him as an itinerant pedlar whose money-making schemes are always let down by some small but vital flaw, such as trying to sell things he doesn't own or that don't work or, sometimes, don't even exist. Quite often they describe him as someone they would like to catch up with.

He is not, strictly speaking, a criminal.

In his natural state – i.e., when not inspired to take advantage of some passing fad or problem in Ankh-Morpork – Dibbler sells meat pies and sausages-in-a-bun from a tray around his neck or, when funds permit, a barrow. There is no need to describe these items, even as food. Dibbler takes the view that anything that has at any time been any part of a pig, or even near a pig, or possibly even within earshot of a pig, can be called pork. His guiding principle is that with enough mustard people will eat anything (his brief foray into ethnic food for trolls, a silicareous species, proved that Dibbler was even capable of finding stale rock).

He is skinny, and when regarding him people are moved to recall that humans have some kind of small rodent somewhere in their ancestry. He speaks very quickly, with many a sidelong glance. He is known to have premises in a cellar near the SHADES in Ankh-Morpork. No one knows where he actually lives. Since going to sleep might involve missing a wonderful business opportunity he possibly never does so.

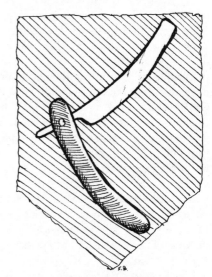

Dibbler's coat of arms

Dibbler is also the seller of mail-order lessons on the Path of the Scorpion, a self-defence system, under the name of Grand Master Lobsang Dibbler. He also served short stints as moving pictures mogul and music industry promoter, two occupations that came as near to suiting his peculiar talents as any he has ever tried.

He feels that it is not his fault that perfectly sound business propositions have a habit of exploding or tasting awful.

Dibbler, Solstice ('Soll'). C. M. O. T. DIB-BLER's nephew. Was heavily involved in the moving picture industry, where he showed a business acumen very nearly equal to that of his uncle. But he has a more modern outlook. Should mobile phones ever be invented on the Discworld, one feels, then Soll will be the first to have one (although he will not have anyone to talk to, of course). [MP]

Didactylos. Ephebian philosopher. This short, bald, blind man in a grubby toga and with a petulant, reedy voice is never-theless one of the most quoted and popu-lar philosophers of all time. His wise sayings are quoted throughout the multi-verse (and include such axioms as 'There'll be another one along in a minute', 'It's a funny old world', 'It'll all end in tears', 'You cannot trust the bas-tards an inch,' and so on). At one time he carried a lantern, telling people that he was looking for an honest man, but this was probably just a pose and an attempt to get money. He lives in a barrel and would probably benefit from bathing rather more often, or at all.

He reasoned that if the Disc is 10,000 miles across and light travels at about the speed of sound, then the sun has to travel at least 35,000 miles in its orbit every day, or twice as fast as its own light. This means that it is, from the standpoint of modern physics, a tachyon (a scientific term meaning magical thing).

He was made a bishop of the Omnian church despite not believing in any gods, although this is perfectly OK for a modern bishop. [SG]

Dil. Embalmer in the Kingdom of DJELI-BEYBI. Thirty-five years' experience in the funeral business. A solid and thoughtful man, with that tranquillity of mind and philosophical outlook that comes from spending most of your work-ing day up to the elbows in a dead king. [P]

Diome. Witch of the Night. An adventur-ess. Probably not a proper witch, because real witches would burst out laughing at the name. [E]

Dios. High Priest in DJELIBEYBI. First Minister and High Priest among High Priests.

Dios was (or is, or will be – certain temporal uncertainties make the choice of tense very difficult) a tall, bald man with an impressive nose. In his role as general adviser to the ruler he spoke (speaks, etc.) softly but carried a big stick, in this case his staff of office – sym-bolic snakes wrapped round an allegori-cal camel prod.

He ate (we will settle on the past tense) no meat, believing that it diluted and tarnished the soul, and lived for 7,000 years by regularly sleeping in a pyramid, which renewed him or, more accurately, recycled him. In fact it could be said that he was only 7,000 years old from the point of view of an external cal-endar; more realistically, he had for most of that time been living the same day over and over again. Since the palace days on Djelibeybi were a complex net-work of rigidly observed ritual, this suited him quite well. There was never any *need* to do anything differently.

Consequently he was a man of tra-dition and organization – indeed, he con-sidered that there are no things more important.

Dios, although a devout priest, was not a naturally religious man. He felt that it was not a desirable quality in a high priest; it affected your judgement, and made you 'unsound'. He felt that the gods were necessary, but he required that they should keep out of the way and leave him to get on with things. [P]

Discworld, the. As all will know, the Discworld is a flat planet – like a geological pizza, but without the anchovies. It offers sights far more impressive than those found in universes built by Creators with less imagination but more mechanical aptitude. It exists right on the edge of Reality; the least little things can break through from the other side. It is allowed to exist either because of some impossible blip on the curve of probability, or because the gods enjoy a joke as much as anyone else. More than most people, in fact.

It was the Ephebian philosopher EXPLETIUS who first proved that the Disc was 10,000 miles across. Viewers from space can appreciate in full its vast, 30,000-mile circumference, garlanded by the long Rimfall, where the seas of the Disc drop endlessly into space. It gives the impression, with its continents, archipelagos, seas, deserts, mountain ranges, that the Creator designed it specifically to be looked at from above.

The Disc revolves at a rate of about once every 800 days. This means that, except at the Hub, a full astronomical year contains eight seasons, or two each of the classical four (*see* CALENDARS).

Its tiny orbiting sunlet, with prominences no bigger than croquet hoops, maintains a fixed elliptical orbit, while the Disc revolves beneath it. The little moon shines by its own light, owing to the cramped and rather inefficient astronomical arrangements.

The Hub, dominated by the spire of CORI CELESTI, is never closely warmed by the weak sun and the lands there are permanently locked in permafrost. The Rim, on the other hand, is a region of sunny islands and balmy days. From the RAMTOPS' highest peaks you can see all the way to the Rim Ocean that runs around the edge of the world, since the Discworld, being flat, has no horizon in the real sense of the word.

There appear to be at least four major continental masses:

The (unnamed) continent of which the STO PLAINS and the Ramtops are a major feature: this stretches all the way to the Hub and finishes, at least in the area of Ankh-Morpork, at the CIRCLE SEA. Less than half of it has been covered in the chronicles, and there must be far more land on the far side of the Ramtops. So far we know only of GENUA and some miscellaneous small countries.

KLATCH (the continent): this is detailed elsewhere, but here and now we might not be far wrong in thinking of Klatch as the Discworld's Africa, with a collection of 'Mediterranean' countries shading into the large, and more or less unexplored, plains of HERSHEBA and HOWONDALAND.

The COUNTERWEIGHT CONTINENT: smaller than either of the above, and occupied by an advanced civilization.

'xxxx': the name as it appears on maps of the mysterious fourth continent, once reached by people from Ankh-Morpork, now lost.

There have been other continents, which have sunk, blown up or simply disappeared. This sort of thing happens all the time, even on the best-regulated planets.

And there, below the mines and sea-ooze and fake fossil bones put there by a Creator with nothing better to do than upset archaeologists and give them silly ideas, is Great A'TUIN.

Chaotic as it sometimes appears, the Discworld clearly runs on a special set of natural laws, or at least on guidelines. There is gravity. There is cause-and-effect. There is eventuality – things happen after other things. After that, it becomes a little more confusing. The following theory can be gingerly advanced:

The Discworld should not exist. Flatness is not a natural state for a planet. Turtles should grow only so big. The fact that it *does* exist means that it occupies an area of space where reality is extremely thin, where 'should be' no longer has the veto it has in the rest of the universe. The Discworld creates an extremely deep well in Reality in much the same way as an incontinent Black Hole creates a huge gravity well in the notorious rubber sheet of the universe.

The resulting tension seems to have created a permanent flux which, for want of a better word, we can call magic. There are several secondary effects, because the pressure of reality is so weak. Things that might *nearly* exist in a 'real' world – back up there on the rubber sheet – have no difficulty at all in existing in quite a natural state in the Discworld universe; so here there *will* be dragons, unicorns, sea serpents and so on. The rules are relaxed.

But there are additional factors which make up Discworld 'physics'. These could be called:

a) Life force
b) The Power of Metaphor and Belief
c) Narrative Causality

Life, it has been said, has a tendency to exist. It has even been argued that the Universe has been *designed* in order that this should happen, although of course it is hard for a life that does not exist to look around and declare that the Universe has clearly been designed not to come into being. Certainly on the Discworld life is a very common commodity. Whatever obstacles there are to

life elsewhere are that much weaker on Discworld. Almost anything can be alive and develop, if not intelligence at least a point of view. Rocks, thunderstorms and even entire buildings can, in the right circumstances, demonstrate their literal vitality.

Then there is metaphor. On Discworld, metaphor has a disturbing tendency to take itself seriously. Death as a robed skeleton is not just a metaphor for the process of mortality; he really *is* a robed skeleton, with a rich existence of his own. On Discworld, belief is a potent force. What is believed in strongly enough is real. (Conversely, what is not believed can't be real regardless of the fact of its existence. For example, the dog GASPODE can talk. But most people cannot hear him when he does because they know, in their soul, that dogs do *not* talk. Any dog who appears to be talking, says their brain, is a statistical fluke and can therefore safely be ignored.) Discworld gods exist because people believe in them, and their power waxes and wanes with the strength of that belief. There is nothing very magical in this. After all, half the power of witches – and wizards, too, for that matter – lies in the fact that they advertise what they are. The pointy hats are a kind of power-dressing; they're no different from the white coats worn by any actor hawking washing powder. If people believe you can do magic you're halfway there already.

Finally there is narrative causality, the power of stories. This is perhaps the strongest force of all and, again, weaker echoes of it are found in this world. Not for nothing do we say: History repeats. History does have patterns, clichés of time. People find themselves again and again in situations where they are playing roles as surely as if a script had been thrust into their hands: the Marital Row, the Job Interview, the Man Behind has Shunted You at the Traffic Lights, the Bastard. And there are the bigger patterns: the rise of empires, the spread of civilizations . . . Again and again humans tread the same dance through life, and with each dance the path becomes deeper and harder to leave.

The sense of predestination permeates Discworld. History Monks observe history to make sure that it happens 'according to the book'. When a princess is saved by MORT, History itself conspires to kill her. The process is focused in Lily WEATHERWAX, who forces the lives of people into stories – and also in DIOS, the high priest of DJELIBEYBI, who has been practising the same daily rituals for so long that he is incapable of dealing with anything new.

On Discworld, the future is set. It's the job of everyone to fight back.

Djelibeybi. (The name means 'Child of the Djel', after the river which flows through this land.) Also called the Kingdom of the Sun and the Old Kingdom. Principal crops: melons, garlic and, since they are increasingly encroaching on the fertile agricultural land, pyramids.

Djelibeybi is two miles wide and 150 miles long and is on the CIRCLE SEA coast of KLATCH. Almost entirely underwater during the flood season and both threatened and protected on either side by stronger neighbours (TSORT and EPHEBE). It was once great, but all that now remains is an expensive palace, a few dusty ruins in the desert, and the pyramids. The entire economic life of the country is, until after the events of *Pyramids*, devoted to building them. As a result, Djelibeybi is permanently bankrupt.

The kingdom is 7,000 years old. In the Pyramid era, even the heat was old. The air was musty and lifeless, pressing like a vice. Time moved slowly in Djelibeybi, and even then only in circles.

And this was, once again, because of the pyramids. Pyramids slow down time and prevent decay, a fact known to ancient Egyptians and modern Southern Californians. So many had been built in the Old Kingdom, however, that their cumulative effect was to act as a temporal brake of major proportions. In fact (again until events chronicled in *Pyramids*) the thousands of pyramids in the necropolis, a city of the dead occupying some of the kingdom's best land and second only to Ankh-Morpork as the biggest city on the Disc, were actually preventing time from moving at all. The pyramids were acting as time accumulators, sucking in fresh time as it occurred and, around sunset, flaring it off from their tips. As a result the kingdom spent thousands of years reusing the same day.

Please note that it was not the same as repeating the same day. People were born, grew and died (and, if they were important enough, they were placed in a pyramid). It was similar to the 'time' in DEATH's domain. Plants grew and flowered. There was an ongoing history. But it took place, as it were, in the temporal equivalent of an unaired room – the stale time could be detected in the kingdom's obsessive reverence for the past and its resistance to, or even ignorance of, the possibility of doing things differently. The more things changed, the more they stayed the same . . .

This impasse was finally broken with the construction of the Great Pyramid, which put so much additional pressure on the local dimensions that the entire kingdom was temporarily removed from them.

The country has an enormous number of local gods, unknown to the world outside. Its ruler, the Pharaoh, is also a god, although in human form. He wears a gold mask (the Face of the Sun) and during his official functions carries the Flail of Mercy, the obsidian Reaping Hook of Justice, the Honeycomb of Increase, the Asp of Wisdom, the Sheaf of Plenty, the Gourd of the Water of the Heavens, the Three-Pronged Spear of the Waters of the Earth, the Cabbage of Vegetative Increase and the Scapula of Hygiene. He may well lose points for dropping any of these.

Under the current ruler, Queen PTRACI I, it is quite likely that the mask has been sold and the money spent on plumbing.

Dog Guild. No motto; no coat of arms, not even a little tartan one. Led by the Chief Barker. The Guild consists of dogs who have all been 'bad dogs'; every dog has to have run away from his or her owner. It controls scavenging rights, night-time barking duties, breeding permissions and howling rotas. [MAA]

Dolly. Kitchen girl at Unseen University. [SM]

Door, Bill. Name adopted by DEATH while temporarily alive and working for Miss FLITWORTH. [RM]

Doorkeeper, Brother. A member of the ELUCIDATED BRETHREN OF THE EBON NIGHT. A baker by trade. [GG]

Dorfl. A GOLEM by species, a butcher by trade. Lives in Long Hogmeat, Ankh-Morpork. [SM]

Downey. White-haired Deputy Master – and later Master – at the ASSASSINS' GUILD. He is an amiable-looking old man whose speciality is giving people poisoned peppermints. [MAA]

Dragons. These exist in two forms – *Draco nobilis* and *Draco vulgaris*, more commonly known as Noble Dragons and Swamp Dragons. There are a number of differences between the two forms, but they can all be summed up succinctly: Noble Dragons are dragons as they are imagined, and Swamp Dragons are dragons as they have to be.

Noble Dragons, although obviously weighing up to 20 tons and with a wingspan of 80 feet, can fly and breathe very hot fire. There is considerable argument about this, but it is believed that they were transmuted from the common swamp dragons during the MAGE WARS, when the intense magical flux allowed the existence of many creatures quite unviable in normal conditions. Any flapping-winged creature weighing 20 tons would, even with the Discworld's amiable natural laws, leave a large hole if it ever tried to get airborne.

When favourable conditions ceased to exist, the theory runs, *Draco nobilis* used its magical nature to exploit an under-used ecological niche – the human imagination. In very exceptional circumstances the dragons can be recalled. They are intelligent, cunning and cruel. The dragon which for a brief period ruled Ankh-Morpork was entirely representative of the breed. They eat meat and do not physically *need* to eat people, but will do so for ceremonial purposes because such things are expected of them and they are sticklers for tradition even if it means having clothing stuck in their teeth.

Their ancestral swamp dragon, on the other hand, is totally real although this state of affairs is often quite brief owing to the explosive nature of their digestive system, which is very unstable. Their internal plumbing can rearrange itself to make the best possible use of any raw materials available for flame-making (although there is at least one recorded case of a dragon being able to flame ventrally for ramjet propulsion). The drawback to this talent is that the swamp dragon is capable of exploding violently if excited, frightened, aroused, surprised or bored. It is prey to a whole host of diseases, including a number only otherwise contracted by the common household oil-fired boiler. Most of its body fluids are corrosive.

It is presumed that the explosive capability is a defence mechanism acting for the good of the species as a whole, since it certainly doesn't work for the individual concerned. Any general advantage is also in doubt. There are many creatures that use bitterness and poisons to discourage predators, but blowing them to pieces serves no useful purpose. A wolf cannot teach its young that 'these things are bad to eat' when it is an expanding cloud of fur.

In the wild places where these dragons are still found, incidentally, the occasional explosion is all part of the normal background noise (hence the Ankh-Morpork saying, used to mean 'Unquestionably!': 'Is the High Priest an Offlian? Does a dragon explode in the woods?').

Nevertheless, there is an occasional vogue for the smaller varieties of swamp dragon as pets. And, as often happens when pets get too big, too difficult or, in this case, explosive, they are frequently abandoned on the streets of Ankh-Morpork. Others are cruelly used as paint-strippers or fire-lighters. The SUN-SHINE SANCTUARY in Morphic Street endeavours to rescue and care for as many as possible of these unfortunates, but the occasional 'bang!' of a lost pet is still heard in the city. On at least one occasion a dragon has deliberately been used as an explosive (MAA) and a handgun (GG).

A typical swamp dragon may reach a length of about 2 feet, tail excluded, although varieties and individuals down to 6 inches and up to more than a yard have been recorded. In the lexicon of dragon breeders a female dragon is a hen, and a male dragon is a pewmet (up to eight months), a cock (eight to fourteen months), a snood (fourteen months to two years) and then a cobb (two years to death). After death a swamp dragon is known as a crater.

Collecting box outside the
Sunshine Sanctuary

Drongo, Big Mad. A student wizard at Unseen University. His real name is Adrian Turnipseed. [SM]

Druellae. Smooth-voiced Dryad encountered by RINCEWIND. She had green flesh and wore nothing but a medallion around her neck. Her long hair had a faintly mossy look about it; her eyes had no pupils and were a luminous green. [COM]

Druids. The Druids of the Disc pride themselves on their forward-looking approach to the discovery of the mysteries of the universe. Of course, they believe in the essential unity of all life, the healing power of plants, the natural rhythm of the seasons and the burning alive of anyone who doesn't approach all this in the right frame of mind.

Their theory of creation is that the universe depends for its operation on the balance of four forces which they have identified as charm, persuasion, uncertainty and bloody-mindedness. Thus it is that the sun and moon orbit the Disc because they are persuaded not to fall down, but don't actually fly away because of uncertainty. Charm allows trees to grow and bloody-mindedness keeps them up and so on. Some druids suggest from time to time that there are certain flaws in this theory, but senior druids explain very pointedly that there is indeed room for informed argument and the cut and thrust of exciting scientific debate, and basically it lies on top of the next solstice bonfire.

The home of druidism is in the small wet country of LLAMEDOS. Druids occupy themselves with the building of large stone circles for computing purposes; these seldom work properly, but the druids always take the view that the problems can be solved only by building a much larger and more expensive circle. Sixty-six-megalith circles are now commonplace.

On this basis, it can be tentatively suggested that the circle at Stonehenge in England, which is actually a number of circles and isolated stones, was originally commissioned by a local tribe who wanted nothing more than a simple circle, suitable for basic calendar use and possibly the occasional sacrifice. Then they met a salesman. He may not have had smoked glass windows and potted plants in his office, and he may not have called himself a consultant, but the effect was the same. [LF]

Drull, Mrs.   A ghoul, and a past member of the FRESH START CLUB. A vague, shy old lady in a shapeless grey dress. Resides at Mrs CAKE's. Now retired, she does children's party catering. [RM, MAA]

Drum, the Broken/Mended.   Principal inn of Ankh-Morpork. Located in Filigree Street, at the junction with Short Street. A battered sign hangs over the door, showing a drum, not very well drawn.

The pub opens straight on to the street at the front (guarded by a troll), and its rear backs straight on to the river. The current landlord is Hibiscus DUNELM, but he probably won't last long – the Drum breaks men, or at least men who are not satisfied with the tavern as it is and have dreams of striped umbrellas and a better class of clientele. You have to take the Drum as you find it, which you do by following the noise of breaking glass . . .

. . . down the stairs into the beamed bar, with its walls stained with smoke and its floor a compost of old rushes and nameless beetles. Its sour beer is not so much purchased as hired for a while (a comment so old that it probably post-dates the invention of beer by an afternoon). But the Drum is famed not for its beer, which looks like maiden's water and tastes like battery acid, but for its clientele. It is said that if you sit long enough in the Drum, then sooner or later every major hero in the Disc will steal your horse.

The atmosphere inside is loud with talk and heavy with smoke. Thick coils of the stuff hang in the air, perhaps to avoid touching the walls. Nevertheless, it is a reputable disreputable tavern. Its customers have a certain rough-hewn respectability – they might murder each other in an easy-going way, as between equals, but they don't do it vindictively. A young woman could happily spend an evening in the Drum without being molested, unless that was her intention. A child could go in for a glass of lemonade and be certain of getting nothing worse than a clip round the ear when his mother heard his expanded vocabulary. On a quiet night, when he's certain that the LIBRARIAN isn't going to come in, the barman is even known to put bowls of peanuts on the bar.

The Drum is now conscious of its near-legendary status as the most famous tavern on the Discworld and is such a feature of the city that, after one bout of unavoidable redecorations, the then owner spent days recreating the original patina of dirt, soot and less identifiable substances on the walls and imported a ton of pre-rotted rushes for the floor.

Drumknott. Clerk in the PATRICIAN'S PALACE. [MAA]

Dryad. (*See* HAMADRYAD.)

Duc of Genua, the. When first encountered, the Duc appeared to be a vain and stupid man with long and well-turned legs and a wide mouth. He wore black silk and smoked glasses, in order to conceal his eyes (a fundamental rule of magical change that even gods have to obey – you can alter your shape, age, sex and species, but the look of your eyes cannot be changed). His bedroom, in the castle in GENUA, was green and full of flies. There was no bed, just a big, wooden cover on the floor with a pond under it.

The Duc was a frog under enchantment, and he met an unfortunate and rather depressing end. He really served only to be on the throne behind which Lily WEATHERWAX was the power. [WA]

Duck Man, the. A beggar in Ankh-Morpork. He has a duck on his head.

At least, everyone else thinks he has a duck on his head. The Duck Man knows he has no duck on his head. The duck's views on this are unrecorded. [SM]

Dunelm, Hibiscus. Current landlord of the Mended DRUM and, like many before him, full of ideas for attracting new customers. The idea of selling good beer cheaply is always the last one they think of. [SM]

Dungeon Dimensions, the. The endless wastelands outside space and time. The sad, mad things that dwell there have no understanding of the world but simply crave light and shape and try to warm themselves by the fires of reality, clustering around it with about the same effect – if they ever broke through – as an ocean trying to warm itself around a candle.

A few have managed to survive in this world in very special circumstances, but for most of them the reality they desire is soon fatal. Insofar as they can be said to have any emotions, the guiding one is hatred of all 'real' creatures. They are jealous of life and all things alive.

They are lured by really heavy concentrations of magic, because these weigh heavily on the frail rubber sheet of reality and present a weak point at which to break through. They can even break through inside a mind, using its owner's voice and brain to further their own ends – and a mind with magic in it shines out for them like a beacon. The number eight is also said to have some attraction for them, which is why wizards are enjoined to avoid saying it.

Dunmanifestin. Abode of the Disc's gods, atop CORI CELESTI. The stuccoed Valhalla wherein the gods face eternity with the kind of minds that are elsewhere at a loss to know what to do to pass a wet afternoon. Your basic home of the gods, with marble pillars and huge, impossible-to-carpet floors.

Dunnykin, Brother. A member of the ELUCIDATED BRETHREN OF THE EBON NIGHT. Seems to consist entirely of a little perambulatory black robe with halitosis. [GG]

Dwarfs. A race of humanoids approximately 4 feet tall. Stocky, bearded, long-lived (c. 300 years) and with a natural attraction for mountains and mineshafts. They provide the STO PLAINS area with most of its miners and 'heavy' engineers.

Unlike TROLLS, it appears that beyond the matter of build there are no major genetic differences between dwarfs and men, any more than there are genetic differences between bulldogs and poodles. Certainly the Discworld's second-greatest lover, CASANUNDA, seems to have met no insurmountable difficulties in his busy schedule.

A flaw in dwarfish nature from a human point of view is their tendency to take things literally. This is a result of their subterranean life. In an environment where there are things always ready to explode or collapse it is vitally important that information be passed on clearly and honestly. The human

language, with its unthinking reliance on metaphor and simile, is a veritable minefi— a complete morass— a fog of incomprehensi— very difficult for dwarfs.

Dwarfs wear up to twelve layers of clothing, including the famous woolly dwarf's vest made from RAMTOPS sheep wool, which is the closest thing possible to natural chain mail. All dwarfs have beards and this, together with the aforesaid clothing, makes gender more or less optional for everyday purposes.

Many of the more traditional dwarf tribes have no female pronouns like 'she' or 'her'. It should be pointed out that they have no male pronouns either – 'he' is considered by them to embrace both sexes equally, as it were, in the same sexless sense as the word mankind (or at least the same sexless sense as the word mankind is considered to have by men). They do, however, adopt a suitable pronoun when they are dealing with men, because of the embarrassment otherwise caused to humans.

A dwarf is not considered old enough to have the facts of life explained to him until he has reached the age of puberty (at about fifty-five). Dwarfs are very reticent about revealing their sex, which most of them don't consider to be very important compared to things like metallurgy and hydraulics. Dwarf courtship consists of finding out, in delicate and circumspect ways, what sex the other dwarf is.

Politically, the dwarfs are ruled by a king, although again the word is shorn of most of its human connotations and really means 'chief mining engineer'. Most mines have a king.

Large numbers of dwarfs have been drawn to Ankh-Morpork, where they are the biggest non-human ethnic group. Usually, they fit in well. All dwarfs are by nature dutiful, serious, obedient and thoughtful, and their only failing is a tendency, after one drink, to rush at enemies, screaming 'Aarrgh!' and axing off their legs at the knee. No one knows why it is that dwarfs, who at home in the mountains lead quiet, orderly lives, forget it all when they move to the big city. Something comes over even the most blameless iron-ore miner and prompts him to wear chain mail all the time, carry an axe, change his name to something like Grabthroat Shinkicker and drink himself into surly oblivion. It is noticeable that the dwarfs in Ankh-Morpork are far more 'dwarfish' (in the clichéd sense of being stroppy gold-

A street in the Shades

obsessed little buggers in iron helmets and chain mail) than they are in their natural environment, but the same statement with minimal adjustments could be made about the Irish in New York, the Welsh in London and Australians everywhere.

Dwarf bread. A dwarfish delicacy and battle weapon. It contains all you need to sustain you for days, mainly by causing you to perform miracles of endurance in order to get somewhere where you don't have to eat dwarf bread. Dwarf cake is similar, but thicker. A properly thrown slice of dwarf bread is a fearsome weapon, especially in view of its boomerang properties.

Dykeri. Ephebian philosopher. Author of *Principles of Navigation*. Got lost trying to find his way out of the bathroom. [SG]

Dysk. VITOLLER's theatre in Ankh-Morpork. Presumably rather similar to London's Globe Theatre, but possibly flatter. [WS]

Eateries. Prominent among Ankh-Morpork's most available places to eat are the CURRY GARDENS (a greasy stick), GIMLET's Hole Food delicatessen, HARGA'S HOUSE OF RIBS and Fat Sally's. The Three Jolly Luck Take-Away Fish Bar in Dagon Street did not make it beyond its opening night (*see* HONG, MR).

Ee. The Lost, or Forbidden, City of Ee was originally sited in the Great NEF, and it was the location of the miraculously preserved first pizza created on the Disc. It appears that Ee is not only a brigadoon but also one of the specialized ones that are not moored to one site but reappear in different places.

Eight. A number of some considerable occult significance on the Disc. In theory it must never be spoken by a wizard, although in fact it is generally safe in and around the University and wizards do seem to be able to get away with it elsewhere. However, outside of magically protected places no sensible wizard will mention it if he can avoid it; the problem lies in finding the sensible wizard. After all, generations of young wizards have accepted, with a frisson of fear, the injunction 'never say the number that comes between seven and nine, otherwise you will be *ate* alive' without wondering how the terrible occult forces were able to distinguish between two identical-sounding syllables without seeing them written down. Nevertheless, there is something about the harmonics of the word that is attractive to the denizens of the DUNGEON DIMENSIONS, and it is the number of BEL-SHAMHAROTH, one of the most successful of them to have maintained form and vitality in the world of reality. There are eight days in a Disc week, and eight colours in a Disc spectrum. [COM]

Eightfold Seal of Stasis. Design on the floor of the room housing the OCTAVO. Generally agreed in magical circles to have all the stopping power of a well-aimed brick. [LF]

Eightpanther. Producer of Captain Eightpanther's Traveller's Digestives. Claimed to have saved many a life at sea. They are rock-hard, and purchasers are not sure whether to use them as a raft or throw them at the sharks and watch the wretched things sink. Although these biscuits originated on the COUNTER-WEIGHT CONTINENT, anecdotal evidence suggests they are very similar to DWARF BREAD. [COM]

Elenor of Tsort (or is it of Crinix? or of Elharib?). Elenor was the cause of the Tsortean Wars. She was kidnapped from the Ephebians (or was it by the Ephebians? She has figured in legend so often that details have become obscured, or possibly she was just a very popular girl). What *is* known is that however legendarily beautiful she may have been at the start of the war, by its conclusion she was plump, good-looking in a slightly faded way, wearing a black dress and with a squint and the beginnings of a moustache. She also had at least seven children and seemed to have become somewhat attached to her captors. In fact she much preferred life there (wherever it was) to life back home (wherever that was). But it's the principle of the thing, isn't it? [P, E]

Elucidated Brethren of the Ebon Night. A group of rather inadequate men who summoned a dragon to help them to overthrow the government of Ankh-Morpork. Almost all of them ended up as little heaps of ash. The thing about Discworld karma is that it often happens real soon. [GG]

Elves. A humanoid race, extending through a number of worlds. They are vain, vapid, cruel and totally without any feeling or regard for any other creatures – but they are also beautiful, and it is a sad fact that the truly beautiful can get away with just about anything despite behaving in a way that would make the Marquis de Sade say 'Ooo, what nasty people.'

Their power derives from the use of a mental ability that could be described as 'glamour' to confuse and overawe people. They can also hypnotize humans with their singing (which is not, as such, musical; elves cannot make music or, indeed, anything else – they traditionally kidnap human musicians for this purpose).

Socially, elves somewhat resemble bees. They have a queen and a king, whose attitude towards one another is chilly contempt most of the time. The sex of the rest of the elves is fairly obscure, and appears to be more or less a matter of personal choice at the time. Nor does there seem to be any great sense of the *individual* elf, except for the royal family and a few retainers.

They also resemble bees, and pigeons, in being very sensitive to weak magnetic fields, to the extent that the magnetic sense is as important to them as taste or smell and gives them their acrobatic poise and their absolute sense of position and direction. Elves always know exactly where they are. It is also the cause of their traditional hatred of iron, because this distorts the local magnetic field and leaves them panicky and powerless. This explains the familiar horseshoes over cottage doors and the legendary power of blacksmiths, and is also the reason for the erection of LANCRE'S DANCERS, whose magnetic field forms a barrier between Discworld and one entrance to the elvish worlds.

Elves have in the past bred with humans and there are some Discworld families with an elvish taint to them. Elves do not seem sexually attracted to other elves, possibly because they know what they're really like.

Elves, King of. A tall, horned man with goat's legs and overlarge hooves. He smells of lions' cages and leaf mould and has a rich, dark voice, like a voice-over for a chocolate advert. Unlike the

Queen, who is constantly seeking new worlds to dominate, he is content to lie up in his sweat lodge and wait for the end of this temporary aberration which seems to have mankind in its grip, i.e. farming with ploughs, the use of metals, civilization and other gewgaws. [LL]

Elves, Queen of. Usually seen as dark-haired, wearing a red dress, but she can make herself appear in whatever form she likes and no stated appearance is definitive. She wears a copper crown in her hair and has exquisitely thin hands. Her true face is almost triangular, with a tiny mouth, an almost non-existent nose and eyes larger than human eyes – but, again, this may not be the face that people see.

The relative positions of the elven royalty are similar to those on the chess board; the queen is ostensibly the more powerful of the two, but ultimately fails without the king. [LL]

Embalmers' Guild (Guild of Embalmers and Allied Trades). Motto: FARCIMINI.

Coat of arms: a shield, per bend sinister. On it, a seringue argent on a field gules et vert.

An ancient and international Guild, with fraternal links to other STO PLAINS cities and even to the countries of KLATCH. Guild historians trace their origins back to the very first shambling creature who dropped a mammoth thighbone and a bunch of flowers on a dead fellow shambling creature in a shallow grave and charged the descendants a big lump of bear.

As is so often the case, the Guild is now the official body for a large number of associated trades, such as undertaking and grave-digging. Unlike other Guilds, many of its members have their practices actually based in the building, so that the smells of camphor and formaldehyde make the Guild easily distinguishable on a dark night.

Embalming is still popular in the city, many inhabitants remaining firm in their belief that you might be able to take it with you. Since the Guild includes some highly skilled experts, many people in Ankh-Morpork are buried looking healthier than they did when they were alive, although this is not difficult to achieve.

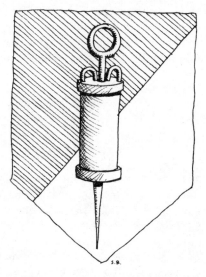

The training school for gravediggers is worthy of note because it includes classes in cackling and graveyard repartee. In the crowded cemeteries of Ankh-Morpork previous incumbents are often exhumed by the digging of new holes and, in the ancient traditions of their trade, the trainee gravediggers are taught morbid philosophy, humorous recitation and – in case they find a particularly well-preserved skull – ventriloquism.

Endless Street, Ghost of. Endless Street, Ankh-Morpork, is the name of the street running entirely around the city centre inside the city wall. It is said to be haunted by the ghost of one Gumler Vode, condemned for eternity to measure its length. Vode's unfortunate sentence began some three hundred years ago.

It is agreed in the city that, since Broad Way is in two sections, Short Street is the longest street in the city. Vode bet a wizard in the Broken DRUM that it was not, and then, with what was considered by bystanders to be a nasty, know-it-all smirk, claimed that the space behind the walls (then unnamed) was a street. The wizard, annoyed at the thought of losing $5, pointed a finger at him and said, simply, 'Measure it, then . . .'

The ghost of Vode, and the clink of his tape measure, can be heard on quiet nights. It is a reminder to everyone that, when dealing with wizards, it is always best to know when not to be right.

Endos. A skinny little man who takes payment for listening to Ephebian philosophers. He doesn't do anything else except listen. This is why he is known as Endos the Listener (although for a small extra sum he may vouchsafe grace phrases like 'That is true', or 'A well-made point, if I may say so.'

In EPHEBE, people who only listen are far rarer than people who only talk. This may be the case everywhere else. [P]

Engravers' Guild. Motto: NON QVOD MANEAT, SED QVOD ADIMIMVS (Not What Remains, But What We Take Away).

Coat of arms: a shield, dimidiation. Sinister an 'I' capitale sable on a field argent. Dexter an 'I' capitale argent on a field sable.

A small, select and solemn bunch of men, whose Guildhouse is on the corner of Short Street and God Street, Ankh-Morpork. They prize practical engraving skills (on wood and metal) above all else, although candidates for membership are also expected to demonstrate lack of imagination, an anal-retentive attention to detail and the ability to think in reverse.

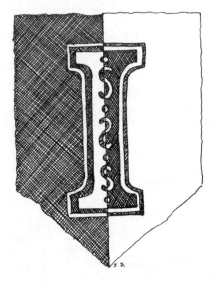

Because of the peculiar informal rules relating to printing in Ankh-Morpork, which effectively ban movable type (see PRINTING) the engravers are responsible for all semi-mechanically printed output in the city, and their prices are high (although, in Ankh-Morpork's flourishing free market, there are a large number of non-Guild engravers). It remains to be seen how long this state of affairs will be allowed to continue.

Eorle, Duke of. Nobleman of Ankh. Appears to be a rather lazy and stupid man with a braying laugh and the mental powers of a dead mole. On the other hand, the Eorles have survived everything life can throw at them for hundreds of years, so it may be that the most intelligent thing they've ever done is to appear stupid on every occasion. [MAA]

Ephebe. Pop. (city and surrounding farmlands): 50,000.

Political system: tyranny (a form of democracy); slavery is a long-established tradition.

Major export: ideas.

General description: The white marble city lazes around its rock overlooking the blue CIRCLE SEA. Blindingly white houses coil all the way up to the top, where a wall runs around the peak like a headband. Beyond that is the famous and ancient labyrinth, full of one hundred and one amazing things you can do with hidden springs, razor-sharp knives and falling rocks. There are six guides – each one knows his way through one sixth of the labyrinth. Alongside the palace within the labyrinth are the remains of the famous library, which used to be the second biggest on the Discworld before it was burned by Omnian soldiery (or so legend has it; but there is a story that the first match was put to it by DIDACTYLOS the philosopher just seconds before the guard arrived, on the basis that setting fire to your own library is more philosophical).

This tiny but influential city state lies on the Rimward coast of the Circle Sea, between DJELIBEYBI and OMNIA. It is the land of the bourzuki (a kind of dog) and retsina (a kind of paint-thinner) and above all the land of philosophy.

Ephebe has more philosophers per square yard than anywhere else on the Disc. It is impossible to throw a brick in Ephebe without hitting a philosopher and, owing to the heightened level of philosophical debate that rages in the city, this often happens. For it is unfortunate that a city whose inhabitants frequently storm the walls of paradox and smash the doors of perception is also beset with that particular dogged Discworld logic which would not recognize a metaphor if it was handed to it in a cornet with chocolate chips on top.

This certainly makes for briskness of thought. Any philosopher who suggests that, logically, an arrow cannot hit a running man (XENO's Arrow Paradox) will be given a short head start before all the other philosophers reach for their bows. This experiment was actually performed and the philosopher did escape unscathed, but after some thought rewrote the statement so that it read that a running man cannot be hit by an arrow *providing it is fired by someone who has been in the pub since lunchtime.*

Which, rather neatly, leads on to the subject of Ephebian food and drink. In short, Ephebians make wine out of anything they can put in a bucket, and eat anything that can't climb out of one. They will drink wine which varnishes the inside of the throat and sometimes their food will try to hold on to the plate. (Plate-smashing is a tradition at the end of an Ephebian meal, although it may be a better idea to smash them beforehand.)

Ephebe has been called 'the cradle of democracy', and it is true that Ephebian democracy could do with its nappy changed. The Ephebians believe that every man should have the vote – providing he isn't poor or a slave or foreign or disqualified by reason of being mad, frivolous or a woman.

The voters (1,300 of them) go to the polls every five years to elect the Tyrant, who is more or less the supreme ruler for his period of office. In order to be considered for election a candidate for Tyrant must prove beyond doubt that he is pure in thought, word and deed, with no stain whatsoever on his character; once elected it is assumed by everyone that he is a criminal madman.

Candidates for Tyrantship are elected by the placing of black or white balls in various urns, thus giving rise to a well-known comment about politics.

A note on slavery: slaves make up more than half of Ephebe's population. Periodically someone suggests that they should be freed, but there is always a tremendous outcry. It comes from the slaves themselves, who have several times risen in revolt against the very idea. The reason lies in the particular status of slaves vs free men in Ephebian society. A free man is, clearly, free – free to sleep in the rain, free to starve, free to suffer whatever vicissitudes the world might drop upon his manumitted head. No one is there to care for a free man. A free man is free to drop dead.

Whereas there are rules for slaves, established over a thousand years. Slaves get three meals a day, at least one with named meat in it. And one day off a week. And two weeks being-allowed-to-run-away every year (it is generally understood that a proper master will pay for his slave to come back from wherever it is he or she has run away to). A slave may not be beaten without a chance to appeal to the Tyrant, and the mistreatment of slaves is a grave crime. A slave is, after all, property. Respect for property is the cornerstone of democracy.

A slave does, of course, have to work, although not work like a slave.

After twenty years as a slave he can automatically become a free man, but most slaves take one look at what freedom entails and, despite the entreaties of a master who may well be living on olive pits in order to feed his household, sign up again for another twenty years.

Slavery would in fact be a huge drain on the economy of Ephebe were it not for the fact that it hasn't got one. The sun shines, ripening the olives and the grapes, there are fish in the sea, there doesn't seem to be any really pressing reason to do anything much except sit and think, and so Ephebe ambles amiably from day to day.

Special notes for the visitor to Ephebe: do not be surprised to see naked old men, dripping wet, trotting through the streets. Most of the really serious philosophizing in Ephebe is done in the bath, and the birth of a new idea will often lead the bather to spring away crying 'Eureka!'* to start work on the theorem right away.

Barrels will be seen dotted around the streets. This is where the philosophers traditionally live, in order to show their disregard of matters in the mundane world. In order to show their love of comfort, however, the barrels are often very large, with enough room for a sauna.

*Lit. 'Give me a towel!'

Erasmus. Great-uncle of Mrs CAKE. Sometimes used to eat his meals under the table on account of werewolf blood. [RM]

Eric. (*See* THURSLEY, ERIC.)

Errol. Goodboy Bindle Featherstone of Quirm, and technically a pedigree dragon. His sire was Treebite Brightscale, a prizewinner bred by Lady Sybil RAMKIN. But it was clear right from the egg that Errol was something unusual. He had a pear-shaped body and a head like an anteater, with nostrils like jet intakes, two tiny spiky ears and a pair of eyebrows almost the same size as his stubby wings, which should never have supported him in the air. He was named Errol by Corporal NOBBS, because of a supposed resemblance to his brother (Corporal Nobbs's, not the dragon's.) In fact Errol, dismissed as a whittle (or runt), was an entirely new sub-species of swamp dragon; his genes realized what could be done with a streamlined body, small wings and a very hot flame, if only the flames could be persuaded to, er, come out of the other end. [GG]

Esk.   Eskarina Smith. Daughter of Gordo SMITH. Eight years old and 4 feet tall, she has long brown hair and a gap in her front teeth, and the sort of features that promise to become, if not beautiful, then at least attractively interesting. She is the eighth child of an eighth son, and was handed, at birth, the wizard's staff belonging to Drum BILLET. She was the first female to be admitted to Unseen University. And the last, so far as records show. Current whereabouts unknown. [ER]

Evil-Minded Son of a Bitch.   Camel who appeared in the moving pictures. Probably the most intelligent mind in HOLY WOOD. [MP]

Evil-Smelling Bugger.   Renowned as the greatest camel mathematician of all time, and yet he spent his entire sad life carrying cargoes of dates and being hit with a stick by a man who couldn't count to twenty without looking at his sandals. [P]

Expletius.   Ephebian philosopher who proved that the Disc is 10,000 miles wide. A lucky guess. More than twenty other philosophers proved that the Disc varied in size from infinite to 'too small to see', and since they turned out to be wrong Expletius got the Top Brain award. [SG]

Ezeriel.   One-time Queen of KLATCH. Every young student of history knows that Ezeriel had a lot of lovers and died when she sat on a snake and used to bathe in asses' milk (they seldom know any more than this). She is a distant ancestor of KELI, which suggests that royalty around the CIRCLE SEA, as in Europe, followed the mix'n'match approach to royal weddings. [M]

Goodboy Bindle Featherstone of Quirm

Famine. An anthropomorphic personification. One of the Four Horsemen of the APOCRALYPSE. [LF, S]

Far-re-ptah. Past Queen of DJELIBEYBI. Grandmother of TEPPICYMON XXVII. A strict and fearsome old woman who was, however, known as 'Grandma Pooney' to TEPPIC. [P]

Fasta Benj. A fisherman from a small nation of marsh-dwelling nomads near OMNIA, who were unknown to the world at large and entirely bypassed by history until by sheer chance his little boat was swept up by the multi-national fleet sent to destroy that country. His only recorded contribution to the very short Omnian war was a hopeful attempt to sell raw fish to all parties. Nevertheless, as a representative of a sovereign nation he went home with his own share of the spoils, which included the secret of fire and the use of metals. [SG]

Fate. Another anthropomorphic personification. A friendly-looking man in late middle age, with greying hair brushed neatly around features that a maiden would confidently proffer a glass of small beer to, should they appear at her back door. It is a face a kindly youth would gladly help over a stile. Except for the eyes, of course . . . while at a mere glance they are simply dark, a closer look reveals that they are holes opening on to a blackness so remote, so deep that the watcher feels himself inexorably drawn into the twin pools of infinite night and their terrible, wheeling stars. [COM]

Febrius. Ephebian philosopher. He proved that light travels at about the same speed as sound, in his famous 'Give us a shout when you see it, OK?' experiment involving two hills, a lantern with a movable cover over it and an assistant with a very loud voice. [SG]

Felmet, Lady. Wife of Leonal, Duke FELMET. A powerful and impressive woman who could not abide slackness or weakness and regarded the whole universe as something to bully. She had a big red face with thick eyebrows and a stubbly chin, and wore red velvet dresses that matched her complexion. Possibly eaten to death by rabbits and other fluffy creatures in the forests of LANCRE. [WS]

Felmet, Leonal, Duke. Murdered his cousin, King VERENCE I of LANCRE. An insect of a man with a thin face and heavily beringed hands, he had a mind that ticked like a clock and, like a clock, it regularly went cuckoo.

He was married for twenty years to the massive Lady FELMET, whom he wed largely because he was fascinated by power, of which she was practically the embodiment. Fell to his death into the river Lancre. [WS]

Fiddler's Riddle. An unpleasant inn in OHULAN CUTASH. No self-respecting goat would endure the smell in the Fiddler's Riddle. It was here that Eskarina SMITH turned a barrel of plum brandy into milk. [ER]

Fido, Big. Chief Barker of the DOG GUILD. A small and rather dainty white poodle with the overgrown remains of a poodle cut and wearing a diamante collar. Big Fido was, to hijack a convenient phrase, barking mad – apparently driven to this state one day by the realization that everything around him (his bowl, his collar, his kennel, his blanket) had his name on it. He ate his blanket, savaged his owner and ran off. The madness seemed to tap some deep pit of primordial rage in his soul which enabled him to fight and kill dogs much larger and theoretically much stronger than him, and thus he became the acknowledged leader of the feral dogs of Ankh-Morpork. To them he expounded, at length and with much excited farting and foaming when he talked, his Dream: that all dogs were wolves at heart, and needed only to band together to overthrow humanity (the 'Master' race) and reclaim their ancient heritage. [MAA]

Fingers, Brother. Member of the ELUCI-DATED BRETHREN OF THE EBON NIGHT.

He used to work as an odd-job man at Unseen University, but is better known to the City WATCH as Bengy 'Lightfoot' Boggis, of the famous thieving family. [GG]

Firefighters' Guild. Not in existence long enough to develop a motto or a coat of arms. Outlawed by the PATRICIAN after many complaints. If you bought a contract from the Guild, your house would be protected against fire. Unfortunately, the general Ankh-Morpork ethos quickly came to the fore and firefighters would go to prospective clients' houses in groups, making loud comments like 'Very inflammable looking place, this,' and 'Probably go up like a firework with just one carelessly dropped match, know what I mean?' Since the disbanding of the Ankh-Morpork Guild of Firefighters the incidence of fires has gone down considerably. [GG]

Flannelfoot, Zlorf. Past President of the ASSASSINS' GUILD, and of rather earthier origins than many of its later members. Broad, honest face, a welter of scar tissue, the result of many a close encounter. Said by some that he chose a profession in which dark hoods, cloaks and nocturnal prowlings predominated because there was a day-fearing trollish streak in his parentage. People who repeated this in earshot of Zlorf tended to carry their ears home in their hats. [COM]

Fliemoe. A student at the ASSASSINS' GUILD, and a bit of a bully. [P]

Flitworth, Renata. Skinny, short-sighted, aged seventy-five, with a face the colour and texture of a walnut. Miss Flitworth never had the chance even to become a widow because of the death of her intended in an avalanche just before their wedding, but she overcame a tendency to mope about this and got on with life in a determined, no-nonsense sort of way. She owned a farm in the plains below the RAMTOPS, not far from SHEEPRIDGE.

Her main claim to fame was as the employer of Bill DOOR (DEATH), who was sufficiently impressed by her to allow her soul to remain in the world just long enough to attend the long-looked-forward-to harvest dance. [RM]

Flora of the Disc. The Discworld has a rich and unusual variety of plants. These include:

Achorion Purple [P]
Aphacia wood [SG]
Bloodwater Lily [ER]
Choke apples [COM]
Devil's Bit Scabious [WA]
Dum-dum [RM]
Earwort [ER]
Fellwort, Woolly [WS]
Floribunda Mrs Shover (a rose) [RM]
Gherkins, Water [ER]
Kzak fruit [M]
Maiden's Wish [ER]
Mandrake, Five-Leaved False [WS]
Maniac [RM]
Mustick [P]
Nervousa gloriosa [RM]
Old Man's Frogbit [WS]
Old Man's Trousers [ER]
Peahane, Greater [ER]
PINES, COUNTING
Purple Bindweed (Love-in-a-Spin) [SM]
SAPIENT PEARWOOD
Snake's Head [WA]
Spikkle [RM]
Syphacia bush [P]
Uloruaha bush [COM]
WAHOONIE
Wasp Agaric [P]
Wormseed, Treacle [WS]

Flume, Lady Odile. A pupil in the fifth form of the QUIRM COLLEGE FOR YOUNG LADIES. Her great-great-grandmother was once seduced by the god BLIND IO in the form of a vase of daisies. So she claims, anyway. [SM]

Fondel. Composer. Wrote the 'Wedding March' and 'Prelude in G Major'. [MAA]

Food and drink. The Discworld is famed for its cuisine. A visitor would be able to eat for a year without needing to repeat a meal, and in most cases without wanting to.

Amanita Liquor [M]

Antipasta. Created some hours *after* the meal, whereupon it exists *backwards in time* and, if properly prepared, should arrive on the tastebuds at exactly the same moment, thus creating a true taste explosion. It costs five thousand dollars a forkful, or a little more if you include the cost of cleaning the tomato sauce off the walls afterwards. [RM]

Banged Grains. Made of corn heated in cooking oil with salt and butter added. Tastes of salt, butter and cardboard. [MP]

Barnacle canapés [COM]

Bentinck's Very Old Peculiar Brandy [RM]

Blowfish, Deep Sea. Safe to eat if every bit of stomach, liver and digestive tract is removed. Better still, to be on the safe side it is wise to remove every part of the fish. [P]

Cakes, Dwarfish (very solid and inedible – see DWARF BREAD)

Carrot and Oyster Pie. Nanny Ogg's recipe. Carrots so you can see in the dark, oysters so you've got something to look at. [LL]

Cheese (Lancre has the holes, Quirm is the one with the blue veins) [SM]

Clooty Dumplings [MAA]

Dark Enchantments (chocolates) [RM]

Distressed Pudding [MAA]

Fikkun Haddock [MAA]

Ghlen Livid. Fermented vul nut drink distilled in the Agatean Empire. Also made in the Rehigreed Province using re-annual plants. It is believed that some is being imported now into Ankh-Morpork. [COM]

Jammy Devils [MAA]

Jellyfish, Crystallized [COM]

Jimkin BEARHUGGER's whiskey – quite strong, and often matured for hours at a time.

Klatchian Coffee. Very strong: goes through an untrained stomach like a hot ball-bearing through runny butter. This strange, thick brew is drunk in thimble-sized cups. It doesn't just sober you up; it takes you through sobriety and out the other side, so that you glimpse the real universe beyond the clouds of warm self-delusion that sapient life usually generates around

itself to stop it turning into a nutcake. Coffee enthusiasts take the precaution of getting thoroughly drunk before touching the stuff. Varieties include Curly Mountain Straight and Red Desert Special. [S, MP, MAA]

Klatchian Delight – a sweetmeat and flypaper [SG]

Klatchian Hots (type of pizza) [GG]

Knuckle Sandwich [MAA]

Merckle & Stingbat's Very Famous Brown Sauce [GG]

Old Overcoat (another fine product from Jimkin Bearhugger's vats) [M]

Orakh. Made from cactus sap and scorpion venom. One of the most virulent alcoholic beverages in the universe. Not drunk for its intoxicating effects, but to mitigate the effects of Klatchian coffee (see above).

Peach Corniche. One of those sticky drinks no barman ever expects to take off the shelf. [M]

Pressed Seaweed biscuits [COM]

SCUMBLE.

Sea Grape wine [COM]

Sea Urchin, Candied [COM]

Shark's Fin soup [LF]

Slumpie [MAA]

Soggy Mountain Dew, C.M.O.T. Dibbler's Genuine Authentic. Despite its name, it is not strong and may not even be alcoholic, its effects being caused by whatever Mr Dibbler thinks might give it some kind of kick – gunpowder, corroded copper, and so on. [MAA]

Spring Cordial [M]

Squid, Crystallized [COM]

Squishi – possibly like sushi, only older [LF, M, P]

Stardrip – plum brandy, brewed in the Ramtops [M]

Starfish, Baby, with Purée of Sea Cucumbers [COM]

Starfish, Candied [COM]

Traveller's Digestives [LF]

Turbot's Really Odd (real ale) [SM]

WOW-WOW SAUCE

Fool, the. Jester at the LANCRE court. A very loyal servant to his masters. On his first appearance he was seventeen years old and wore a red and yellow costume with silver bells on his hat and a red and yellow hankie, also decorated with bells. He looked a sad and thin little man with runny eyes, although he was in fact of at least average height, but he made himself look small by hunching his shoulders, bandying his legs and walking in a half-crouch.

He was a Fool like his father and grandfather before him, and was raised by his stern grandfather following his father's abrupt departure from Lancre. He was soon sent away to the FOOLS' GUILD in Ankh-Morpork, where he had the traditional education and, by employing application and hard work to make up for lack of talent, actually passed out as a very respected Fool.

His real name was VERENCE, and he was half-brother to and slightly older than TOMJON, who was acknowledged as the son and heir of King VERENCE I. It is believed in Lancre that the Fool's father was also King Verence I, who had a somewhat old-fashioned approach to the young women of the kingdom, and that he had been christened Verence by his late mother in memory of that royal, er, connection.

However, the witches of Lancre have a slightly different, if unspoken, view of events. King Verence I was indeed a ladies' man, but so was the Fool's official father, who achieved with kind words and a fetching manner what the King achieved by hammering on the door with his sword. They also recall that the man left town hurriedly shortly after the birth of Tomjon, and that the Queen was a rather lonely lady who may well have appreciated a little gentle attention on those long nights when her husband was exercising his droit de seigneur around the kingdom. The witches are also midwives, and can count rather better than she could. They're quite certain that Tomjon and the Fool are half-brothers, though . . .

Further evidence that the Fool (now ruling Lancre as VERENCE II) is the son of a commoner and had no genetic tradition of kingship in his bones may be gathered from the fact that he is hardworking, intelligent, conscientious, humble and kind. His only failings, if such they be, are a tendency to try to better the lot of his fellow men even if they are happy with the lot they've got – and he has no sense of humour whatsoever, and a strong aversion to custard. There is something about the regime at the FOOLS' GUILD that can do that to a man. [WS, WA, LL]

Fools' Guild (Guild of Fools and Joculators and College of Clowns). Motto: DICO, DICO, DICO.

Coat of arms: a shield, bisected dancette. The upper half, sable with a roundel, gules. Each lower point decorated with a clochette d'or. The lower half is bisected vertically, the right half being azure, the left half, argent.

The Guildhouse is located on the corner of God Street and Widdershins Broadway. One of the more recent Ankh-Morpork Guilds, although like the ASSASSINS' GUILD and Unseen University it is a major exporter of its graduates and has ancient origins among the circus fraternity.

The Guild was founded some 150

years before the present by Charles Nixon, former Fool to the Duke of Quirm. As with most of the Guilds it is also a hospital, craft standards enforcer, fraternal society and school – although unlike the other Guilds it will not accept for education boys not firmly apprenticed to clownship or Foolhardiness. It takes the sons of clowns and Fools, and it is also a charity school insofar as there is always a place and a custard pie in the face for any young boy with an amusing hump, speech impediment or other laughable deformity.

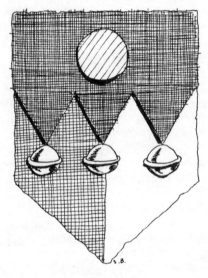

It is strange but instructive to contrast the Guild with the Assassins' Guild next door. One is a pleasant, airy building, whose corridors echo with the laughter of students and hum with the quiet activity of people working hard in a job they love – the other is gaunt, forbidding and silent except for the occasional muffled sob. One leaves its gates open most of the time and its graduates are considered to brighten up any party – the other operates its wretched craft behind locked doors and its members are regarded with disdain by right-thinking people. One

turns out people who, admittedly, must in the course of their duties sometimes stab, poison or otherwise inhume their patients – but at least they never ask them to believe that pouring whitewash down someone's trousers is funny.

One important function of the Guild is the maintenance of the Hall of Faces, which is primarily for the clown members. Clowns are not particularly identified by their names, which serve more to identify the *variety* of clown, but by their faces. No two clowns are allowed to have the same make-up, and the Hall of Faces contains hundreds of eggs, each one painted with the face of a Guild member. It is said to be a very unpleasant place in which to spend the night.

Forest of Skund. Enchanted forest Rimwards of the RAMTOPS. The only forest in the entire universe to be called 'Your finger, you fool', the literal meaning of the word *Skund*. When the first explorers from the warm lands around the CIRCLE SEA travelled into the chilly hinterland they filled in the blank spaces on their maps by grabbing the nearest native, pointing at some distant landmark, speaking very clearly in a loud voice and writing down whatever the bemused man told them. Thus were immortalized in generations of atlases such geographical oddities as Just a Mountain and I Don't Know, What? This is known as the 'surly native' technique of map-making. [LF]

Fox, Cassandra. Pupil at the QUIRM COLLEGE FOR YOUNG LADIES. A rather horsy gel. [SM]

Frank, Mister. Card sharp on the Vieux River riverboats, until he played CRIPPLE MR ONION against Granny WEATHERWAX. [WA]

Fresh Start Club. Motto: UNDEAD, YES – UNPERSON, NO. A club for those who are having difficulty in relating to being undead, founded by Reg SHOE, a zombie; it meets at 668 Elm Street, Ankh-Morpork, on the first floor, above a tailor's shop. The entrance to the club is via an alleyway, at the end of which is a wooden door with a notice saying: 'Come In! Come In! The Fresh Start Club. Being Dead is only the Beginning!!!' Club slogans, all devised by Reg, include: 'Dead Yes! Gone No!', 'Spooks of the World Arise, You Have Nothing to Lose but your Chains', 'The Silent Majority want Dead Rights' and 'End Vitalism Now!' A sad place. Most of its members are embarrassed by the whole business but keep coming along so as not to upset Reg; the club is his whole life. Or would be, if he still had one. [RM]

Fresnel's Wonderful Concentrator. Spell used to create the flying lens on which RINCEWIND and TWOFLOWER are taken to KRULL. The spell calls for many rare and unstable ingredients, such as demon's breath, and it takes eight fourth-grade wizards to envision. The lens itself is 20 feet across and totally transparent, with rings on to which passengers and the twenty-four HYDROPHOBES strap themselves, and a stubby pillar dead centre. [COM]

Fri'it, General Iam. Officer who ran most of the Omnian Divine Legion. He clicked his knuckles when worried, which was often. History remembers him as a fairly honest soldier who fell among priests and politicians. [SG]

Frord, Grisham. Leader of the Grisham Frord Close Harmony Singers, a cappella assassins and crack enforcers for the MUSICIANS' GUILD. [SM]

Frottidge, Violet. One of DIAMANDA's coven in LANCRE. (*See also* MAGENTA.) [LL]

Fruni. Prophet of the Omnian religion. [SG]

Fruntkin. Dwarf who worked as a short-order chef in Nodar BORGLE the Klatchian's canteen in HOLY WOOD. [MP]

Fullomyth. An invaluable aid for all those whose business is with the arcane and hermetic. It contains lots of things that don't exist and, in a very significant way, aren't important. Some of its pages can be read only after midnight, or by strange and improbable illuminations. There are descriptions of underground constellations and wines as yet unfermented (*see* RE-ANNUAL PLANTS). For the really up-to-the-epoch occultist, who can afford the version bound in spider skin, there is even an insert showing the London Underground with three stations they never dare show on public maps. [S]

Furgle. Dwarf owner of a horn which sounded itself when danger was near . . . and also in the presence of, for some reason, horseradish. [SM]

Galena. A troll who worked in the clicks in HOLY WOOD. His screen name was Rock Cliffe, although he had been considering calling himself Flint and having a cement nose-job. (In MAA, a Flint was working in the armoury and later joined the WATCH, but there are not a great many troll names and it might well be a different Flint.) Galena has pointed ears, a nose which looks like Neanderthal Man's first attempt at an axe, and a fist the size and hardness of a foundation stone. [MP, MAA]

Gamblers' Guild. Motto: EXCRETVS EX FORTVNA. (Loosely speaking: 'Really Out of Luck'.)

Coat of arms: A shield, gyronny. On its panels, turnwise from upper sinister: a sabre or on a field sable; an octagon gules et argent on a field azure; a tortue vert on a field sable; an 'A' couronnée on a field argent; a sceptre or on a field sable, a calice or on a field azure; a piece argent on a field gules; an elephant gris on a field argent.

The arms represent the eight suits of the classic Ankh-Morpork pack of cards.

The Guildhouse is in the Street of Alchemists. Current President (chosen by the draw of a card) is Scrote Jones.

Guild membership is small, because it is restricted to professional gamblers. The Guild mainly exists to enforce rules about marked cards, loaded dice, shaved billiard balls and so on. Note that it does not *ban* them, it merely regularizes the size of marks and weight of dice and closeness of shave. (Since all professional gamblers use these items a game between any two of them means that they are cancelled out and the contest

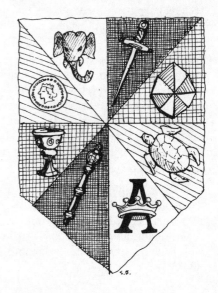

becomes, perforce, a matter of skill and luck.) The Guild also very strictly controls the amount of money a member may take from a non-member (a 'mark') in any game; in the words of Scrote Jones, 'If you want to make money out of keeping sheep you don't rip their hides off all in one go.' There are plenty of customers in Ankh-Morpork, where the basic gambling survival rules appear to be unknown.*

*Never Find the Lady, play cards against anyone named after a city, or gamble in any game against anyone called Doc.

Games. Disc games include:

Aargrooha. Troll game, played with obsidian boots and a human head. Not played any more, of course, except in remote mountain regions. [SM]

Aqueduct (or is it Fishing Line/Weir/Dam?) Rules include mention of trumps, ruffs, trump return, trump lead, contract, psychic bids, rebiddable suit, double finesse, grand slam and rubbers. [LF]

BARBARIAN INVADERS

Chase My Neighbour Up the Passage. Details have never been given, but it appears to be a simple game like Old Maid or Happy Families. [WA]

Craps. Dice game played with three eight-sided dice, and probably similar in general rules and terminology to our craps, although since it is played on the cobbles of Ankh-Morpork the name may have a rather more honest origin. [M]

CRIPPLE MR ONION

Darts. Effectively the standard British game, although the Ankh-Morpork rules specifically ban leaning out over the oche and hammering the darts in with your fingertip while exclaiming 'Ook!' [RM]

Exclusive Possession. Game once played by Death instead of the symbolic chess game. Reference is made to another player getting 'three streets and all the utilities'. One of the playing pieces is a boot. We can only guess at what the board looks like . . . [RM]

Pond. Game played on a table with holes and nets around the edge and, in rural areas, balls carved expertly out of wood. [RM]

Significant Quest. Very popular among gods, demi-gods, demons and other supernatural creatures. [S]

Wallgame. Played at the Assassins' Guild, usually two or three storeys above street level. [P]

Gancia. Leader of the gang of mercenaries led by HERRENA on their mission to capture RINCEWIND for Ymper TRYMON. A fairly long explanatory note for someone whose job was, basically, to die at the right time. [LF]

Gander, Adab. Trail boss of the caravanserai that transported ESK from ZEMPHIS to Ankh-Morpork. An impressive figure in a trollhide jerkin, rakishly floppy hat and leather kilt. Trollhide as a type of hard-wearing leather – in fact, a flexible type of stone – is certainly not politically correct wear in Ankh-Morpork these days. [ER]

Gargoyles. An urban species of troll, which has evolved a symbiotic relationship with gutters, funnelling run-off water into their ears and out through fine sieves in their mouths. They speak strangely because they cannot close their mouths. Gargoyles often spend years without moving from one spot and do not have names so much as locations (see CORNICE OVERLOOKING BROADWAY). When they do move it is in a jerky fashion, like bad stop-motion photography. Few birds nest on buildings colonized by gargoyles, and bats also tend to fly around them. [LF, S, MAA]

Garhartra. Guestmaster of KRULL. His job is to make sacrificial victims feel comfortable, at least up to the point just before they are sacrificed. A wizard, with a cracked yet cheerful voice. [COM]

Garlick, Magrat. A witch in LANCRE. The youngest member (comparatively speaking) of the coven that Granny WEATHERWAX swears she has not got. Magrat has a cottage in Mad Stoat, but she now lives in LANCRE CASTLE, as Queen to VERENCE II, after a romance which was always on the point of foundering because the principals were invariably too embarrassed to speak to each other.

Magrat is the daughter of Simplicity Garlick, now deceased. Her grandmother was Araminta Garlick, and her aunt Yolande Garlick. None of her relations was a witch, which is unusual. Although by tradition witches do not train their relations, witchcraft tends to run in families. Magrat is an original.

She was selected and trained by Goodie WHEMPER, a methodical and sympathetic witch with a rather greater regard for the written word than is common among the Lancre witches. Goodie was a research witch; she may have had some long-term aim in mind.

In a certain light, and from a carefully chosen angle, Magrat Garlick is not

unattractive. Despite her tendency to squint when she's thinking. And her pointy nose, red from too much blowing. She is short, thin, decently plain, well-scrubbed and as flat-chested as an ironing-board with a couple of peas on it. She has the watery-eyed expression of hopeless goodwill wedged between a body like a maypole and hair like a haystack after a gale. No matter what she does to that hair, it takes about three minutes to tangle itself up again, like a garden hosepipe left in a shed. She likes to wind flowers in it, because she thinks this is romantic. In some other kind of hair it might be.

Magrat has an open mind. It is as open as a field, as open as the sky. No mind could be more open without special surgical implements. As a result, it fills up with all sorts of things. For example, Magrat is one of those people who firmly believe that wisdom is wiser if it comes from a long way away (see WISDOM). A lot of what she believes in has the word 'folk' in it somewhere (folk wisdom, folk dance, folk song, folk medicine), as if 'folk' were other than the mundane people she sees every day. She plays a guitar badly and sings wobbly folk songs with her eyes shut in a way that suggests she really believes them. She thinks it would be nice if people could just be a bit kinder.

She is a relentless doer of good works, whether or not anyone needs them or wants them to be done. She rescues small lost baby birds and cries when they die; at various times, trying to get into the swing of it, she has tried to keep a magical familiar – generally some small creature that wanders away or dies or just gets the hell out of it at the earliest opportunity.

She is, however, more practical than most people believe who see no further than her vague smile, startlingly green silk dress (which would be both revealing and clinging if Magrat had anything for it to reveal or cling to) and collection of cheap occult jewellery. She is incidentally a great believer in occult jewellery – she has three large boxes of the stuff. Although she has a black cloak lined with red silk, she hardly ever wears a pointed hat. She's just not a pointy-hat person.

As Queen of Lancre, Magrat has a whole kingdom to be nice to. Things can only get worse.

Gaskin, Herbert 'Leggy'. A member of the City WATCH. Killed in the line of duty. His widow lives in Mincing Street, Ankh-Morpork. [GG, MAA]

Gaspode (the Wonder Dog). Small, bow-legged and wiry; basically grey but with patches of brown, white and black in outlying areas. Gaspode has fleas, hardpad, scurf, crusted yellow eyes, arthritis, rotting teeth and horrible bad breath, and is probably the only dog to contract Licky End, which is usually restricted to sheep. He is host to so many doggy diseases that he is surrounded by a cloud of dust and, all in all, smells like a privy carpet.

He is named after the original 'famous' Gaspode, who belonged to an old man in Ankh many years ago. When his owner died and was buried, the dog lay down on his grave and howled and howled for a couple of weeks, growling at everyone who came near. Then he died. He was considered a paragon of doggy faithfulness and loyalty until it was discovered that his tail had been trapped under the stone.

Gaspode was thrown into the river with a brick in a sack when he was a pup. Luckily, it was the ANKH, so he walked ashore inside the sack, forming for several days a certain confused relationship with the brick.

Gaspode encapsulates the essential

schizophrenia of all dogs. On the one hand, he desires nothing more than to be owned, to have a master and in general have a very secure warm place in front of the fire of life; on the other hand, he rebels against the very idea of ownership and any restriction on his freedom to roam Ankh-Morpork, eating and rolling in whatever he likes. Gaspode's tragedy is that, unlike other dogs, he is aware of this conflict.

Oh, and he can talk. But not many people pay any attention, because everyone knows that dogs can't talk. [MP, MAA]

Geas. A bird, with a head like a flamingo, a body like a turkey and legs like a Sumo wrestler. It walks in a jerky, bobbing fashion, as though its head were attached to its feet by elastic bands. Its prime means of defence is to cause a predator to laugh so much that it can run away before the predator recovers. *Geas* is also a word meaning curse or obligation. [S]

Genetics. The study of genetics on the Disc has never been very organized. The wizard Catbury (some 300 years before the present) is on record as having noticed, while strolling in his garden, that some plants were taller than other plants and, interestingly enough, that some plants were shorter than other plants. The response to his monograph on the subject can be summed up as

'Yes? Well? So what?', because Ankh-Morporkians have a logical and common-sense approach to life which means that Science is beaten before it starts.

Nevertheless, Catbury's writings remain in the LIBRARY and there were, later, some experiments based on his simple observations. These failed at an early stage, however, when wizards tried the experimental crossing of such well-known subjects as fruit flies and sweet peas. Unfortunately, they didn't quite grasp the fundamentals, and the resultant offspring – a sort of green thing that buzzed – led a short, sad life before being eaten by a passing vegetarian spider.

In any case a more dispassionate study of the evidence suggests that on the Discworld heredity is more mental than genetic, and certainly owes more to Lamarck than Mendel. The observation of the current ARCHCHANCELLOR, Mustrum RIDCULLY, that heredity means 'that if your father has a good brocade waistcoat you'll probably end up getting it' contains a certain amount of truth. In *Soul Music*, DEATH becomes encumbered with a granddaughter (daughter of his adopted daughter YSABELL and MORT) who has certainly acquired his powers of invisibility and memory. On Discworld, cutting off the tails of mice might well lead to them having tail-less offspring. And probably vengeful ones, too.

Genua. The Magical Kingdom, the Diamond City, the Fortunate Country. Genua was originally a pleasant and relaxed place in which to live but, under the iron rule of Lily WEATHERWAX, it became a fairytale city; this meant that people had to smile and be joyful the livelong day – at spearpoint, if necessary.

Genua nestles on the delta of the Vieux river, surrounded by swamp. It is a wealthy kingdom, having once controlled the river mouth and taxed its traffic. It has always been rich, lazy and unthreatened. From a distance, it looks like a complicated white crystal growing out of the greens and browns of the swamp.

Close to, there is an outer ring of small buildings, an inner ring of large, impressive white houses and, at the centre, a palace – tall, pretty and multi-turreted, like a toy castle. Under Lily, everything was very clean. Even the cobblestones had a polished look. The city was guarded by tall soldiers in red and blue uniforms. The place looked, in fact, like a fairytale city . . . with all the horrors that implies.

Both before, during and since the Weatherwax period Genua has also been a city of cooks. They don't have much to cook there, so they have learned to cook everything. A good Genuan cook can more or less take the squeezings of a handful of mud, a few dead leaves and a pinch or two of some unpronounceable herbs and produce a meal to make the gourmet burst into tears of gratitude and swear to be a better person for the rest of their entire life if they could just have one more plateful. [WA]

Geoffrey. One-time Secretary and Chief Butt of the FOOLS' GUILD. A Fool. He has eyes like two runny eggs and a very nervous disposition, as is often the case when you do not know where the next custard pie is coming from. [RM]

Gern. Apprentice embalmer in DJELI-BEYBI. A plump young man with a big, red, spotty face. He is fond of all the practical jokes you can play with the sad remnants of mortality, such as the disembodied handshake gag and all the other little delights so familiar to generations of medical students. [P]

Gibbsson. Apprentice guitar-maker in the employ of Blert WHEEDOWN. [SM]

Gimick. One of many cousins of Lance-constable CUDDY. A manufacturer of pins. [MAA]

Gimlet. A dwarf with a famously penetrating gaze who runs a café and delicatessen in Cable Street, Ankh-Morpork. It used to be for dwarfs only but under the influence of civic decency, a sense of the brotherhood of all sapient species and a desire to get some of the 'troll dollar', it has subsequently catered for that species as well. Try their rat and cream cheese.

Ginger. (*See* WITHEL, THEDA.)

Glod. A dwarf, the tangential victim of a curse placed on the Seriph of AL-YBI. His son, Glod GLODSSON, later found employment as a horn player in Ankh-Morpork. [WA, SM]

Glodsson, Glod. A dwarf. Small, even for a dwarf. Cousin of MODO. He has lodgings behind a tannery in Phedre Road and plays a large bronze horn. A member of the BAND WITH ROCKS IN and considers himself to be an extremely professional musician, in that money is always on his mind. [SM]

Glwenda. The daughter of a garlic farmer in DJELIBEYBI. Romantically linked with GERN the apprentice embalmer. [P]

Gnolls. A variety of troll, but without the latter's intelligence and noble disposition. [ER]

Gnomes and goblins. A more or less interchangeable term (a gnome is merely a goblin found underground, a goblin is merely a gnome coming up for air) for the Discworld's smallest (4'–9") humanoid species. Seldom encountered, not because of their rarity but because of their speed and natural desire to keep out of the way of creatures to whom they would merely be something sticky on the sole of the boot. They are generally hunters and gatherers, usually of property belonging to someone else.

Goatfounder, Hilta. A witch in OHULAN CUTASH, where she sells thunderdrops and penny wishes at a small, covered, market stall. Small and fat, Hilta wears an enormous hat with fruit on it and gives the impression of a mass of lace and shawls and colours and earrings and ordinary rings and so many bangles that a mere movement of her arms sounds like a percussion section falling off a cliff. She laughs like someone who has thought about life for a long time and has now seen the joke.

Her lodgings are over a herbalist and behind a tannery, offering splendid views over the rooftops of Ohulan. Among her 'back of the stall' preparations are: Tiger Oil, Maiden's Prayer, Husband's Helper, ShoNuff Ointment, Stay Long Ointment and Madame Goatfounder's Pennyroyal Preventatives. She performs an important function in the town, although no one talks very much about what that actually is. The only clue is that, if Hilta wasn't there, the town would be a good deal larger. [ER]

Godmothers, Fairy. A specialized form of witch with particular responsibility for the life of one individual or a number of individuals. They use wands – probably a modification of the wizard's staff – and tend to have an interest in travel. Fairy godmothers develop a very deep understanding of human nature, which makes the good ones kind and the bad ones powerful. [WA]

Gods, the. The Discworld has gods in the same way that other worlds have bacteria. There are billions of them, tiny bundles containing nothing more than a pinch of pure ego and some hunger.

Most of them never get worshipped. They are the small gods – the spirits of lonely trees, places where two ant-trails cross – and most of them stay that way. Because what they lack is belief. A handful, though, go on to greater things. Anything may trigger this. A shepherd, seeking a lost lamb, for example, may find it among the briars and take a minute or two to build a small cairn of stones in general thanks to whatever spirit might be around the place.

Despite the splendour of the world below them, the Disc gods are seldom satisfied. It is embarrassing to know that one is a god of a world that only exists because every improbability curve must have its far end; especially when one can peer into other dimensions at worlds whose Creators had more mechanical aptitude than imagination. No wonder, then, that the Disc gods spend more time bickering than in omnicognizance.

They are quarrelsome and somewhat bourgeois gods, who live in a palace of marble, alabaster and uncut moquette three-piece suites they chose to call DUN-MANIFESTIN. It is always a considerable annoyance to any Disc citizen with pretensions to culture that they are ruled by gods whose idea of an uplifting artistic experience is a musical doorbell.

The gods don't play chess, they haven't got the imagination. They prefer simple, vicious games, where you 'Do Not Pass Transcendence but Go Straight to Oblivion'; a key to the understanding of all religion is that a god's idea of amusement is Snakes and Ladders with greased rungs.

They are great believers in justice, at least as far as it extends to humans, and have been known to dispense it so enthusiastically that people miles away are turned into a cruet.

The trouble with gods is that, if enough people start believing in them, they begin to exist. People think the sequence is: first object, then belief. In fact it works the other way. Belief sloshes around in the firmament like lumps of clay spiralling into a potter's wheel. That's how gods get created. They clearly must be created by their own believers, because a brief resumé of the lives of most gods suggests that their origins certainly couldn't be divine. They tend to do exactly the things people would do if only they could, especially when it comes to nymphs, golden showers and the smiting of your enemies.

Gods and humans are inseparable. Because what gods need is belief, and what humans want is gods. (*See also* DEITIES.)

Gogol, Mrs Erzulie.   A voodoo woman in GENUA, who smokes a pipe and is known to have made use of zombies when household chores need doing. She is tall, handsome, middle-aged, and wears heavy gold earrings, a white blouse and a full red skirt with flounces. She has a black cockerel, Legba, as her familiar. She used to be romantically linked with Baron SATURDAY, who was later a zombie, and is the mother of Ella SATURDAY.

For practical purposes she can be considered a witch, although perhaps with a slightly different moral sense from the classic RAMTOPS craftswomen.

She foretells the future ostensibly by staring into bowls of jambalaya (but probably by relying on close observation and a deep study of human nature – all witches understand the need for a little magic in people's lives).

She lives in a house in the swamps close to Genua. From the river it looks like a simple affair of driftwood, roofed with moss and built over the swamp itself on four stout poles. They end in four large duck feet on which the house can, when necessary, move around the country. [WA]

Golems.   One of the rarest of Ankh-Morpork's minority groups, and unique in that it has not yet been found anywhere outside the city. It can hardly be called a 'species', since golems are created by priests or holy men from clay animated by a spell (or holy word). The word or spell is carved on their forehead and is in effect their life force.

No such creation has been attempted for a thousand years, it being held to be a little tasteless, but there is a third group that can create golems and that is golems themselves. All they need is some more clay and a Word. There are no such things as golem children, merely golems who are younger than other golems.

Even trolls look down on golems, who tend to be (physically) larger and more shapeless even than computer programmers and (mentally) withdrawn and rather sad yet very alert creatures doomed to do the jobs that men disdain and trolls don't want; not for nothing are they called 'horny-handed tons of soil'.

Gorphal.   A bearded, elderly diplomat in Ankh-Morpork. Famed as a student of AGATEAN EMPIRE affairs. [COM]

Gorrin the Cat.   A thief in Ankh-Morpork. B12 was his code identification from YMOR. Called the Cat because of his tendency to sleep a lot and not do much work. [COM]

Gortlick.   A writer of dwarf songs with HAMMERJUG. Songs are important to the dwarf community and new ones are commissioned for birthdays, weddings, and so on. Cynics say that the word 'gold' will inevitably turn up somewhere. [SM]

Gorunna Trench. An undersea chasm in the Disc's surface that is so black, so deep and so reputedly evil that even the krakens go there fearfully, and in pairs. In less reputedly evil chasms the fish go about with natural lights on their heads . . . in Gorunna they leave them unlit and insofar as it is possible for something without legs to creep, they creep. No living thing knows what lies down there; those who have found out have not been in a position to tell. [COM]

Granny's Cottage. Home to Granny WEATHERWAX. A witch's cottage so typical that, if there were any kind of tourist organization in the RAMTOPS, it would be given a grant. The description can be taken to apply to a greater or lesser extent to all rural witch cottages, although as indicated this one can be considered a witch's cottage *par eldritche*.

It nestles in the woods. It leans against itself for support. It's of the architectural style known as 'the vernacular', i.e. somebody swearing, and by now it gives the impression of having grown in place rather than having been built.

Access to the cottage is exclusively via the back door, but it is first worth taking some time to look at the garden. In the front of the building is a bit of lawn, with a forlorn windsock on a pole, although the cottage is largely surrounded by unruly beds of herbs which seem to move, even on windless days. There are also some leggy soft fruit bushes and, in front of the Rimward wall, a bleached wooden bench to catch the sun. Such shrubs and flowers as are otherwise found are all cuttings or spare clumps given to Granny Weatherwax by neighbours. A witch would never dream of *buying* anything for the garden. Around the side is a water butt and a walled paddock for her goats when they are not turned loose in the forest (witches prefer goats to cows). In a corner are half a dozen beehives.

Marking a boundary of the herb garden is a tree stump, beyond which is Granny Weatherwax's privy. Apart from the usual offices, the privy also contains the key to the cottage (on a nail), half a copy of an *Almanack and Booke of Dayes* (also on a nail), a stump of candle on a shelf and a chrysalis (this shelf tends to be a repository of things Granny Weatherwax has found on her walks and which appear to be interesting: oddly shaped stones, strange roots, fossils, and so on). Next to the privy is a large beech tree.

A key sign that this is the garden of a witch is the lack of a wall. Creatures of the forest could wander across it at any time. They very seldom do.

And now, the cottage . . .

Through the back door is the hall, with Mss Weatherwax's official witching hat hanging on a hook. This leads through into the stone-flagged kitchen, dominated by its wide chimney and inglenook fireplace, with its firedogs and hook over the fire for a big black kettle. Over the mantelpiece hang a small key, and a clock, kept mainly for its tick; in front of it are a rag rug and a rocking chair.

The room is otherwise furnished with a kitchen table and chairs, a dresser and an old chest. There is also a small speckled mirror. None of the furniture is new. None of it even looks as though it could ever have *been* new.

Off the kitchen is the scullery, which contains the walk-in pantry, a well (topped with a stone slab and a pump) and a big copper still. Shelves containing bottles and jars of ingredients suggest quite correctly that this is where some of the more physical, take-one-spoonful-at-night-and-another-if-you-wake-up-in-the-morning aspects of witchcraft are carried out. A door in the scullery leads to the lean-to where the goats are bedded down in bad weather.

Back in the kitchen is a small door opening on to the cramped staircase which leads to the bedroom. The plaster on the bedroom ceiling is cracked, and bulges like a tent. On the wash stand are a jug and a basin with a fetching rosebud pattern which also matches another china item under the bed. On the bed itself is a patchwork quilt which looks like a flat tortoise. It was made by Gordo SMITH and was given to Mss Weatherwax by ESK's mother one HOGSWATCHNIGHT. On the quilt is Granny Weatherwax, lying very still and holding a card saying 'I ATE'NT DEAD'.

Er . . .

Don't all rush for the stairs . . .

Granny Whitlow. A witch. She used to live in the gingerbread cottage encountered by RINCEWIND and TWOFLOWER. [LF]

Grateful, Lady Sara. A pupil at the QUIRM COLLEGE FOR YOUNG LADIES. Another horsy gel and an INTERCHANGEABLE EMMA. [SM]

Great Pyramid of Tsort. A now-derelict ancient wonder of the Discworld. Made of 1,003,010 limestone blocks, ten thousand slaves were worked to death in its construction. It is a maze of secret passages, their walls reputedly decorated with the distilled wisdom of ancient TSORT. In the circumstances the most important of these wise sayings must have been: Don't be a Slave.

It took sixty years to build. Its height plus its length divided by half its width equalled exactly 1.67563, or precisely 1,237.98712567 times the difference between the distance to the sun and the weight of a small orange. [LF]

Greebo. Nanny OGG's cat. A huge, one-eyed tom who divides his time between sleeping, eating and fathering the most incestuous feline tribe. He is technically a mottled grey but is covered with so much scar tissue that he looks like a fist with fur on it. He can only be said to have ears because there's no other word for the things left on top of his head.

Greebo's good eye, his left one, is yellow. The other one is pearly-white. He radiates genuine intelligence. He also radiates a smell that could knock over a wall and cause sinus trouble in a dead fox. Although he is addressed by virtually everyone as 'Yarrgeroffoutofityahbarstard', to Nanny Ogg he is still a cute little kitten and still sleeps on her bed when not out at night looking for something to fight, rape, eat (or all three). The way he affectionately tries to claw her eyeballs out in the morning is as good as an alarm clock.

When Greebo was briefly transformed into a human in GENUA, he was 6 feet tall, broad shouldered and leather clad, with rippling muscles under his shirt. He had a beard, a mane of black hair, a broken nose and a black patch over his bad eye. His other eye glittered like the sins of angels and his smile was the downfall of saints (female ones, anyway). He exuded a kind of greasy, diabolic sexuality. He was, in short, Greebo. [WS, WA, LL]

Greetling. Master Greetling is the Head of the Teachers' Guild. [GG]

Greggs, Miss. Teaches History at the QUIRM COLLEGE FOR YOUNG LADIES. [SM]

Greicha the First. Lord of the WYRMBERG.

He was killed by his daughter LIESSA but, because he was also a powerful wizard, he resolved to remain alive unofficially until only one of his children was left to conduct the funeral. [COM]

Gretelina. (*See* MELLIUS.)

Grimnir. Queen Grimnir the Impaler (1514–53, 1553–7, 1557–62, 1562–7, 1568–73). A vampire Queen of Lancre. The phrase 'the Queen is dead, long live the Queen' is particularly apposite in her case. [WS]

respected Guilds, the largest and most senior of which are micro-societies in their own right. A Guild may well, in return for a tithe, oversee all aspects of a member's life practically from the cradle to the grave (particularly in the case of the ASSASSINS' GUILD) and possibly beyond (in the case of the Guild of Priests, Sacerdotes and Occult Inter-mediaries). The oldest and richest guild is the Beggars'; the most stylish the Assassins'; the largest the Thieves' (although there is popularly supposed to be a Rat Guild).

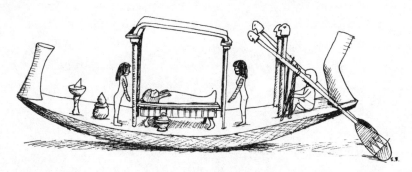

Grinjer. Maker of grave models in DJELI-BEYBI. He is twenty-six, acne'd and still lives with his mother because he cannot find a girl who shares his interest in glue. [P]

Gritz. A troll hotel in Ankh-Morpork. Considered very high-class by trolls, since water is piped to every room and there are carpets, or at least something soft, on the floor. The dining room, with its fine selection of clays, is particularly noted. [SM]

Grodley, Sister. A witch from the Skund area. Drops her aitches and sticks her little finger out when she drinks her tea. [WS]

Guilds. Ankh-Morpork is the home of many of the Disc's oldest and most

The smallest Guild is, most people are surprised to learn, the Guild of C.M.O.T. Dibblers, membership one. It nevertheless qualifies, under ancient rules that were changed almost immediately after Mr Dibbler discovered them, for full Guild status.

Almost all the schools and most of the hospices in Ankh-Morpork are Guild-run. The 300-odd Guilds to be found in the city include:
ALCHEMISTS' GUILD
ASSASSINS' GUILD
Bakers' Guild [GG]
Bandits' Guild [LL]
BEGGARS' GUILD (Fellowship of Beggars)
CONJURERS' GUILD
Dibblers, C.M.O.T., Guild of
DOG GUILD [MAA]
EMBALMERS' GUILD (Guild of Embalmers and Allied Trades)

ENGRAVERS' GUILD

FIREFIGHTERS' GUILD

FOOLS' GUILD (Guild of Fools and Joculators and College of Clowns)

GAMBLERS' GUILD

Haberdashers' Guild [P]

Handlemen's Guild [MP]

Lawyers' Guild [WS]

MERCHANTS' AND TRADERS' GUILD

PLUMBERS' GUILD (Guild of Plumbers and Dunnikindivers) [P]

Priests', Sacerdotes' and Occult Intermediaries' Guild

SEAMSTRESSES' GUILD

Smugglers' Guild [P]

STRIPPERS' GUILD

Teachers' Guild [GG]

THIEVES' GUILD (Guild of Thieves, Burglars and Allied Trades)

Gulta. One of the sons of Gordo SMITH, and brother of ESK. [ER]

Gurnt the Stupid. A past king of Lancre. He had a plan for an aerial attack force of armoured ravens. It never got off the ground. [LL]

Hakardly, Ovin. A seventh-level wizard and a one-time Lecturer in Lore at Unseen University. He was an elderly wizard, who gave the impression of being as fragile as a cheese straw. [S]

Hamadryad. Tree-dwelling species. The females have green skin and long, mossy hair. The males are tall and have skins the colour of walnut husks, with muscles bulging like sacks of melons. Their eyes are luminous green and have no pupils. Hamadryads do not wear clothes. They live not exactly in the tree, as squirrels do, but inside what can only be called the psyche of the tree. [COM]

Hamesh. A farmer. Brother to LEZEK and thus MORT's uncle. [M]

Hammerhock, Bjorn. A dwarf craftsman in Ankh-Morpork, with a workshop in Rime Street. Killed by the march of weapons technology. [MAA]

Hammerjug. A writer of dwarf songs with his partner, GORTLICK. [SM]

Hamstring, Goodie Ammeline. Address unknown, but almost certainly the RAM-

TOPS. A witch, bent with age, like a bow. White hair, and a cracked and quavery voice, but her eyes were bright and small as blackcurrants.

After death, her soul was no longer bound by the body's morphic field and her hair unwound itself from its tight bun, changing colour and lengthening. Her body straightened up, her wrinkles dwindled and vanished and her grey dress changed to something leaf-green and clingy. Her voice became suggestive of musk and maple syrup. A prime example of the Discworld truth that what you look like isn't who you are. [M]

Harebut the Provision Merchant. Father of NIJEL the Destroyer. [S]

Harga, Sham. Owner of HARGA'S HOUSE OF RIBS in Ankh-Morpork. Sham, with his beefy hands and well-padded vest, is an expansive if grubby advert for his own carbohydrate merchandise. He has run a successful eatery for many years by always smiling, never extending credit and realizing that most of his customers want meals properly balanced between the four food groups: sugar, starch, grease and burnt crunchy bits. He runs:

Harga's House of Ribs. An eatery down by the docks in Ankh-Morpork. It is probably not numbered among the city's leading eateries, catering as it does for the type of clientele that prefers quantity and breaks up the tables if it doesn't get it. HARGA's All-You-Can-Gobble-For-a-Dollar menu is famous wherever huge appetites gather and mountainous stomachs rumble.

The fat in the pan has a geological history all of its own. Bits of ancient sausage and nodules of bacon from pig varieties long extinct are still in it somewhere. Nor does the coffee jug ever get cleaned out – the coffee is like molten lead, but it has this in its favour: when you've drunk it, you have overwhelming feeling of relief that you've got to the bottom of the cup. Normally the only decoration in the café is on Harga's vest, which also acts as a sort of unofficial menu.

The city's dogs have also noted that Sham Harga puts out his rubbish at midnight. This would come as a surprise to his clientele, who thought he cooked it.

Hashimi. A prophet of the Omnian church. It is said that he was given the *Book of Creation* by the Great God OM. They all say this. [SG]

Hashishim. The original assassins. A band of mad killers, who were feared throughout Hubward KLATCH, and were led by the first CREOSOTE, Seriph of AL

Buildings along the Ankh

118

KHALI. They derived their name from the huge quantities of hashish they consumed. They were unique among killers in being both deadly and, at the same time, inclined to giggle, groove to interesting patterns of light and shade on their terrible knife blades and, in extreme cases, fall over. [S]

Hedge wizards. Hedge wizardry is a very honoured and specialized form of magic that attracts silent, thoughtful men of the druidical persuasion and topiaric inclinations. If you invite a hedge wizard to a party he will spend half the evening talking to your potted plant. And he will spend the other half listening to it. These wizards do not have anything to do with Unseen University, where they would be considered in dire need of dried frog products. [ER]

Heliodeliphilodelphiboschromenos. Disc town mentioned in the song 'The Ball of Philodelphus'. A sort of architectural equivalent of Colonel Bogey. [E]

Hell. There are, almost by definition, an unlimited number of Hells – potentially at least a personal one for every living sapient being.

However, humans are impressionable, gregarious creatures (one famous definition of Hell, after all, is that it is other people). Hell tends to look like they have come to expect and what they expect is often conditioned by what they've read and seen, so that for people around the CIRCLE SEA there is a kind of general, consensus Hell. This is the one described quite fully in *Eric*, where rather dull demons mindlessly apply physical torture to non-physical bodies and there is a general wailing and gnashing of teeth subsequent to a handout of free, badly fitting false teeth for those who die toothless.

The unremarkable horror of the place is somewhat ameliorated by the lack of imagination of the demons who run it. For example, a forbidding door leads to it, with a sign on it saying, 'You Don't Have To Be "Damned" To Work Here, But It Helps!!!', and the three exclamation marks and quote marks around a word that patently does not need it suggest a type of dreadfulness all their own. It also has a doorknocker – black, horrible and tied up so that it can't be used. There is a doorbell next to it, which plays a jolly little chime. For anyone with any interest in music, Hell starts right there.

As you might expect – in fact, precisely because you would expect – the broad steps leading up to Hell are made of good intentions, carved in stone. (*See also* DEMONS.) [E]

Henderson, Fred 'Mr Harpsichord'. Musician and council member of the MUSICIANS' GUILD. [SM]

Henry, Coffin. A professional beggar in Ankh-Morpork. Is paid money not to attend important social occasions. If people don't take this small but essential precaution, he sidles ingratiatingly into the party and invites guests to inspect his remarkable collection of skin diseases. He also has a cough, which sounds almost solid, and is known for his volcanic spitting. Apart from this, he can be recognized by his sign on which is chalked: 'For sum muny I wunt follo you home. Coff Coff.' [SM]

Here'n'Now. An unlicensed thief and stool pigeon in Ankh-Morpork. The worst thief in the world (worst as in not good at it). A very small, raggedy man, whose beard and hair are so overgrown and matted together that he looks like a ferret peering out of a bush. Called Here'n'Now because of his nervous inability to master anything but the present tense, so that his speech is therefore on these lines: 'So I'm standing outside the Mended Drum when who is coming up to me but Flannelfoot Boggis who tells me he is seeing where the De Bris gang are robbing the jewellers' shop in Gleam Street, but I am reticent because I know this to be nothing but an untruth . . .' [MAA]

Herne the Hunted.   God of all small furry creatures whose destiny it is to end life with a brief, crunchy squeak. Herne is about 3 feet high with long, floppy, rabbit ears and very small horns. He has an extremely good turn of speed. Found in the mountains and forests of LANCRE, moving extremely fast. [WS, LL]

Heroes.   Most of the Disc's classic heroes are from the barbaric tribes nearer the frozen Hub, which have a sort of export trade in heroes, which shows that the leaders of these tribes are by no means stupid because their sons are usually suicidally gloomy when sober and homicidally insane when drunk. They tend to acquire magic swords, a forthright attitude to women, and a complete disrespect for other people's property. Some of the Disc's best-known heroes include COHEN the Barbarian, HRUN the Barbarian, Erig Stronginthearm [COM], Black Zenell [COM], Codice of Chimeria [COM], and Cimbar the Assassin [LF]. Stronginthearm is a dwarf name, but presumably they have heroes just like everybody else.

Herrena the Henna-Haired Harridan.   An adventuress. A good swordswoman who has amassed a modest fortune for a future which will certainly include a bidet if she has anything to do with it. She is usually sensibly dressed in light chain mail, soft boots and a short sword, and

would look quite stunning after a good bath, a heavy-duty manicure and the pick of the leather goods in Woo Hun Ling's Oriental Exotica and Martial Aids on Heroes Street, Ankh-Morpork. [LF, E]

Hersheba.   Small desert kingdom Rimwards of KLATCH, practically on the more-or-less vague boundary with HOWONDALAND. Said to be ruled by a queen who lives for ever.

History, nature of.   (*See* MONKS, HISTORY.)

Hodgesaargh.   Castle falconer at LANCRE. Hodgesaargh is not his original name, but he is regularly attacked by his birds just as you speak to him, and this has led to a common misunderstanding. An amiable, good-natured man, whose love and care for his charges is only surpassed by their own fervent desire to eat his eyeballs. [LL]

Hogfather, the.   Now considered to be a kind old gentleman with whiskers and boots who arrives, to the sound of hog bells, with a sack of toys on HOGSWATCH-NIGHT. Children leave out a glass of wine and a pork pie for him. They decorate their houses with an oak tree in a pot and strings of paper sausages; on Hogswatchday they wear paper hats while they eat their pork dinner.

However, this is a light modern version of a darker myth. The original Hogfather is a winter god associated with the pig-killing that is customary in country districts in the month before Hogswatchnight. According to legend – at least in those areas where pigs are a vital part of the household economy – the Hogfather spends the year in his secret palace of pig bones, emerging on Hogswatchnight to gallop from house to house on a crude sledge drawn by four tusked wild boars to deliver presents of sausages, black puddings, pork scratchings and ham to all the children who have been good. He says 'Ho Ho Ho' a lot. Children who have been bad get a bag full of bloody bones (it's these little details that tell you it's a tale for children). There is a song about him, which includes the line: 'You'd Better Watch Out . . .'

The kinder version of the Hogfather is said to have originated in the legend of a local king who, one winter's night, happened to be passing, or so he said, the home of three young women and heard them sobbing because they had no food to celebrate the midwinter feast. He took pity on them and threw a packet of sausages through the window – badly concussing one of them, but there's no point in spoiling a good legend.

However, it is clear that the root of the story goes back much, much further.

Hogswatchnight. The one night of the Disc's long year when witches are expected to stay at home. Occurs at the turn of the Disc year. By tradition, shops do not open on Hogswatchday.

Hoki (Hoki the Jokester). A nature god in the RAMTOPS. He manifests himself as an oak tree, or as half-man and half-goat, or in his most common aspect as a bloody nuisance. He is found only in deep woods and likes to haunt the Ramtops. Hoki was banished from DUNMANI-FESTIN for pulling the old exploding mistletoe joke on BLIND IO.

Hollow, Desiderata. A fairy godmother, which is a very specialized form of witch. A kindly and intelligent soul, who lived in LANCRE. Although blind for thirty years, she was blessed or possibly cursed with second sight and always saw what she was doing just before she did it.

Her cottage was stuffed with old books, maps and curios from Foreign Parts. Her friendship with Magrat GAR-LICK, who has rather more respect for book learning than her fellow witches, led to Magrat inheriting her magic wand and, directly, the confrontation between the WEATHERWAX sisters. [WA]

Holy Wood. A wind-blown old forest, a temple and some sand dunes about 30 miles turnwise of Ankh-Morpork, on a sun-drenched spit of land where the CIRCLE SEA meets the Rim Ocean. There is a legend that a city on the site was destroyed by the gods for some unspeakable crime against them or mankind, and given what the gods (and mankind) get up to all the time without any kind of punishment at all, it must have been something pretty awful.

For a while, Holy Wood was the focus for creatures from the DUNGEON DIMEN-SIONS, who tried to use the magic of the area to break into the real world during the time that moving pictures were being made there. [MP]

Hong, Mr. Owner of the short-lived Three Jolly Luck Take-Away Fish Bar, which was built on the site of an old temple on Dagon Street. No one really knows what happened to him in that terrible five minutes just after he opened for business. [MAA]

Hopkins, Chickenwire. A farmer in the RAMTOPS who once threw a rock at Granny WEATHERWAX just after she'd helped a local troll. Soon afterwards his barns were mysteriously flattened. [WA]

Horse People. The Horse Tribes of the Hubland steppes are born in the saddle, despite the inconvenience, and are particularly adept at natural or witch magic. They live in yurts heated by burning horse dung; this makes good fuel, but the Horse People have a lot to learn about air-conditioning – starting with what it means. They eat horse cheese, horse meat, horse soup, horse black pudding, horse d'oeuvres and drink a thin beer you wouldn't want to speculate about. When he's not working elsewhere they tend to be joined by COHEN the Barbarian, who enjoys their easygoing attitude to life, or at least to other people's lives. [LF]

Howondaland. When people talk of the 'dark and mysterious continent of KLATCH' it is Howondaland they are referring to. Its borders are imprecise, since they begin where those of the other countries on the Hubwards coast of Klatch fade away (that is to say, where surveyors don't come back and mapmakers are found nailed upside down to a tree). Indeed, it is hardly correct to call it a country – it has a name simply because cartographers don't like vast expanses of empty paper. A few hardy souls trade there, but it remains one of the biggest genuinely unexplored areas of the Disc, and is widely believed to be even more dangerous for the unwary traveller than Shamlegger Street, Ankh-Morpork, on a Saturday night.

Hrun the Barbarian. Hrun of CHIMERIA. One of the CIRCLE SEA's more durable heroes. Not exceptionally bright, but exceptionally unimaginative. Nevertheless, practically an academic by Hub standards in that he can think without moving his lips.

Hrun has the statutory wide chest and neck like a tree trunk, but a surprisingly small head, with bushy eyebrows and stubbly chin under its wild thatch of black hair – the effect is like putting a tomato on a coffin. His skin has a coppery gleam and there is much gold about his person in the shape of anklets and wristlets that once belonged to someone else, although he is otherwise naked apart from the usual leopardskin loincloth. (He killed the leopard with his teeth, according to legend, or his breath, according to likelihood.) For a while at least he carried the magical sword KRING. [COM]

Hub, the. The centre of the Disc and site of CORI CELESTI. [COM]

Humptemper. Author of *Names of the Ants*. A strange book, half magical treatise and half autobiography. The title apparently derives from an account of the time Humptemper, who was highly skilled in the discipline witches call 'borrowing' and wizards called *psychoproicio* (lit. 'throwing away the mind'), spent inside the group mind of a nest of ants in the University's walls. [E]

Humptulip. Author of the 2,000-page *Howe to Kille Insects*. Frequently confused with HUMPTEMPER, although the former lived several centuries before. [MAA]

Hwel. A dwarf, banished from his tribe, not only because of his claustrophobia but also because of his tendency to daydream (both undesirable, not to say fatal, traits if you work in a mine). He has a very receptive mind for raw inspirations and is still one of the Discworld's premier playwrights, writing for VITOLLER's troupe of players. He has a hairy bullet head and stubby legs and, at the time of *Wyrd Sisters*, was 102 years old – the prime of life for a dwarf. [WS, LL]

Hydrophobes. Also known as Loathers. Wizards who loathe water; the very idea of it revolts them. A really good hydro-phobe has to be trained on dehydrated water from birth. Although they make great weather magicians (rain clouds just give up and go away), they are mainly used on the kingdom of KRULL to power the flying lens means of transport, which can be suspended over water by the sheer power of revulsion from the hydrophobes strapped to the lens' rim. They wear distinctive black and dark blue robes and all wear ingrained expressions of self-revulsion at their own body fluids. They die young; they just can't live with themselves. [COM]

Ibid. Ephebian philosopher and author of *Discourses* and *Civics*. Tall and willowy with an indefinable air of authority, he is a well-known expert on everything except geometry, interior decorating and elementary logic. [P, SG]

Ice Giants. The size of large houses, craggy and faceted, glinting green and blue in the light. Their eyes are tiny and black and deep-set, like lumps of coal (although this is the only way in which they resemble the idols built, in response to ancient and unacknowledged memories, by children in snowy weather).

The Ice Giants have been engaged in an eons-old battle with the gods and are currently imprisoned inside a wall of mountains at the Hub. They probably began as a metaphor for glaciers, but we know what happens to metaphors on the Disc.

Technically, the Ice Giants are probably a type of troll. [LF, S]

Iconoscope/iconograph. The iconograph is a picture-making box. Operates via a small demon imprisoned inside with a good eye for colour and a speedy hand with a paintbrush.

Introduced to the STO PLAINS by TWOFLOWER the tourist, it was subsequently developed in Ankh-Morpork; by the time of the moving picture craze in HOLY WOOD it was possible to achieve motion pictures by using a lot of demons and getting them to paint very fast by means of a handle attached to a lot of tiny whips. And by the time of *Men At Arms*, Corporal CARROT – even on a Watchman's salary – was able to buy a small iconograph, by then known, because of the demon inside, as a 'brownie'. [COM, LF, MP]

Iesope. An Ephebian, and another contender for 'Greatest Teller of Stories in the World'. The one about the fox and the grapes went down very well among the farmers who know how important it is to lock up their grapes every night. [P]

Igneous. A troll who owns a pottery in Ankh-Morpork. [GG]

Illuminated & Ancient Brethren of Ee. Secret society in Ankh-Morpork. You never hear about all the charity work they do because they don't do any. [GG]

125

Imp y Celyn. A bard from LLAMEDOS. A tall, eighteen-year-old harpist with dark, curly hair, who went to Ankh-Morpork to seek his fortune after falling out with his father, a strong-minded druid. Until the city and certain other things worked their magic on him he had been a good, circle-going boy from the valleys, who didn't drink, didn't swear and played the harp at every druidic sacrifice.

He became a member of the pop music group The BAND WITH ROCKS IN, adopting the stage name 'Buddy' because his real name, 'Imp', means 'small shoot' or 'bud'. 'y Celyn' means 'of the holly'; it was obvious that anyone with a name like 'Bud of the Holly' would find this a drawback in the music business. [SM]

Incessant, the Hon. Douglas. An assassin, a guest at the ball in GENUA on Samedi Nuit Mort. [WA]

Inn-sewer-ants. An Agatean concept: people pay money against the odds of a disaster occurring. The importation of this idea is allegedly the reason behind Ankh-Morpork's most recent fire, which destroyed much of the city. [COM]

Inns. Known drinking-houses on the Disc include:

Blue Lias (Holy Wood) [MP]

Broken/Mended DRUM (Ankh-Morpork)

Bucket (Ankh-Morpork) [MAA]

Bunch of Grapes (Ankh-Morpork) [GG]

Crimson Leech (Ankh-Morpork) [COM]

FIDDLER'S RIDDLE (Ohulan Cutash)

Goat & Bush (Lancre) [LL]

Jolly Cabbage (Scrote) [SM]

Quene's Hed/Duke's Head (Sto Helit) [M]

Troll's Head (Ankh-Morpork, in the SHADES) [S]

Insider, the. An old dark god of the NECROTELICOMNICON. As the name suggests, probably yet another DUNGEON DIMENSIONS inhabitant who managed to enter Reality and stay there. [ER]

Inspirations. A fundamental particle in the Discworld universe. It is harder to describe them than it is to describe their effect, which is to create ideas – or, more accurately, sudden insights – in the human brain.

It has been postulated that untold millions of inspirations constantly sleet through the universe. They can pass through absolutely anything and also seem to be able to travel, tachyon-like, through time. However, the human or near-human brain contains a receptor which, while it doesn't stop an inspiration, can be fired up by the passage of one (causing, in that telling phrase, 'a flash of inspiration' – and not for nothing do we say 'I was struck by an idea').

This causes the throwing out of an idea. It may be for a play, an invention or something insubstantial, such as a theory of genetics. Since inspirations are not restricted in time, it may also be for something quite anachronistic. Presumably the brighter proto-hominids went to sleep in their trees and were occasionally awakened and mystified by the idea of pre-sliced bread or cold fusion for hundreds of years before the more immediately useful one involving the idea of hanging on more tightly happened to be shooting past.

According to Ponder STIBBONS of Unseen University, inspirations also *originate* in the human brain. In some rare individuals an inspiration may excite the inspiration node, causing it to throw off new inspirations. There is certainly anecdotal evidence for this. Everyone knows people who are not only brilliant in themselves but also generate ideas in other people around them.

Which, given the Discworld's love of opposites, must also mean that there are people who are an 'ideas *sink*'. And, again, common observation suggests that this is the case – there are certainly people who, humdrum in themselves, cause humdrumity in others as well. It is as if they act as a lightning rod for any originality around them, diverting it to earth.

For some reason, these people quite often end up in positions of power . . .

Interchangeable Emmas. Captain VIMES's name for the well-bred young women who muck out, dose, worm and exercise the dragons at Ankh-Morpork's SUN-SHINE SANCTUARY – and, by extension, that large army of Alice-banded sisters who do much the same job at stables and kennels all over the universe. It's a strange fact that the more highly born the family, the more likely the young female members are to be doing something smelly with a big fork.

Invisible writings. The study of invisible writings is a new discipline in Unseen University made available by the discovery of the bi-directional nature of Library-Space. The thaumic mathematics are complex, but boil down to the fact that all books, everywhere, affect all other books. This is obvious: books inspire other books written in the future, and cite books written in the past (as is the case this very moment). The General Theory of L-Space suggests that, in that case, the contents of books as yet unwritten can be deduced from books now in existence.

The Reader in Invisible Writings is currently Ponder STIBBONS. [LL]

Iodine. Fourth former at the QUIRM COLLEGE FOR YOUNG LADIES. Her father liked the sound of the word. [SM]

Ipslore the Red. A wizard. Eighth son of an eighth son – powerful and of course wearing a pointy hat. He fled the halls of magic and fell in love and got married (not necessarily in that order). He had eight sons: the first seven were at least as powerful as any wizard in the world; the eighth was a sourcerer. (*See* COIN and MAGIC.) [S]

Irexes. Ephebian philosopher who found that sandstone is stone pressed out of sand, which suggested to him that grains are the fathers of mountains. [SG]

Ironfoundersson, Mr. 'King' Ironfoundersson, of COPPERHEAD in LANCRE. CARROT's adoptive father. He made the crown for the Queen of Lancre. As is usual among dwarfs, the royal title is merely a technical term and has few of the connotations that it carries among humans, viz., people are likely to try to take sneaky pictures of you with your clothes off. [LL]

Ishkible. Prophet of the Omnian religion. [SG]

Ixolite. The last surviving banshee. A member of the FRESH START CLUB, who stays at Mrs CAKE's lodging house. Tall, with a long, sad face, he is usually seen wrapped in something which may be a long cloak but could possibly be wings. He has a speech impediment and is shy of meeting people, so instead of sitting on rooftops screaming when people are about to die he just writes them a suitable note ('OooeeeOooeeeOoooeee') and slips it under the door and runs away. Technically, banshees should be female; this might be one of the reasons for his sadness. [RM, LL, MAA]

Jackson, 'Tonker'. An old army pal of Sergeant Fred COLON. [MAA]

Jade, Princess. A troll schoolfriend of SUSAN at the QUIRM COLLEGE FOR YOUNG LADIES. She has bad eyesight, knits chain mail in handicraft class and has a note excusing her from unnecessary sunshine. Comes from the COPPERHEAD area of LANCRE. Anti-siliconism is still a feature of Discworld affairs and she was probably accepted because snobbery beat speciesism; the headmistress said a princess, even a troll one, would add *ton* to the school. In Jade's case she was right to within a few pounds. [SM]

Jaims. A son of Gordo SMITH and another brother of ESK. [ER]

Jape, Brother. Lecturer at the FOOLS' GUILD. He has a soul like cold boiled string and teaches juggling. [WS]

Jerakeen. One of the four giant elephants supporting the Discworld. [COM]

Jimbo. Best friend to CRASH. Plays the bass guitar, or at least moves his hands on one, in Crash's musical group – originally called Insanity. [SM]

Jimi. God of beggars. Panhandles prayers.

Johnson, Bergholt Stuttley ('Bloody Stupid Johnson'). A broadly incompetent landscape gardener, but also considerably unskilled in the fields of civic statuary and large musical instruments.

Also known as 'Bloody Stupid "It Might Look A Bit Messy Now But Just You Come Back in Five Hundred Years' Time" Johnson', or 'Bloody Stupid "Look, The Plans Were the Right Way Round When I Drew Them" Johnson'.

It would be wrong to call him completely unskilled, because some of the creations for which he'll be remembered must surely have taken considerable skill. It was just not the right skill.

Fundamental to his approach was blindness to the significance of, and more importantly the difference between, such things as feet and inches and ounces and pounds. He never let this get him down, however, and was relentlessly cheerful in the face of disappointment.

Among his achievements were an artificial hillock built from 2,000 tons of earth in front of Quirm Manor because 'It'd drive me mad to have to look at a bunch of trees and mountains all day long, how about you?'; he also designed the commemorative arch celebrating the Battle of Crumhorn, which is kept in a small cardboard box, the Quirm Memorial, the Hanging Gardens of Ankh and the Colossus of Morpork (all pocket-sized), and the ornamental cruet set for

example, he built the great organ of Unseen University, which has the widest range of any musical instrument known to man or devil.

Strangely enough, Johnson's renowned lack of aptitude brought him considerable fame and quite a few commissions in later life. There are always

Mad Lord Snapcase. Four families live in the salt shaker, and the pepper pot is used for storing grain (both in Upper Broadway).

Johnson was never a man to let inexperience or incompetence in any field stand in his way, and with his near-godlike ineptitude often achieved effects that a genius might find hard. For

very rich people looking for fashionable and amusing ways of spending their money, and Johnson was for a while much in demand by those who found that oversized ornamental temples at the bottom of small lakes, or tree-lined avenues 4 feet long, brightened up their day. It became quite the thing 'to have been Johnsoned'.

Johnson can be summed up as being on the opposite end of the scale which, at the other end, contains people like LEONARD OF QUIRM. The high spot of his career is thought to be the PATRICIAN'S PALACE grounds. [MAA]

Jorgen. A cousin of Acting-constable CUDDY. A dwarf, and a watch-maker. [MAA]

Judy. A goblin. Works, reluctantly, with Chas SLUMBER. [TOC]

Keeble, Liona. A job broker in Ankh-Morpork. [M, RM]

Keli. Princess Kelirehenna of STO LAT. When first encountered, she was a slim, red-haired girl of fifteen with a strong jawline; not beautiful, being over-endowed in the freckle department and, frankly, rather on the skinny side. Her role in life was to fail to be killed by an assassin owing to the gland-led incompetence of MORT.

She eventually became Her Supreme Majesty, Queen Kelirehenna I, Lord of Sto Lat, Protector of the Eight Protectorates, and Empress of the Long Thin Debated Piece Hubwards of Sto Kerrig. [M]

Ken, Stalling. A beggar on the streets of Ankh-Morpork. He had the privilege of supping with DEATH, or at least of supping with Death and getting up the next morning. [SM]

Kepple. A past sergeant of the Night WATCH in Ankh-Morpork. He was head of the Watch when Sam VIMES was a recruit. [MAA]

Khat-leon-ra-pta, Queen. A past monarch of DJELIBEYBI, during the Second Empire. She conquered HOWONDALAND, but it was subsequently sold back to its inhabitants to pay for yet more pyramids. [P]

Kheneth XIV. Past monarch of DJELIBEYBI. [P]

Khuft. Accidental discoverer of the subsequently mighty land of DJELIBEYBI. A small, dark man in a loin cloth and with two blackened stumps of teeth. He fled into the desert to escape disgruntled purchasers of his sub-standard camels. [P]

Kings, Ankh-Morporkian. These have included:
Aguinna IV (Queen) [MAA]
ARTOROLLO
Cirone IV [MAA]
Coanna (Queen) [MAA]
LORENZO THE KIND
Ludwig the Tree
Paragore [MAA]
Tyrril [MAA]
Veltrick III [MAA]
Webblethorpe the Unconscious [MAA]
(*See also* MONARCHY.)

Klatch. The name of both an individual country and the great mysterious continent, between the CIRCLE SEA and the Rim Ocean, which is its hinterland. Klatch too once had an empire and ruled, more or less, the greater part of the continent . . . hence the name has lingered on, at least as far as the people of Ankh-Morpork are concerned.

It has to be said that the words 'Klatch' and 'Klatchian' are used by people of the STO PLAINS as practically interchangeable with 'foreign', in the same way that the fierce D'reg nomads in the Klatchian desert use the words 'foreigner' and 'traveller' interchangeably with the word 'target'.

The sovereign countries of TSORT, DJELIBEYBI, EPHEBE and even OMNIA are all on the Klatchian coast.

Klatch the country is a prosperous trading nation with a proud and venerable civilization, whose capital city is now AL KHALI. Its tongue is said to have all the subtlety of a language so ancient and sophisticated that it had fifteen words meaning 'assassination' before the rest of the world caught on to the idea of bashing one another over the head with rocks. Klatch has a big trading fleet, and is also known for its 'bhong' music, its blue-black-skinned people and its cuisine (curry, boiled fish, dark green sauce, rice, etc.).

Klatch is the nearest 'foreign' nation to Ankh-Morpork. Technically, of course, Pseudopolis and QUIRM and STO HELIT are all independent city states and much closer, but they are really for all their protestations economic and social satellite states of Ankh-Morpork. Klatch, however, is clearly a rival and is also obviously foreign, and there is therefore that strange love-hate relationship that always exists between two nations whose fortunes are historically intertwined (cf. England and France, the United States

North and South, Western Australia and the rest of Australia, Scotland and Scotland, etc., etc.). Traditionally, this means that Klatchians are regarded as being at one and the same time incredibly cunning and irredeemably stupid, bone-idle and deviously industrious, highly cultured and obstinately backward . . .

The continental hinterland consists of deserts, jungles and rain forests. It also contains lost kingdoms of Amazonian princesses, volcanoes, elephants' graveyards, lost diamond mines, strange ruins covered in hieroglyphics and hidden plateaux where reptilian monsters of a bygone era romp and play. On any reasonable map of the area there's barely room for the trees.

Klatchian Foreign Legion, the. A special force set up by KLATCH (the country) to defend its rather vague desert borders against predatory neighbours and also

against the D'regs, a desert tribe. It is, however, open to recruits from any country and traditionally is a refuge for the disgraced, the fugitive and the lovelorn.

It is well known that people join the Klatchian Foreign Legion to forget (everything except sand) and this seems to work, because no one in the Klatchian Foreign Legion can remember why they are there.

Or their name. Or their rank.

The Klatchian Foreign Legion has a famed drinking and marching song, which goes 'Er . . . '.

Klopstock. Mr Klopstock is the proprietor of the Bull Pit in Pseudopolis, a crude theatre. [SM]

Knibbs, Lettuce. Lady's maid to Queen MOLLY of the BEGGARS' GUILD. Killed in error for Queen Molly. As was remarked by Lance-constable ANGUA, she was one of those people whose chief role in life is to die. [MAA]

Knurd. Knurd is the opposite of drunk. It should not be mistaken for sobriety. Sobriety is merely the median state; knurdness is a sort of super-sobriety. By comparison, sobriety is like having a bath in warm cotton wool.

Knurdness strips away all the illusion, all the comforting pink fog in which people normally spend their lives, and lets them see and think clearly for the first time ever. Then, after they've screamed a bit, they make sure they never get knurd again.

Klatchian coffee makes you knurd.

Koomi. Koomi of Smale. A religious philosopher and author of *Ego-Video Liber Deorum*. [SG]

Koomi, Hoot. Bald-headed Djelibeybian

High Priest of Khefin, the Two-Faced God of Gateways. [P]

Kring. A magical, talking, black sword. Forged from thunderbolt (meteoric) iron. It has highly ornate runic inscriptions running up the blade, a couple of rubies set in its pommel, a slight nick two-thirds of the way up the blade and what it would really like to be is a ploughshare.

Kring speaks in a voice like the scrape of a blade over a stone. Once owned by HRUN the Barbarian, but present whereabouts unknown. [COM]

Krona, Heme. The owner of the Camels-R-Us livery stable in DJELIBEYBI. [P]

Krull. A secretive island kingdom. Geographically, it is a large island, quite mountainous and heavily wooded, with pleasant white buildings visible among the trees. The land slopes gradually up towards the Rim, so that the highest point in Krull slightly overhangs the Edge.

The island not only gets higher as it nears the Edge, it gets narrower, too. Here at the very lip is its major city, also called Krull. At the very edge of the city is a large amphitheatre, with seating for several tens of thousands of people. Its rimmost mountains project over the RIMFALL . . . in fact a large part of its coastline sticks out over the Edge, so native Krullians need to look where they are going and avoid sleepwalking at all costs.

Since building materials on Krull are largely salvaged from the CIRCUMFENCE, their houses have a distinctly nautical look. Entire ships are morticed together and converted into buildings.

The city rises, tier upon tier, between the blue-green ocean of the Disc and the soft cloud sea of the Edge, the eight colours of the RIMBOW reflecting in every window and in the many telescope lenses of the city's multitude of astronomers.

Krull is known to the rest of the Discworld but it generates little commerce or trade. It does have a magical university, far smaller than Unseen University. Krullians have a far more practical attitude to magic, and it is frequently employed for everyday purposes.

The Krullians once had plans to lower a vessel over the Edge to ascertain the sex of the Great A'TUIN. [COM, M]

Ksandra. A young woman, employed at Unseen University to do laundry duties and dusting. [ER, MP]

K!sdra. A dragonrider from WYRMBERG. His steed is Bronze Psepha. He wears general dragonriders' clothing: a pair of high boots, a tiny leather holdall in the region of his groin and a high-crested helmet. [COM]

Ku. A continent that slipped into the ocean several thousand years ago. It took thirty years to subside; the inhabitants spent a lot of time wading. It went down in history as the multiverse's most embarrassing continental catastrophe. [E]

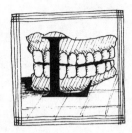

Lackjaw. Dwarf jeweller. He made COHEN the Barbarian's dentures. Current whereabouts unknown, but he is probably a floating piece of onion in the great melting-pot that is Ankh-Morpork. [LF]

Laddie. A pure-bred RAMTOP hunting dog who found fame in HOLY WOOD as Laddie the Wonder Dog. A friendly personality, but in the opinion of his manager (GASPODE) he was as dim as a ha'penny candle. [MP]

Lady Jane. An ancient and evil-tempered gyrfalcon in LANCRE. [LL]

Lady, the. (*See* LUCK.)

Lancre. A kingdom on the STO PLAINS side of the RAMTOP mountains.

Coat of arms: two bears on a black and gold shield.

Pop. (inc. humans, trolls, dwarfs and miscellaneous): approx. 500. (Dwarfs and trolls do not formally acknowledge the Crown of Lancre, but the three species get along quite amicably, or at least seldom practise open warfare within shouting distance of the border.)

Pop. for tax purposes: 17

Size: technically it has a border some 100 miles in length. The actual acreage of the kingdom is hard to calculate because of its mountainous nature and, in any case, it backs on to the Ramtops themselves and areas that are claimed by no man, troll or dwarf. The fact that there are at least two gateways into other dimensions in the country could also be held to give it a possibly infinite area.

Imports: none, except for various minor items (rare herbs, some manufactured goods). The people of Lancre are smugly self-sufficient.

Exports: iron ore and gold (from the dwarfs) and people (from mothers and fathers). People are Lancre's greatest export; the tiny kingdom has produced many wizards, at least one ARCHCHANCELLOR of Unseen University, one possible king of Ankh-Morpork and a vast number of industrious dwarfs and humans who have gone off to seek their fortune and send some of it back to their mum every week, regular. Lancre is one of those places, like A-Town-You've-Probably-Never-Heard-Of, Iowa, in which are generated people who go off somewhere and become famous.

Geography: Lancre occupies little

more than a ledge cut into the side of the Ramtop mountains. Behind it, towering peaks and dark, winding valleys climb to the massive backbone of the central ranges. In front, the land drops to the Sto Plains. Most of Lancre is thus cruel mountainside with ice-green slopes and knife-edge crests, or dense, huddled forests. As has been indicated, it gives visitors the feeling that it contains far too much geography. There are few places in the kingdom where you could drop a football and not have it roll away.

On the Hubward side of the country are glacier lakes and alpine meadows. This end of the kingdom is dominated by COPPERHEAD – by no means the biggest of the Ramtops, but an impressive mountain whose slopes and foothills are home to many dwarfs and trolls.

The kingdom has a number of human habitations: Lancre Town, where most human inhabitants live, and the villages of BAD ASS, Slippery Hollow, Razorback and, of course, Slice.

Slice is in a deep forested cleft in the mountains, and contains both the original Rock and a Hard Place, and the Place Where the Sun Does Not Shine. The inhabitants of Slice are considered strange even by the lax standards of the rest of Lancre. We are talking twenty-toe country here; we are talking the kind of place where you may have to learn to play the banjo to survive and marrying your cousin is considered posh.

Other features of note include the DANCERS, a circle of standing stones on a small area of moorland not far from the town, and the LONG MAN, an assemblage of one long and two round barrows, now badly overgrown. Both of these features contain secret entrances to the world of the ELVES and, in the case of the Long Man, also to Lancre Caves.

The caves are rumoured to run everywhere in the kingdom; it is widely believed that there is a secret entrance in the castle. But they are also one of those features that are not bound by the laws of time and space. Travel far enough in the caves and you will find mythical kings, asleep with their warriors; you will hear the roar of the Minotaur and the sheep of the Cyclops. Walk far enough and you will meet yourself, coming the other way . . .

Politics: in theory, under VERENCE II, a constitutional monarchy. This is not running smoothly because the citizens of Lancre, bloody-minded monarchists to the bone, feel that if someone is supposed to be king he should damn well get on with it. They don't expect the king to tell them how to farm or thatch, and so don't see why he should expect them to tell him how to king.

Verence and his queen, Magrat (Magrat GARLICK), have devoted themselves to the well-being of their subjects, instituting a number of social, agricultural and educational improvements which the people of Lancre seem to be surviving by dint of ignoring them all as politely as possible.

State religion: none. However, various wandering monks and priests tour the mountains for those who need them. The Nine Day Wonderers and the Priests of Small Gods are generally welcome, if only because their religions hinge on the uncertainty of knowing anything at all.

Lancrastians, however, do instinctively practise a kind of civil religion. It is felt right and proper to have some kind of religious service to mark births, marriages and deaths, without much attention being paid to which god or goddess is actually involved, and a regular feature of the Lancre calendar is the harvest festival, when the people give thanks – not to anyone, exactly, but in general terms.

Lancre Castle. The most striking thing about the castle is that it is much bigger than it needs to be. This may be a relic of the time when elves – as has been said, Lancre contains at least two dimensional doorways into their worlds – made more incursions than they do now.

It is built on an outcrop of rock, leaning vertiginously over the river Lancre and immediately overlooking the town square. It is in very bad repair, and one

Other outside staff, who in many ways pursue their own jobs with only a mild interest in whatsoever is actually running the place, consist of HODGESAARGH the falconer and Mr BROOKS the beekeeper.

Lancre river. A shallow and very fast river, a tributary of the Ankh. As it curves around the town it foams over a series of rapids and weirs, but further into the mountains there are occasional

View of Central Lancre

of the first jobs of the staff in the morning is to see what parts of the castle have fallen down during the night.

Under the present monarch the staff have been reduced somewhat, and now consist of Mrs SCORBIC the cook, SPRIGGINS the butler, Millie CHILLUM the maid and Shawn OGG (Commander-in-Chief of the Army, the rest of the Army, Captain of the Guard, the Guard, the Seneschal, the kitchen boy, the armourer, the odd-job man, the herald, the gardener, the gatekeeper and Lord Privy of the Privy).

hidden water meadows and quiet pools. Lancre Bridge, over which travels the road to the Plains, is three miles from the castle, upstream of the town of Lancre Gorge. The road from the bridge to the town curves between high banks, with the forest crowding in on either side.

Lancre Town. The town is a stone's drop from the river. Technically it would barely pass anywhere else as a village, but by dint of being that much bigger than anywhere else in Lancre it acts as though it were a city. A town rule is that all mummers, mountebanks, etc., must be outside the gates by sundown. This is not a problem as the town has no walls to speak of, and after sundown they just come back again. It boasts a tavern (the Goat & Bush) on the main square, plus an old forge and a lodging house.

Lankin. An elf. High cheekbones, a perfect nose and a ponytail. He wears odds and ends of rags and lace and fur, confident in the knowledge that anything looks good on an elf. Like all elves, totally self-confident and immensely cruel – but with style, so that's OK. [LL]

Lasgere. A former prince of TSORT. Killed by a slave during an experiment in 'learning while you sleep'; the slave's duty was to read to him all night. What Lasgere presumably did learn was that it was not a good idea for the slave to be armed with a knife. [SG]

Launch Controller. Official of KRULL responsible for the planning of the launch of the POTENT VOYAGER from Krull. He was a practical magician, rather than a diplomat. [COM]

Lavaeolus. The finest military mind on the continent of KLATCH. When first seen, he was wearing tarnished armour and a grubby cloak. The helmet plume looked as though it had been used as a paintbrush. He was skinny, with all the military bearing of a deckchair.

His genius consisted of realizing that, if there has to be a war, the aim should be to defeat the enemy as quickly and with as little bloodshed as possible – a concept so breathtaking in its originality that few other military minds have been able to grasp it, and it shows what happens when you take the conduct of a war away from skilled soldiers.

He was a hero of the Tsortean Wars, which he ended by bribing a cleaner to show him a secret passage into the citadel of TSORT. So not many people actually died, which means it couldn't have been that much of a victory, really.

It is possible that he is an ancestor of RINCEWIND. [P, E]

Lavatory, Sir Charles. Owner of C. H. Lavatory & Son, Mollymog Street, Ankh-Morpork, and president of the PLUMBERS' GUILD. Invented the first really efficient flushing toilet, which was therefore named after him. Of course, flushing a lavatory in Ankh-Morpork is not likely to make things any better.

A remarkable parallel with Thomas Crapper, the Victorian sanitary engineer who also lent his name to the more modern version of the privy (although the term 'crapper' in that sense dates back at least to the sixteenth century. Perhaps Thomas got teased a lot at school and decided that if he was going to bear this name through life, then he'd damn well see to it that it was one to be proud of). [SM]

Laws of Ankh-Morpork. There aren't any.

Well . . .

Not entirely true. There aren't any now, except in the almost iconographic memory of Captain CARROT of the City WATCH. There are Guild laws, administered by the various Guilds and often the cause of friction between them (see VETINARI, LORD), but laws in the modern sense have gone out of fashion in the last several hundred years. The city is not, however, lawless. It more or less runs on the 'Patrician's Rules'. Lord Vetinari takes the unvoiced view that most citizens are guilty of something, or just generally guilty in a low-grade way. If there is a crime, then there ought to be seen to be a punishment; if the punishment can involve the actual perpetrator of the crime then this is a happy state of affairs, but it is not essential. Anything that threatens the city in any way – be it a man, a philosophy or a device – is 'against the law'.

Beyond that, Lord Vetinari believes in a common or natural law; if a man can sell short-weight bread and get away with it, then get away with it he does. If, however, his defrauded customers decide to nail him to his own ceiling, then that is fine, too.

The known and somewhat fossilized laws of Ankh-Morpork are:

Being Bloody Stupid Act, 1581
Decency Ordinances, 1389
Dignity of Man (Civil Rights) Act, 1341
Domestic & Domesticated Animals
  (Care & Protection) Act, 1673
Gambling (Regulations) Acts
General Felonies Act, 1678
Industrial Processes Act, 1508
Licensed Premises (Hygiene) Acts,
  1433, 1456, 1463, 1465 and 1470–1690
Privacy Act, 1467
Projectile Weapons (Civil Safety) Act,
  1634
Public Ale Houses (Opening) Act, 1678
Public Forgatherings (Gambling) Act,
  1567
Public Order Act, 1457

They are listed merely for completeness.

THE SYSTEM OF JUSTICE

1. Criminal Justice
As explained, there is none.

Although the current system in Ankh-Morpork consists almost entirely of 'Guild Justice' enforced by the city's Guilds, it is still the case that criminals taken by the Watch may opt to stand for trial before the PATRICIAN.

The accused may, if they have money, employ a member of the Guild of Lawyers (motto: LVCRE SERMAT [Money Talks]) to speak on their behalf. If they wish to be found not guilty they will often need large reserves of money. The long-held principle is very clear – the more money you have, the more likely you are to be innocent. This is considered right and proper by the Guild, because rich people are an asset to society and there are far too many poor people around in any case, and they're probably all criminals.

If the accused has no money, then their only hope is if the Patrician decides in their favour. He quite often does so, because he finds it instructive to all concerned.

As indicated elsewhere, there is no formal system of criminal law in the city. Nor is there any recognized scale of punishment. Imprisonment is viewed as a school for criminals and a drain on the state, and so therefore most punishments are a fine or a flogging. There are a number of specialized punishments, of which the scorpion pit is the best known, but for offences of a sexual nature, particularly against minors, the usual recourse is the traditional tree, jar of honey and herd of cows.

Occasionally – but rarely – other ancient punishments are resurrected for deserving cases. A classic one is tying the offender to one of the pillars of the Brass Bridge at low tide and untying him 24 hours later, at which point he is free to go.

The death penalty is usually reserved for treachery to the city, continuing to commit murder after being told not to, irredeemable stupidity while not being a troll, and persistent street theatre.

2. Civil Justice
A state whose citizens are as perennially indignant and argumentative as are Ankh-Morpork's is bound to have a thriving Civil bench, and this is where

the Guild of Lawyers make their real money. Cases are usually heard before a Court of Magisters (for poor people) or before a senior member of the Guild who has been appointed by the Patrician to serve as a judge.

(Since this is a fixed salary post, this means that the appointee suffers an effective drop in income, barring bribes, of course. Thus appointment to the role of judge is usually used by the Patrician as a form of mild rebuke to lawyers who have failed him in one way or another.)

3. The Historical System

In the very early days of Ankh-Morpork justice was dispensed by the ARCHCHAN-CELLOR's Court (*see* UNSEEN UNIVERSITY). There then followed a system set up under the city's monarchy, and many of today's traditions and titles date from that period. A three-tier system of justice prevailed:

i. Small cases, involving the common citizens, would be heard by the Court of Magisters (or Justices of the King's Peace), made up of men of the city's ruling classes. These JKPs would carry a nosegay into court, to ward off the offensive smell of the lower orders. As Ankh-Morpork got bigger, sometimes three or four people were needed to carry the flowers.

ii. Larger cases, involving the wealthier members of society, would be pleaded on their behalf by trained legal experts from the Guild of Lawyers. These experts, known as pleaders (who wore robes with a purse sewn into the upper-left back, so that their fee could be dropped in without them having to be seen handling filthy lucre), carried the title of Serjeant (a corruption of their old title of *servientes Regis ad legem*). They were the only people entitled to plead cases before one of the King's Judges. The King's Judges were reputed to be

The Ankh-Morpork Armoury

142

the finest judges that money could buy and they were often employed by other kings and queens in the STO PLAINS.

iii. Ultimate recourse was to the King, who would hear their pleadings in the Rats Chamber (so called because of the fresco of dancing rats painted on its ceiling). A vestige of this system still prevails in that the Patrician is the last court of appeal.

Reference is still made to the 'Inns of Court'. These were the ale-houses surrounding the Court House from which accused people would try to entice drunken lawyers with offers of hard cash.

COURTS AND PRISONS

The old and derelict Ankh-Morpork Court House was taken over by the THIEVES' GUILD as their headquarters in the time of Lord Vetinari. Large and probably profitable court cases are now heard in a courtroom within the Guild of Lawyers.

There used to be a large prison (now private houses) around Sybil Lane near Hen and Chickens Field. The field got its name from the frequent processions to the gallows there, when the priest of choice would walk ahead of the gaggle of warders and accused, like 'a hen and her chicks'. This is how proper old cities name their places; they wouldn't *dream* of calling something First Avenue just because they'd got a lot of avenues and it was the first.

For the few individuals whom it is necessary to lock up, the modern prison, originally a royal palace called Tintement but now known as The Tanty, is on the Rim Bank. Its current head warder is an enlightened man who practises an intensive counselling and caring approach, subsequent to which many prisoners apply briskly for the cow and honey cure.

Legba. A large, black cockerel. Familiar of Mrs GOGOL. [WA]

Legibus. An Ephebian philosopher and author of *Geometries*. A little man with a beard you could camp out in. He is quite old, and resembles a frog that has been dried out for some time. Something about him generally makes people think of the word 'spry'. [SG]

Lemon, Satchelmouth. The recruiting and enforcement officer for the MUSICIANS' GUILD, Ankh-Morpork. [SM]

Leonard of Quirm. (Aka Leonard da Quirm.) A painter and inventor; the greatest Discworld technological genius of all time. He had a house in the Street of Cunning Artificers, Ankh-Morpork, but currently resides in a cell in the PATRICIAN'S PALACE.

This may be considered cruel, but in many ways it is quite impossible to imprison someone like Leonard. Give him enough wood, wire, paints, drawing materials, food, a potty and a window through which he can watch the birds and it's unlikely that he will even notice.

In appearance, he is clearly one of those people who started to look old around the age of thirty. He is not exactly bald. His head has just grown up through his hair.

One of his achievements is the well-known painting the *Mona Ogg* (her teeth are said to follow you round the room), currently in the PATRICIAN's collection. It is believed that Nanny OGG has not as yet visited Ankh-Morpork; this may be some other Ogg which, considering the fecundity of the Ogg tribe, is quite likely.

Leonard's true genius, however, lies in seeing inherent in the common world the obvious things that men have never seen before. He watches the swirl of water over weirs, the intricate movements of musculature, the gliding of birds and the play of light through prisms and, then, fills up notebook after notebook with ingenious devices for killing whole cities by means of hot oil, explosions, etc. He has never in his life

Leshp, Brass Gongs of. The legendary Brass Gongs can be heard far out in the CIRCLE SEA on stormy nights, as the currents stir the drowned towers of the city of Leshp, three hundred fathoms below. [M]

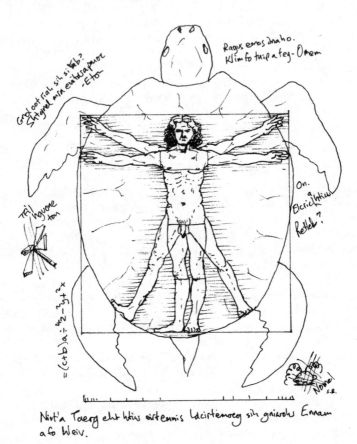

harmed a living creature, and would be greatly surprised and terribly shocked to think that anyone would take these doodles (with their carefully numbered components and cutaway diagrams) seriously. Inventions of his, lying unnoticed in obscure places or drawn as idle sketches in the margins of otherwise unremarkable books, lie around Ankh-Morpork like razor blades in a ham sandwich. [WS, SM, MAA]

Lezek. MORT's father. Bearded, shorter than his son, he made a haphazard living as a farmer. [M]

Liartes. Brother of LIO!RT Dragonlord and LIESSA Dragonlady, and son of GREICHA the First, Lord of the WYRMBERG. [COM]

Librarian. The Librarian of Unseen University is an orang-utan. This was not always the case. He was magically transformed by the events chronicled in *The Light Fantastic* – but since then no member of the University staff can remember who he was beforehand. In addition, a page was torn out of the relevant year book; no one knows why, or why the place was marked with a banana skin. There is a rumour that the Librarian was once Dr Horace Worblehat, B. Thau, D.M., but no one utters this out loud. Dr Worblehat is dimly remembered as being quiet, polite and generally the kind of person you cannot remember in the school photo.

It is clear that whatever he once was the Librarian is now blissfully happy in himself, reckoning that the prehensile toes and extra-long arms are very helpful in his role. In a sense, say the wizards, it is as though he always was the Librarian and whatever inoffensive human shape he had for the first several decades of his life, he was merely marking time until he could become his own self.

In looks he has the red-haired-rubber-sack-filled-with-water look of a very well grown (300lb) male, although he has not developed the overlarge cheek pads that are a feature of a dominant male orang. This is because he is not, strictly, a dominant male – he is an ex-officio member of the college council and a member of the faculty and he therefore quite rightly regards the ARCHCHANCELLOR as the dominant male, even though the Archchancellor does not often sit high up in trees with a large leaf on his head.

Habits and habitat: he has a book-lined nest in a cubby hole under the desk in the middle of the Library. He hides there under his tattered blanket when he is worried. He appears to want nothing more than soft fruit, a regular supply of index cards and the opportunity, every month or so, to hop over the wall of the PATRICIAN's private menagerie. (This is a puzzle. There are no orangs in the menagerie. Nor are there any other kinds of ape.) He is generally naked but he does wear an old green robe when he's had a bath or modesty really requires it.

The Librarian is, of course, very much in favour of reading in general, but readers in particular get on his nerves. There is something sacrilegious about the way people keep taking books off the shelves and wearing out the words by reading them. He likes people who love and respect books, and the best way to do that, in the Librarian's opinion, is to leave them on the shelves where Nature intended them to be.

In short, he is a useful and well-respected member of the University staff, his only failing being a tendency to educative violence if referred to as a 'monkey'. During the evenings he can often be found enjoying a quiet pint and, if the landlord is not wary, every single bowl of peanuts in the Mended DRUM, where his iron grip and ability to swing from the rafters adds an extra dimension of terror to bar-room brawls.

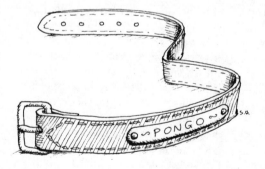

Libraries, nature of. Even big collections of ordinary books distort space and time, as can readily be proved by anyone who has been around a really old-fashioned second-hand bookshop, one of those that has more staircases than storeys and those rows of shelves that end in little doors that are surely too small for a full-sized human to enter.

The relevant equation is Knowledge = Power = Energy = Matter = Mass; a good bookshop is just a genteel Black Hole that knows how to read. Mass distorts space into polyfractal L-space, in which Everywhere is also Everywhere Else.

All libraries everywhere are connected in L-space by the bookwormholes created by the strong space-time distortions found in any large collection of books. Only a very few librarians learn the secret, and there are inflexible rules about making use of the fact – because it amounts to time travel.

The three rules of the Librarians of Time and Space are: (1) Silence; (2) Books must be returned no later than the last date shown, and (3) the nature of causality must not be interfered with. (*See also* BOOKS and INVISIBLE WRITINGS.)

Library, the. Books play a major role in the Discworld. In Discworld reality as well as in general magical theory the Name is often nearly identical to the Thing itself; to know the Name is to control the Thing. Books on the Discworld often do far more than merely record its history and the concerns of its inhabitants; they often are the script on which the unfolding drama is based.

Books can also be affected by their contents, and a book containing powerful magic spells can become, for all practical purposes, alive.

The Library at Unseen University therefore has to deal with problems rather greater than readers writing 'Rubbish!' in the margins and using slices of bacon as a bookmark.

From the outside, the Library of Unseen University is a low, brooding building, with high, narrow, barred windows and a glass dome high above its centre. There clearly is a centre, because it is quite possible for someone to walk from the door to the middle of the floor.

However, all four of the standard dimensions are, in this place, plaited like soft clay by the presence of the very high thaumic field generated by the magic in the books coupled with the pressure on space-time from the books themselves. Because of the distortions caused by the vast amount of assembled knowledge, the Library has a diameter of about 100 yards but an infinite radius. The interior is a topographical nightmare; the sheer presence of so much stored magic twisting dimensions and gravity into the kind of spaghetti that would make M. C. Escher go for a good lie down, or possibly sideways. The floor seems to become the wall in the distance, shelves play tricks on the eyes and seem to twist through more dimensions than the usual three. There are even some shelves up on the ceiling.

The Library is the greatest assemblage of magical texts anywhere in the multiverse; over 90,000 volumes weigh down its shelves. (This may not sound like many, but it should be borne in mind that most of the books are fully two feet high and six inches thick and some are much larger. And these are merely the *magical* books. The Library also houses an uncounted number of less volatile texts, in the occult sense at any rate; indeed, if the L-space theories are correct, the Library contains every book everywhere, including the ones that never actually got written.)

Magic is volatile. A spell may be pinned to the page like a butterfly, but it still tries to escape, to have form, to take control, to be said. In a sense, the books in Unseen University's library are semi-alive. At UU, your homework could eat the dog . . .

Great care has to be taken to ensure that this magic causes no harm. As the raw magic crackles from the spines of the magical books, it earths itself harmlessly in the copper rails nailed to every shelf for that very purpose.

In most old libraries the books are chained to the shelves to prevent them being damaged by people; in the Library of Unseen University, of course, it's more or less the other way around.

Faint traceries of blue fire crawl across the bookcases and there is a sound, a papery whispering, such as might come from a colony of roosting starlings. In the silence of the night, the books talk to one another.

It is always warm in the Library, because the magic that produces the OCTARINE glow also gently cooks the air.

In the lower levels are the maximum security shelves where the rogue books are kept – the books whose behaviour or mere contents demand a whole shelf, a whole room, to themselves. Cannibal books. Books which will read you rather than the other way about. Books which, if left on a shelf with their weaker brethren, would be found in a 'Revised, Enlarged and Smug Edition' in the morning.

Down in these dark tunnels, behind heavily barred doors, are also kept the . . . er . . . erotic books, in vats of crushed ice. Also kept in the Library of Unseen University is the OCTAVO, originally in the possession of the CREATOR of the Discworld.

And, as indicated before, there is L-space. Somewhere beyond the common shelves lies an entire library universe, peopled by creatures that have evolved in the immense biobibliographical field, such as kickstool crabs and the wild thesaurus. It should be possible eventually to find your way into any other library at any point in time, and it is known that the LIBRARIAN made use of this feature to rescue some of the more interesting works from the burning library of EPHEBE (in *Small Gods*).

Various legends are linked to UU's library. There is the persistent story of the Lost Reading Room, for example. Wise students in search of more distant volumes take care to leave chalk marks on the shelves, and tell friends to come looking for them if they're not back for supper.

Even wiser students don't go in at all.

Liessa Wyrmbidder. Liessa Dragonlady. Lady of the WYRMBERG. Sister to LIO!RT and LIARTES and daughter of GREICHA the First. She is a magnificent sight, with waist-length red hair, flecked with gold. She is almost naked, apart from a couple of mere scraps of the lightest chain mail, and riding boots of iridescent dragonhide. In one boot is thrust a riding crop – unusual in that it is as long as a spear and topped with tiny steel barbs. She has a slim, black dagger in her belt. She is heavily into jewellery, with a diamond spangle in her navel, tiger-rubies adorning her toe-rings, and large, incredibly rare blue-milk diamonds adorning the rings on her fingers. They just don't make heroines like her any more. For one thing, they force them to wear more clothes. [COM]

Lifton. Landlord of the inn near Miss FLITWORTH's farm and father of SAL, the little girl rescued from a fire by Bill DOOR (DEATH). [RM]

Light Dams. Some of the tribes in the Great NEF region construct mirror walls in the desert mountains to collect the Disc sunlight, which they then use as a currency. This is possible because of the strange nature of light in the Discworld's magical field. [M]

Light, nature of. As far as can be determined, there are three distinct types of light on the Disc. For the sake of discussion they could be called common light, meta-light and 'the light fantastic'.

Meta-light is almost an idea rather than a phenomenon. It is the light by which darkness can be seen, and therefore is always available, everywhere. If it didn't exist, darkness could not be visible. It is widely used in the film industry for shots in caves and mines.

Common light undergoes some important changes in the Discworld's vast and ancient magical field. It slows down considerably (and variably, but generally to about the speed of sound) and, at the same time, becomes very slightly heavier than air and also – by assumption – soluble. (It pools in deep valleys but has gone by midnight, so it either sinks into the ground or is soluble in darkness.)

The speed of common light was established by FEBRIUS, the Ephebian philosopher.

The combined effect of these changes can be seen by watching a Discworld day from a convenient point in space. The disc is 10,000 miles across. The sunlight strikes point A and proceeds towards point B at about 600 mph, producing a rather pleasing effect similar to an incoming tide. When it strikes a mountain range (C) it piles up on the dawn side, so that dawn will be postponed in the 'light shadow' of the mountain until either the light flows over the top or around the sides.

The light fantastic is perhaps best evidenced by the dull, sullen light which fills the room where the OCTAVO is kept. Not strictly light at all but the opposite of light. Darkness is not the opposite of light, it is simply its absence. The light fantastic is the light that lies on the far side of darkness.

Ordinary light passing through a strong magical field is split into not seven but eight colours, and the eighth – OCTARINE – is generally associated with things magical. It can be described in terms of other colours about as readily as red can be described in terms of green, yellow and blue, but if some description is really insisted on then octarine is a rather disappointing greeny-purple-yellow colour.

Lilith, Lady. Lady Lilith de Tempscire. (*See* WEATHERWAX, LILY.)

Lily, Iron. Nickname for the woman who teaches games at the QUIRM COLLEGE FOR YOUNG LADIES. The girls say that she shaves, and lifts weights with her teeth. She is well known for her hearty bellows from the touchline during sports matches: 'Get some ball, you bunch of soft nellies!' – and so on. [SM]

Lio!rt Dragonlord. Brother of LIESSA and LIARTES, and son of GREICHA the First. A lord of the WYRMBERG. [COM]

Listeners, the (or Listening Monks). The oldest of the Disc's religious sects –

although even the Gods are divided as to whether Listening is really a proper religion.

The Listeners are trying to work out precisely what it was the CREATOR said when he made the universe: clearly nothing the Creator makes can ever be destroyed, so those first syllables must still be around somewhere, bouncing and re-bouncing off all the matter in the cosmos but still audible to a really good listener.

The monks dwell in a temple shaped like a great white ammonite at the end of a funnel-shaped valley. Eons ago the Listeners found that ice and chance had carved this one valley into the perfect acoustic opposite of an echo valley, and built their multi-chambered temple in the exact position that the comfy chair always occupies in the home of a rabid hi-fi fanatic. Complex baffles catch and amplify the sound that is funnelled up the chilly valley, steering it ever inwards to the central chamber where, at any hour of the day or night, three monks always sit.

This hidden valley is accessible only by a narrow staircase. There is a village in a lower valley a few miles from the temple. [M]

Llamedos. A small, mountainous country, where it rains continuously except for brief periods of drizzle and snow. Rain is the country's main export. It has rain mines. Only holly grows there – everything else just rots.

The Llamedese are a musical but quite strict people of the druidical persuasion. They are in fact the centre of druidical expertise, and stone-circle builders from Llamedos are found wherever megalithic circles are not quite working properly. The Llamedese are also famed and feared for their singing, and in more warlike times their massed male voice choirs

and reinforced harps laid waste the land wherever they appeared. The bardic tradition is now a little less warlike. Central to it is the annual Eisteddfod: three days of poetry, singing and superb bladder control. [SM]

Lobsang, Abbott. Leader of the LISTENERS. A small and totally bald man, with more wrinkles than a sackful of prunes. Currently he is the eighty-ninth Abbott, but he is the victim of reincarnation. He is constantly reincarnated in a child conceived at the moment of his death. Each time an Abbott dies, the monks go down to the village to look for a boy child conceived at the hour that the old Abbott died. That boy is then made the new Abbott, and so it goes on. Only in the brief time between death and conception is Lobsang allowed to be aware of the true situation: that he is, in fact, in a kind of karmic loop. [M, GG]

Long Man, the. A collection of three burial mounds in a very old part of the forest in LANCRE. They comprise two round mounds at the foot of a long one.

In the old days, the men of Lancre would come up to the Long Man for strange rites. They used to build sweat lodges and drink SCUMBLE and dance around the fires with horns on their heads, and so on. This may have been a very ancient rite, or possibly just a response to man's age-old desire to get out of the house and have a jar and a few laughs.

At the foot of the long mound three large irregular stones form a cave, inside which is a flat rock carved with the symbol of a horned man and an inscription in Oggham (a runic alphabet). The inscription as translated by Nanny OGG reads: 'I've got a great big tonker' although this may be her idiosyncratic spin on one central theme of all fertility and Nature cults.

Below the stone is one entrance to the Lancre Caves, which run all through Lancre and also lead to one world of the elves. [LL]

Loremaster. An hereditary official of the WYRMBERG. [COM]

Lorenzo the Kind. The last king of Ankh-Morpork. A fat and elderly man with unspecified and possibly unspeakable predilections. He was beheaded by 'Old Stoneface' VIMES, who didn't say much. [MAA]

Lu-Tze. A senior History Monk. Reputed to be 6,000 years old, because for History MONKS time is a resource to manipulate rather than an amber in which they are imprisoned. Lu-Tze eats nothing but brown rice and drinks nothing but green tea with a knob of rancid butter in it. However, this is simply because he likes the stuff. There's nothing particularly holy about rancid butter.

Lu-Tze also grows BONSAI MOUNTAINS. [SG]

Luck (the Lady). The Goddess Who Must Not Be Named. She appears beautiful, with bright green eyes – the green of fresh emeralds and iridescent as a dragonfly. Like all gods and goddesses she can change her appearance at will, but cannot change the look of her eyes.

Those who seek her never find her yet she is known to come to the aid of those in greatest need. Then again, sometimes she doesn't. She does, it may be gathered, have a soft spot for last, desperate million-to-one chances, but it would be unwise to depend upon this.

Although she is arguably the most powerful goddess in the entire history of Creation, there are no temples to her. She doesn't like the clicking of rosaries, but is attracted to the sound of dice. [COM]

Ludorum, Arthur. A fellow student of TEPPIC's at the ASSASSINS' GUILD. One of only two worshippers of the Great Orm (a god who, therefore, must no longer be that great) and a son of Johan Ludorum – one of the greatest assassins in the history of the Guild. Arthur's innocent, friendly smile and boyish complexion are frequently the last thing some people see. [P]

Luggage, the. In appearance: a largish, metal-bound chest which is capable of extruding a large number of little legs to help it move about. It is made of SAPIENT PEARWOOD, a magical timber which can cause its constructs to portray characteristics similar to that set of characteristics known as 'life'.

Pearwood constructions can be set to do small tasks, such as carry water or guard property. Since it is a magical substance sapient pearwood is impervious to magic, and in the STO PLAINS is much sought after for the manufacture of wizards' staffs, since its capacity for storing magic is up to ten times greater than that of other leading timbers.

In the case of the Luggage, built to serve as self-propelled travel accessory and bodyguard, one of the set of characteristics known as 'life' is a particular characteristic known as 'faithfulness' and another is one known as 'murderous intent'.

When it opens its lid – often in order to snap it hard on something it considers to be threatening its owner – the luggage may reveal clean laundry, or a king's ransom in gold. As often as not, though, it displays teeth like bleached beechwood and a tongue as large as a palm leaf and red as mahogany.

Although it has a keyhole, it cannot be opened when it is in a locked mood. The Luggage will follow its owner everywhere. The word is an absolute – *everywhere*. One use for sapient pearwood in the AGATEAN EMPIRE – where it is quite common – used to be the manufacture of grave goods that the dead could be certain of taking with them.

The Luggage is currently owned, or at least chooses to follow, the wizard RINCEWIND (whereabouts unknown). Its progress across the Disc is marked by debris, people who get nervous at the sound of hurrying footsteps, and communities who are unusually polite to strangers.

No other item in the entire chronicle of travel accessories has quite such a history of mystery and grievous bodily harm.

Lully I. A past king of LANCRE. A bit of an historian and a romantic, which is a polite way of saying that he invented most of Lancre's history and several of its monarchs and almost all of its printable folklore. Of course, this does not mean that the history he invented was untrue, only that it did not, in actual fact, happen. In fact this is generally the case everywhere. History is what people believe; therefore, what people believe is history. [LL]

Lupine. A wereman. That is to say, the exact opposite of a werewolf. He is a 7-foot-tall, muscular, hairy, young man with long canines, pointy ears and yellow eyes – during full moon. The rest of the time he is a real wolf. Last seen leaving Ankh-Morpork in the company of Ludmilla CAKE, a female werewolf. They appeared to have worked out a satisfactory *liaison* despite being the same shape for only one week per month. [RM]

Ly Tin Wheedle. Arguably the Disc's greatest philosopher (well, he always argued that he was). Someone once asked him at a party 'Why are you here?' and the reply took three years. Wheedle is a citizen of the AGATEAN EMPIRE on the COUNTERWEIGHT CONTINENT, where he is regarded as a great sage because of his peculiar smell. His many sayings about respect for the old and the virtues of poverty are often quoted by the rich and elderly. [LF, M, S]

Magazines. If you're reading this book in order, you'll already know that the Disc has a wide variety of book titles. Magazines are a newer phenomenon, but already they include:

Beaks & Talons [LL]
Bows & Ammo [LL]
Popular Armour [LL]

All the above are crudely printed woodblock broadsheets produced in Ankh-Morpork, all at the same address. Nothing is known about the company concerned, but there is a distinct possibility that the name C.M.O.T. DIBBLER is not far away.

Mage Wars. Took place shortly after the Creation. In those days magic in its raw state was widely available, and was eagerly grasped by the first men in their battle against the GODS.

The precise origins of the Mage Wars, as this period was known, are lost in the fogs of time, but Disc philosophers agree that the first men took one look at their situation and understandably lost their temper. And great and pyrotechnic were the battles that followed – the sun wheeled across the sky, the seas boiled, weird storms ravaged the land, small white pigeons mysteriously appeared in people's clothing and the very stability of the Disc was threatened. This resulted in stern action by the OLD HIGH ONES, to whom even the gods themselves are answerable. The gods were banished to high and deserted places, men were re-created a good deal smaller and much of the old, wild magic was sucked out of the earth.

In those places on the Disc that had suffered a direct hit by a spell the magic faded away very slowly over the millennia, releasing as it decayed a myriad sub-astral particles that severely distracted the reality around it. [COM]

Magenta. One of DIAMANDA's coven in LANCRE. [LL]

Magic [including wizards and witches]. Magic and the Discworld go together like cheese and more cheese. Magic permeates the very substance of the place. But it can be tentatively divided into five types: Intrinsic, Residual, Induced, Wizard (including Sourcery) and Witch.

INTRINSIC MAGIC

This is the magic that derives from the very nature of the Discworld universe, and has a certain similarity to some of the matters discussed in quantum physics (physicists who seriously postulate extra dimensions that are curled up on themselves and are too small to see would be right at home in Unseen University). It is the intrinsic magic of Discworld which, for example, is responsible for the slowing down of light but at the same time makes it possible to see light coming. Intrinsic magic is the equivalent of God, thinking.

RESIDUAL MAGIC

A powerful force, which needs some background explanation.

Most magic as used by wizards and witches is a simple channelling of the intrinsic magic of the world. It can be stored – in accumulators such as staffs, carpets, spells and broomsticks – and can be thought of as a slowly renewing resource, like geothermal energy. It is subject to certain laws similar to those of the conservation of energy. A wizard can, for example, cause fires and apparitions and coloured lights quite easily, because these require very little energy. In the same way, a person may quite easily be turned into a frog by causing their brain to reprogram their own morphogenetic field. The effect is temporary but embarrassing.

But a wizard can rise vertically in the air only by locating a large solid object of similar weight in a high place that can be dislodged without much force, so that the descent of the object largely propels the rise of the wizard.

No common magic is powerful enough to cause, for example, a pork pie to come into complete, permanent existence. This would require quite a large amount of new energy to be created within the universe – as much energy, in fact, as would be necessary to create a one-hundredth of a pig, one-ten-thousandth of a baker, one hundred-thousandth of a cleaver, several pounds of flour, salt and pepper to taste, and a couple of hours of baking.

All this can, however, be easily achieved by a sourcerer, who can channel raw creative force and may be thought of as the human equivalent of a white hole. A sourcerer in fact pretty much conforms to the classic picture of a wizard – he can create and destroy by a mere thought.

Fortunately sourcerers are now very rare on Discworld and only one is known to have arisen during the entire period of the chronicles [S]. But they were far more common in much earlier times. And, since power corrupts, and sourcerers were as naturally sociable as cats in a sinking sack, they engaged in vast magical wars which left whole areas (for example, the FOREST OF SKUND and the WYRMBERG) so lousy with magic that the Discworld's fairly lax laws of cause and effect no longer apply even today. Many of the Disc's stranger species, and some of its most potent magical artefacts, probably derive from that period. While such residual magic can be discovered and exploited, in the same way as other worlds exploit the deposits of coal and oil which are similarly stored forms of the energy of earlier periods, the results are likely to be unpredictable, i.e., predictably fatal.

INDUCED MAGIC

An often neglected but very powerful form, and available for use even by non-practitioners. It is the magic potential created in an object, or even a living creature, by usage and belief.

Take, in its simplest form, royalty. It needs but a royal marriage to turn a perfectly ordinary girl that no one would look at twice into a Radiant Right Royal Princess and fashion icon. Similarly, the ARCHCHANCELLOR'S HAT actually became quite magical in itself simply from having been worn on the heads of generations of Archchancellors and thus being only inches away from brains buzzing with magic.

The armour of the warrior Queen YNCI of Lancre had clearly absorbed enough potency to stiffen the resolve of Magrat GARLICK when she wore it (the fact that the armour was a complete fake is quite beside the point – it is association and belief that are important). Mirror magic, as exemplified by the practices of Lily WEATHERWAX, also comes into this category. Witches believe that if they stand between two mirrors their personal power is multiplied by their reflections. This is clearly a primitive folk superstition, which by sheer luck happens to be true.

Possibly the most interesting example was the sword of CARROT Ironfoundersson of the Ankh-Morpork City WATCH. It was not a magic sword. It had no mystic runes. It quite failed to light up in the presence of enemies or anything else. But it had clearly been used by the royal heirs of the city's throne for generations and had become magical in a very subtle way – it had become more and more sword-like, until it was both a thing and the symbol of a thing.

WIZARD MAGIC (AND WIZARDS)

Largely, these days, the province of graduates of Unseen University, Ankh-Morpork. There are eight orders of wizardry and eight grades associated with UU. In practical terms the affairs of academic wizardry as a whole are run by the ARCHCHANCELLOR and faculty.

There are many other schools of wizardry on the Disc, some considered arcane even by wizard standards, and there is nothing to stop anyone calling themselves a wizard of the ninth grade except the fact that if they meet a real wizard they're likely to end up sitting sadly by the pond waiting for a short-sighted princess with a thing about the colour green.

Grades of up to twenty-one have been reported, but this is considered to be just foreigners being excitable, and they impress the Unseen wizards as much as the porcupine-sized epaulettes on the shoulders of a shifty-eyed banana republic Generalissimo impress a battle-hardened soldier.

Wizard magic generally consists of illusion, a little weather-making, fireballs and the occasional darning of the Fabric of Reality. Fundamental to its use is the wizard's staff, usually about 6 feet long with the proverbial knob on the end. Daily rituals with the staff accumulate magical power which can be discharged very quickly at need, or stored in spell books and triggered by the syllables of the spell. People often make jokes about the knob on the end and wizards never understand why. It is a truism that the more senior the wizard, the less likely he is to do any showy or practical magic. Senior wizards' time in the University is taken up with sleeping, eating at least four large meals a day, University administration and generally, well, just existing and being a wizard just as hard as they can. Since UU and its LIBRARY probably hold enough accumulated magic to end the universe, it is just as well that it is sat on by large, contented and stable personalities (with the exception of the Bursar, who is as mad as a spoon, and the Dean, and the Senior Wrangler, and the Chair of Recent Runes . . .).

A sourcerer is the eighth son of an eighth son, and his father must be a wizard. Unlike wizardry which, shorn of the coloured lights and fireballs, largely consists of persuading the universe to do it your way, sourcery is the immensely powerful magic of the storybook wizard – he can stop the sun, make the sea boil and all the other things such wizards feel they have to do. He is a channel through which magic flows into the universe, and the human equivalent of a white hole. Much that is strange on the Discworld (*see* Residual magic) is the result of wars fought between sourcerers long before the present age; they are absolutely incapable of united effort.

It was fears of the occurrence of sourcerers that led to the practice of, and then the insistence on, celibacy among UU wizards, although most of them are quite old and find even celibacy is a bit too exciting. Celibacy has no physical effect on magic ability. Gravity doesn't care if you're good or bad and, likewise, celibacy *per se* has no relevance to the magical act, otherwise Nanny OGG would be a washerwoman.

A sourcerer can only be beaten by another sourcerer. This belief held sway for hundreds of years and it was only when the first sourcerer for millennia appeared on the Disc (in *Sourcery*) that it was realized that this only applied where direct magical contest is involved. A half-brick wielded in a sock is otherwise perfect for the job. (*See also* RINCEWIND.)

WITCH MAGIC (AND WITCHES)

Unlike wizards, witches are solitary creatures. They enrol in no schools and have no formal system of regulation. The informal coven of Granny Weatherwax, Nanny Ogg and Magrat Garlick in LAN-CRE is extremely unusual – witches generally get together only rarely, on sites such as Lancre's Bear Mountain, to exchange gossip and discuss the affairs of the region. Contrary to salacious popular belief, there is no question of them doing anything without their clothes on, with the possible exception of Nanny Ogg. Most serious witches are elderly and keep several layers of flannelette between themselves and the outside world at all times, except Nanny Ogg. Witches have in fact a very strict and ancient moral code, although Nanny Ogg's is rather more ancient than the others'.

Witches are trained by other witches, one to one, with one of the trainees taking over the area when her teacher either dies or quits the world in some other definite way. This means that over time an area may see a succession of witches of a roughly similar strain. The basic unit of witchcraft is the cottage, which may be inhabited by witches for several centuries. Magrat's cottage, for example, is traditionally the home of research witches. Another significant difference lies in the attitude to books. Most witches can read and write but place no particular value on books; wizards without a library would just be fat men in pointy hats.

The three main Lancre witches exemplify aspects of Discworld witchcraft. Granny Weatherwax's personal power is built on a considerable practical knowledge of psychology ('headology'), an iron will, an unshakeable conviction that she is right and some genuine psychic powers, which she distrusts. She is respected, but not liked. She would prefer to look like a crone, because ugliness engenders fear in the beholder and someone who is frightened of you is already in your power (Granny Weatherwax has never claimed to be nice). Unfortunately, she has a clear skin and excellent teeth, which despite her deliberate consumption of sugar show no signs of falling out. She is a traditionalist; she believes that progress is an excuse for making bad things happen faster.

Nanny Ogg is amiable and broad-minded to the point where she could pull it out of her ears and knot it under her chin. Of the three, she seldom does any magic in the normally accepted sense – her role is more one of a highly informal social worker and jobbing wise woman.

Magrat Garlick has a soul of hopeless niceness and welcomes new ideas. Occult candles, cards, mystic philosophies from distant regions – she approaches all these things with an open mind which, unfortunately, then fills up. She does, however, have a natural talent for herbal remedies and, like many small harmless animals, a vicious streak when cornered.

All three of course fulfil the usual daily functions expected of a rural witch: midwifery, the laying out of the dead (and sitting up with them at night, possibly playing cards with the more unusual cases) and folk medicine. Their approach to this last again represents three aspects of witchcraft –

Magrat: will give patients a specific remedy which careful observation over the years has suggested is most efficacious for that complaint;

Nanny Ogg: will give patients a stiff drink and tell them to stay in bed if they want to;

Granny Weatherwax: will give them the first bottle of coloured water that comes to hand and tell them it can't possibly fail. Her success rate is notable.

Their magical philosophies can be summed up as variations on the traditional sour mantra, Do What Thou Will –

Magrat: If it harms no one, and doesn't make, you know, too much noise or unnecessary stickiness or a mess or anything, do what you will, if you really want to. Um.

Granny Weatherwax: Don't do what you will, do what I tells you.

Nanny Ogg: A little bit of what you fancy does you good.

Witches are nominally matrilinear, but in areas around the RAMTOPS, where people are fairly rare and therefore recognized and understood as individuals in their isolated communities, even this system is a bit haphazard and has more to do with an individual's perceived standing than any hard and fast rule. It is certainly the case that all the children of Nanny Ogg and her various husbands are Oggs. Strictly speaking, the children of her sons should not be Oggs but should take their mother's surname. However, this would mean that a daughter-in-law would have to explain this to Nanny Ogg, a woman who once coined the phrase: 'Over your dead body.'

There is no Discworld concept of white/black magic. There is simply magic, in whatever form, which may be used in whatever way the user decides. Suggesting that there is any type of magic that is intrinsically good or bad would make as much sense to a Discworld wizard as suggesting that there is good and bad gravity. (Of course, from a subjective point of view there are such things as good and bad gravity; the gravity which causes an aircraft to crash is obviously different from the gravity which stops everything flying off into space.) (*See also* RESEARCH WITCHCRAFT.)

Magicians. The term is sometimes used interchangeably with 'wizards', but strictly speaking true magicians are mere magical technologists with defiant beards and leather patches on their elbows, who congregate in small groups at parties. Mostly they are failed students of Unseen University, who have nevertheless opted to stay on the fringes of the profession, where they perform menial but essential tasks such as setting up equipment, obtaining magical supplies, and so on. They carry out pretty much the same 'lab tech' functions for wizards as people called Igor do for pioneering brain surgeons.

But even magicians can look down on CONJURERS. [ER]

Malachite, Tubul de. A wizard, and a great student of dragon lore. Author of *The Summoning of Dragons*. Died in a mysterious fire which left half his workshop completely melted. There were the tracks of something like a large wading bird in the ashes, and on the charred wall someone had apparently painted an outline of a wizard with his hands upraised protectively. This was put down to sunspot activity. [GG]

Malich, Alberto. Albert. DEATH's manservant, but also Alberto Malich the Wise, the founder of Unseen University (1222–89 by the city count of that time).

Although in real years he is only about sixty-seven, he has been alive while two thousand years have passed on the Disc.

The generally held belief is that Alberto, one of the most powerful wizards alive at the time, tried to outwit Death by performing the Rite of ASHK-ENTE backwards. Insofar as his charred notebooks hold any clue, he seemed to believe that he could obtain another sixty-seven years of life.

In fact he disappeared, apart from his hat. Unseen University tradition is that he blew himself into the DUNGEON DIMENSION, which is the usual destination of those whose magic gets out of control; in reality, he ended up alive in Death's own country. The price of immortality, it turns out, was immortality. As explained elsewhere, real time does not pass in Death's house; there is, instead, a sort of endlessly recycled day.

It seems, however, that this entirely suits someone like Albert. Endless days filled with the same routine are something that makes a University wizard feel entirely at home. And he is, after all, a hierarchical creature. Wizards usually are.

Back on the Disc, Albert would have had only 91 days, 3 hours and 5 minutes left to live. That is now down to a handful of seconds, since most of it has been frittered away on shopping trips and holidays back in the world. When in Ankh-Morpork, Albert stays at the Young Men's Reformed Cultists of the Ichor God Bel-Shamharoth Association, where he nicks the soap and towels (Death has not got the knack of making towels, or soap, or anything to do with plumbing).

In appearance, Albert is a small hunched old man. This merely shows that first impressions can be wrong. Second impressions suggest quite a tall, wiry man who merely walks like the third illustration along in the usual How Man Evolved diagram. He has a red nose which drips so much that people talking to him blow their own noses out of sympathy. [ER, M, RM]

Malik, Nudger. A late member of the KLATCHIAN FOREIGN LEGION. [SM]

Maltoon, Skully. (Sometimes known as Muldoon; spelling is not a prerequisite for WATCH membership.) A member of the Palace guard. He used to live in Mincing Street with his mother, who made cough sweets. She died one day in a freak accident involving a wet floor, the cat, and a vat of the basic mixture for Mrs M.'s Expectorant Lozenges ('Don't They Make You Want to Spit'). Although she was subsequently pulled out there were nasty rumours that the family didn't want to waste the mixture and sold the lozenges anyway, so Skully grew up under cruel street taunts like 'Hey, these sweets have got some body in them' and 'There's a button in mine'. Lives in Easy Street. [GG]

Mante, Bay of. Scene of a famous shipwreck. [M]

Maps. Map-making has never been a precise art on the Discworld. People tend to start off with good intentions and then get so carried away with the spouting whales, monsters, waves and other twiddly bits of cartographic furniture that they often forget to put the boring mountains and rivers in at all.

Ankh-Morpork has, of course, been mapped. It is a mercantile city, after all, and people getting lost wastes time and money.

Marchesa. A fifth-level (female) wizard who commanded the flying lens which transported RINCEWIND and TWOFLOWER to KRULL. She is a woman with skin as black as the deep black of midnight at the bottom of a cave. Her hair and eyebrows are the colour of moonlight, with the same pale sheen about her lips. A graduate of Krull's own college of wizards. [COM]

Maroon, Mrs. The widow of a Watch-man, Sergeant Maroon. Secretly the recipient of a small pension paid personally by Captain VIMES. [MAA]

Marrowleaf. Wizard and author of *The Theory of Thaumic Imponderability*. This says that it is impossible to know exactly what any magical spell will do until afterwards, when it will be too late, although the Theory itself takes ninety closely written pages. [SM]

Maurice. The Amazing Maurice and His Educated Rodents. He ran a very remunerative operation by infesting a city with rats and then charging the city a large sum to get rid of them. [RM]

Mazda, Fingers. A sort of mythic hero to thieves everywhere. He was the first thief in the world; he stole fire from the gods. He was unable to fence it. It was too hot. [MAA]

M'Bu. Twelve-year-old assistant to Azhural N'CHOATE, a HOWONDALAND livestock exporter. He also has one of the best organization brains in the world, which was entirely necessary to get one thousand elephants all the way to Ankh-Morpork (a trek which at one point included sledging them down mountains). [MP]

Medicine. Discworld medicine is occasionally sophisticated but always erratic.

It might be thought that the practice of medicine would be simple in a world where magic is commonplace, and in purely diagnostic terms this is often the case. But Unseen University wizards, certainly, are expressly forbidden to use magic to cure. Magic is tricky stuff and can have a mind of its own – using it to perform a complex operation might solve the immediate problem but it might also present the patient with a range of new, and probably worse, ones. An analogy would be bringing in a wolf to keep the foxes away from your sheep. It *would* work, but . . .

Putting back an arm by magic would not be difficult, but getting it to do what its new owner wanted – since it would now be a creature of magic – would be hard and would involve a lot of embarrassment and the probable wearing of a boxing glove at night.

So in Ankh-Morpork, for example, the term 'surgical precision' still means 'to within an inch or two, with a lot of sawdust about, and a bucket of hot pitch in the corner'. However, wizards can be used as anaesthetists in preference to the usual large hammer.

Outside the cities of the STO PLAINS the stricken usually resort to witches. Techniques vary, ranging from Keep the Patient Amused While Nature Takes Its Course (since people often get better from things that don't actually kill them) to serious if haphazard knowledge of the genuine healing properties of herbs.

Chiropracty in particular is a witch art – many a witch knows the amazing healing properties of a good prod in the right place. Few other people understand this; throughout the history of the universe people gained an inconvenient reputation for messiahdom merely by demonstrating a useful knowledge of the common slipped disc. (*See also* RETRO-PHRENOLOGY.)

Mellius and Gretelina. The Disc's greatest lovers, whose pure, passionate and soul-searing affair would have scorched the pages of History had they not been born 200 years apart on different continents. [M]

Mended Drum, the. (*See* DRUM.)

Merchants' Guild. Motto: VILIS AD BIS PRETII.

Coat of arms: a shield, quartered. In the top-right quarter, a jeune coq, gules, on a field d'or; in the bottom-left quarter, a tête de boeuf, gules on a field d'or. In the top-left quarter, a vaisseau d'or on a field, azure; in the bottom right quarter, a bourse d'or on a field, azure. Superimposed on the shield, a morpork holding an ankh.

The youngest of Ankh-Morpork Guilds, founded in self-defence by the city's traders and shopkeepers when they realized that their role in the great scheme of things was to be robbed. 'Robbing fat merchants', it seemed, was a perfectly socially acceptable thing for even *heroic* heroes to do. 'Ah, yonder lies a fat merchant,' they'd cry, using the special Landlord-a-flagon-of-your-finest-ale hero talk, 'let us relieve him of some of his ill-gotten gains, 'pon my scalliard!' And *this* to a man who'd been up all night carefully mixing sand with the sugar, and who regularly gave small sums to the less smelly beggars.

The Guild was thus formed to peacefully further the aims of its members, advertise the civic charms of Ankh-Morpork and beat seven kinds of hell out of anyone with a leather loincloth. It is now one of the city's more talkative pressure groups.

It is particularly hot in pursuit of those misguided people who publicly fail to recognize the many attractive points of their fine city. The merchants now hire large gangs of men with ears like fists and fists like bags of walnuts to point out that Ankh-Morpork is, on the contrary, a marvellously clean and decent city in which to live, a process whose on-going nature might be swiftly curtailed if that person does not shut up right now.

The Guild has an annual knife-and-fork supper, held in the upper room of the Mended DRUM. [M]

Mericet. A tutor and examiner at the ASSASSINS' GUILD. He lectures on Strategy and Poison Theory every Thursday afternoon. An old, bald man with a tiny, dried-up smile that had all the warmth boiled out of it long ago. And one of the city's most skilled assassins. [P]

Mica. A bridge troll encountered by COHEN the Barbarian. [TB]

Michael, Cumbling. A member of the BEGGARS' GUILD. [MAA]

Mims, Terpsic. An angler in KRULL, rescued from drowning in the Hakrull river by DEATH because he had fallen in too soon. [M]

Modo. The dwarf gardener at Unseen University. He used to be the assistant gardener at the Palace. He smokes a pipe, and is often found in a secluded area behind the High Energy Magic building where he lights his bonfires, keeps his compost heaps, his pile of leaf mould and the little shed where he sits when it rains. He is a great believer in compost – his compost heaps heave and glow faintly in the dark, perhaps because of the possibly illegal ingredients Modo feeds them. ARCHCHANCELLORS have come and gone, UU has been destroyed and rebuilt, various dire horrors have visited the city, and Modo has still managed to mow the lawns every Friday. [RM]

Molly, Queen. Head of the BEGGARS' GUILD. She walks with a stick and wears layers and layers of rags. Her hair looks as though it has been permed by a hurricane and her face is a mass of sores and warts (which have sub-warts, and they have their own hair). A very sharp woman. [MAA]

Monarchy, Ankh-Morporkian. For most of its history Ankh-Morpork has been a monarchy. An important distinction, however, must be made between the kings of Ankh-Morpork and the kings of Ankh. The original kings of Ankh are enshrined in city mythology as 'real' kings (i.e., wise, powerful, charismatic, etc.), while the later kings of Ankh-Morpork are remembered as, well, real kings (i.e., power-mad, unjust and inventively evil).

Little is really known of the line of the kings of Ankh. It came to an end approximately 2,000 years ago and its period is generally thought of as a 'golden age' – i.e., a time so long ago that no one can remember how wretched it was. Its physical remains are few: there are the ancient sewers, the ruins of what was possibly a castle on the hillock known as The Tump, a throne so worm-eaten that it would become a cloud of dust if sat upon and – according to legend – a sword.

There followed seventeen centuries of

monarchy of a sort, where the crown was available to anyone with enough soldiers and a strong stomach; the history of the Ankh-Morpork monarchy is a litany of betrayals, massacres, ambushes, poisonings, imprisonments in towers, wars, people staggering around battlefields looking for their horse, family feuds and assassinations and wars. Of these last, the longest continued on a low-key basis for two centuries and the shortest, between the followers of Blad, Scourge of Dolly Sisters, and those of Mad Eric the Peaceful, is known as the .002 Years' War.

Compared to the legendary kings of Ankh, all the later kings of Ankh-Morpork were pretenders. Most of them had as much interest in good government as the Borgia popes had in divinity and most of the big families in Ankh-Morpork were 'royal' for a time. Not many lines survived for more than two or three generations and a number did not make it to the end of the coronation feast (in fact the shortest reign on record was that of Loyala the Aaargh, at 1.13 seconds). For a week Ankh-Morpork was technically ruled by a wasp, and for several days by the left foot of the then High Priest Of Io, who'd dropped the crown on it during the crucial point of the ceremony.

The legend of the sword figured very largely in the whole business. It was vaguely understood by the general population that possession of 'the sword' was the badge of the true king, and over the years any amount of 'true swords' were produced. In the case of Blad, it was two bits of wood hurriedly nailed together but for some reason, possibly to do with spikes and things, no one pointed this out for fifty-one years. It is now assumed (if not actually believed) that the sword is lost.

The last civil war, and execution and revelation of the personal habits of LORENZO THE KIND in 1688, marked the final end of any kind of monarchy in the city. The citizens did not object to rulers, even to cruel ones, but they did draw the line at being told that the various imbeciles and bloody-handed tyrants were there by the will of the gods.

And so the rule of kings gave way to the rule of the PATRICIANS. In a kind of mirror image of democracy, they have tended to get into power by lies, trickery and deceit but remain in power only by a very crude democratic process; if they make too many enemies, they'll be out of office, power and probably their corporeal form. It seems to have worked, possibly for the reason advanced by the current Patrician in his treatise on the art of government, *The Servant*: 'If it continues for long enough, even a reign of terror may become a fondly remembered period. People believe they want justice and wise government but, in fact, what they really want is an assurance that tomorrow will be very much like today.'

Monflathers, Lord. The first Duke led 600 men to a glorious and epic defeat at the Battle of Quirm, which somehow therefore has managed to become one of the great and proud moments of Ankh-Morpork's military history. [MAA]

Monks, Balancing. Little has been revealed of this rather strange order, although they do run a charity hospital in Ankh-Morpork.

Central to their faith is a belief that the Discworld will wobble if things aren't perfectly balanced, and the monks spend much of their time moving small weights around according to rituals in one of their holy books. The weights can sometimes be found in the most inaccessible places, the monks travelling thousands of miles to put just one rather small weight in one place on some otherwise insignificant mountain. The weights seldom exceed a pound or two and it is possible – although not necessarily wise – to assume that the whole thing is merely ceremonial.

Monks, History. An order of humans, but with attributes that almost put them in the realm of anthropomorphic personifications. They are the keepers of the History Books – huge, lead-bound volumes held in a secret cave in their hidden valley near the Hub.

The key to understanding the function of the monks is the fact that these books are not chronicles of history, but instructions for it – they are, as it were, the script. Every significant fact – and from the point of view of the historical narra-tive, many quite small events can have tremendous significance – is written down. Why, and who by, is not known to the monks; it is a question which, to them, makes about as much sense as 'Why is yellow?' The History books just are.

The role of the monks lies in the very important distinction between History and what might be called sequential events.

History, in order to happen, has to be observed *by people who know they are observing History*. Skilled people, in fact. It's no good just anyone being there. It is well known that vast areas of the planet Earth had no history whatsoever until explorers turned up and brought History with them. Geography is similar in this respect; the fact that some lake, waterfall or continent is known to millions of people who live there is really of no significance compared to the arrival of an explorer who knows what Geography is.

History on the Discworld generally unfolds according to the patterns laid down in the books and has a natural tendency to spring back into shape, and for most of the time the monks merely have to observe. However, quantum uncertainty means that occasionally they have to intervene, usually in the most subtle of ways. In the same way that the placing of a 2oz weight can (possibly) affect the balance of the Discworld (*see* MONKS, BALANCING), the course of history can be changed by the mere misplacing of a pebble in a stream. These apparently trivial actions can send the whole world rushing down a different leg of the TROUSERS OF TIME.

The monks are, however, quite human and occasionally sentimental, and it is suspected that they will occasionally guide History down the 'wrong' leg and alter the books themselves with whatever is the temporal equivalent of Liquid Paper.

Since they are by definition outside History the monks are invisible to normal people except when they are performing some role in the unfolding drama (it is sometimes necessary to go into History in order to steer it). They experience time on a continual basis but age only when taking on these roles.

They are also skilled in martial arts and possess the secret of being able to walk for many hours in the sub-zero temperatures of the high mountains (known as the Double-Knit Woollen Combinations with the Reinforced Gusset and Trapdoor).

Monolith. A troll folk-hero, who first wrested the secret of rocks from the GODS. Believed to have been the first-ever troll. Apparently, the secret of rock is that if you pick one up you can throw it at someone. This knowledge was jealously guarded by the gods. [MP]

Mooner, Dr. The owner of Dr Mooner's Travelling Take Your Breath Away Emporium. [P]

Mooty, Zebbo. A thief, third class, in Ankh-Morpork. The first person for hundreds of years to have been killed by a dragon. But not the last. [GG]

Morecombe. A vampire. The solicitor of the RAMKIN family. Scrawny, like a tortoise; very pale, with pearly, dead eyes. [MAA]

Morraine. A troll who acted in moving pictures. (After the collapse of the industry a Morraine is known to have worked at the Armoury, and later joined the Ankh-Morpork militia.) [MP, MAA]

Mort. Mortimer. Youngest son of LEZEK. Tall, red-haired and freckled, thin, white face, with the sort of body that seemed to be only marginally under its owner's control; it appeared to have been built out of knees. He had the kind of vague, cheerful helpfulness that serious men soon learned to dread. Despite these drawbacks Mort was chosen by DEATH to be his apprentice, and during that time became considerably less undirected and considerably more serious. Mort married YSABELL and became Duke of STO HELIT.

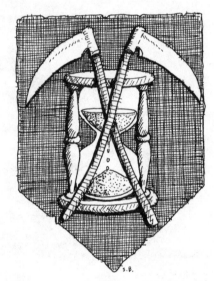

As duke, his coat of arms was faux croisé on a sablier rampant against a sable field. His motto: NON TIMETIS MESSOR. [M, GG]

Moutarde, Colonel. A guest at the Samedi Nuit Mort ball in GENUA. [WA]

Moving Pictures, Production Companies.
Century of the Fruitbat Moving Pictures
Fir Wood Studios
Floating Bladder Pictures
Microlithic Pictures
Untied Alchemists

Moving Pictures, Titles of.
Bad Menace of Troll Valley

Beyond the Valley of the Trolls
Blown Away
Bolde Adventurer, A
Burninge Passiones
Dark Forest
Exciting Study of Pottery Making, An
Golde Diggers of 1457
Golde Rushe, The
High Jinks at the Store
King's Ransom, A
Mystery Mountain
Night at the Arena, A
Pelias and Melisande
Shadowe of the Dessert
Sons of the Dessert
Sword of Passione (or *The Interestinge and Curious Adventures of Cohen the Barbarian*)
Tales of the Dwarfes
Third Gnome, The
Turkey Legs
Valley of the Trolls

Murduck, Brother. A missionary member of the brethren in the Citadel in OMNIA. His death was used to incite conflict between EPHEBE and Omnia. [SG]

Murune. A past King of LANCRE (709–745). He met a terrible fate involving a red-hot poker, ten pounds of live eels, a 3-mile stretch of frozen river, a butt of wine, a couple of tulip bulbs, a number of poisoned eardrops, an oyster and a large man with a mallet. Some people just don't seem to get along with others. [WS]

Muscara. Née Susan. One of the members of DIAMANDA's coven in LAN-CRE. [LL]

Musicians' Guild. Motto: ID MVRMVR-ATIS, ID LVDAMVS.
Coat of arms: a shield, azure, bisected by a band wavy, argent et melodieux.

Sinister a trousseau des clés, or. Dexter a cor, or.

The Guild has a very small office in Tin Lid Alley, Ankh-Morpork (a couple of poky rooms above a barber shop). On the wall of its poky, brown-walled waiting room is a sign: 'For Your Comfort and Convenience YOU WILL NOT SMOKE'. Unlike most of the other Guilds it does not involve itself in education or social work, but does involve itself very deeply and sincerely in collecting very high membership fees and imposing very high performance rates to pay for them. It is not compulsory for a musician to belong to the GoM. On the other hand, it is not *compulsory* for a musician to breathe and see out of both eyes. Although most members of its senior council were once practising musicians, their contact with the Muse these days is generally limited to the notes you can obtain by hitting the human skull quite hard.

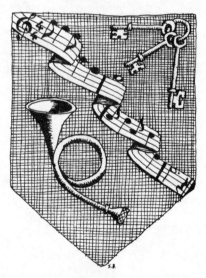

Mwnyy, Owen. Owner of a legendary harp which, according to Llamedese legend, sang when danger threatened. [SM]

N'choate, Azhural. A Klatchian stock dealer. [MP]

Necrotelicomnicon. (Also known as the *Liber Paginarum Fulvarum*.) A book, written by ACHMED THE MAD, which lists all of the old, dark gods of the Disc. The first edition is kept in the LIBRARY of Unseen University, between iron plates, behind a balanced stone door, with its name hacked on to the lintel over the door. The page headed 'About the Author' combusted shortly after his death. Legend says that any mortal man who reads more than a few lines of the original copy will die insane; it is also said that it contains illustrations that could make a strong man's brain dribble out of his ears. Usually, people only read tenth or twelfth hand copies.

There was once a wizard who started to read it and let his mind wander. Next morning they found all his clothes on the chair and his hat on top of them and the book had . . . a lot more pages. [ER, MP]

Nef, Great. An incredibly dry desert region of the Disc, Rimwards of KLATCH, at the heart of which is the DEHYDRATED OCEAN. It is so dry that it has a negative rainfall. It is the site of the Lost City of EE and the Light Dams of the Sorca people. [COM, P]

Nesheley. An inhabitant of Inkcap, in the RAMTOPS. His claim to fame is that he once nearly ran over Granny WEATHERWAX in his cart and is still alive. [WS]

Nhumrod, Brother. Novice Master in OMNIA. A kindly (by the standards of Omnia, anyway) old man, waxy-skinned, with thin, blue-veined hands. He walked with a cane and was also a mass of nervous tics, but perhaps this was due to the fact that he has survived in the Omnian citadel for fifty years and has spent every night wrestling with the evil temptations of the flesh. [SG]

Nijel. Nijel the Destroyer, son of HARE-BUT the Provision Merchant. To say that he is lean would be to miss a perfect opportunity to use the word 'emaciated' – he looks as though toast racks and deckchairs have figured in his ancestry. He has a shock of lank, ginger hair, eyes like boiled grapes and a face that is a battleground for its native freckles and the dreadful invading forces of acne.

Short-sighted, with a weak jawline and a tendency to asthma attacks, Nijel does not conform to the normal perception of a Disc hero. He does, however, dress like one: a few studded leather thongs, big furry boots, a little leather 'holdall' and goosepimples. The woolly underwear doesn't really work, but he promised his mother.

And, indeed, he acts like a hero, too. In fact Nijel has every necessary attribute for the classical hero except strength, charisma and skill. [S]

Nine Turning Mirrors. Grand Vizier of the AGATEAN EMPIRE. Grew old in the service of several Emperors, whom he regarded as being a necessary but tiresome ingredient in the successful running of the Empire. He did not like things out of place – his view was that the Empire was not built by allowing things to get out of place. He had very clear views about who should run the country – e.g. that it should be him. Met his end during his attempt to poison a young Emperor who was handier with a pair of chopsticks. [COM, M]

Ninereeds. The rather unpleasant Agatean Master Accountant to whom TWOFLOWER was once apprenticed. It was also the name given by Twoflower to the dragon he conjured from his mind at the WYRMBERG. [COM]

Nitt, Agnes. (*See* PERDITA.)

Nivor, Grunworth. A tutor at the ASSASSINS' GUILD. Fat, jolly and fond of his food. TEPPIC's housemaster, who lectured about traps and deadfalls on Tuesdays. [P]

Nobbs, Corporal C. W. St J. (**Cecil Wormsborough St John**). A Corporal in the Ankh-Morpork Night WATCH. Known as Nobby. A 4-foot-tall, pigeon-chested, bandy-legged man, with the muscle tone of an elastic band and a certain resemblance to a chimpanzee. The only reason you can't say that Nobby is close to the animal kingdom is that the animal kingdom would move further away. Nobby is actually smaller than many dwarfs.

He is rumoured to have terrible personal habits, although these appear to be no more than a penchant for petty theft (usually from people too unconscious or, for preference, too dead to argue), an ability to do tricks with his facial boils, and a liking for folk dancing.

Men like Nobby can be found in any armed force. Although their grasp of the minutiae of the Regulations is usually encyclopaedic, they take good care never to be promoted beyond, perhaps, Corporal. He smokes incessantly, but the weird thing is that any cigarette smoked by Nobby becomes a dog-end almost instantly and remains a dog-end indefinitely or until lodged behind his ear, which is a sort of nicotine Elephants' Graveyard.

Nobby's normal method of locomotion is a species of sidle; in times of

danger he has a way of propelling himself from place to place without apparently moving through the intervening space. And he tends to speak out of the corner of his mouth. In fact there is something altogether very corner-y about Corporal Nobbs.

Nobby is known to have served as a quartermaster in the army of the Duke of Pseudopolis. There are rumours that he had to join the Watch after items missing from the stores were found in his kit. Since the items were the entirety of the store inventory, Nobby's kit at the time consisted of two warehouses.

He lives in the New Watch House in Pseudopolis Yard, Ankh-Morpork, moving from room to room as he fills them up.

Noddy. A friend to Crash and a member of his music group, originally called Insanity. He was the Other One – you know, the one who isn't the lead guitarist, the bass guitarist or the drummer. The one who jumps around on the stage sweating and drinking beer. [SM]

Nork the Impaler. A regular at the Mended DRUM. No one has ever dared ask how he got the nickname. [GG]

Notfaroutoe, Count and Countess. Formerly just common old Arthur and Doreen WINKINGS. Members of the FRESH START CLUB and vampires, by inheritance. Arthur had been in the wholesale fruit and vegetable business before he inherited the title and, with it, a ruined castle and vampirism. At least, so he believes. And that is the important thing.

Vampirism sits uneasily on the middle class. The difficulty the couple face is that they feel there are established ways vampires should look and behave, and they do their best to behave that way.

The snag is that these details – the wearing of evening dress at all times, and so on – were designed for people a good deal taller, thinner and, well, more inherently stylish than Arthur and Doreen. But since the only vampires they've ever heard of wear posh clothes and live in castles, they set out with a sort of resigned and dogged unimaginativeness to fit the stereotype.

The Countess, for example, is basically a pear-shaped, amiable woman who is trying to look like a consumptive and mysterious lady two feet taller. She wears a figure-hugging black dress, long dark hair cut into a widow's peak and very pallid make-up. Nature, however, designed her to have frizzy hair and a hearty complexion. She speaks with an affected foreign accent except when she forgets. Vampires are always foreign, she believes.

The only vampire trait not embraced by Arthur is the one involving climbing into the bedrooms of young women and sucking their necks. Doreen put her foot down about this. He has to have rare steak and black pudding and like it. This disappointment is on top of his shaving problem; his face is a mass of small cuts, because it's very hard to shave when you can't see yourself in the mirror.

Their four-roomed terraced house at 14 Masons Road, Ankh-Morpork, boasted a crypt, a vault (the Winkings haven't worked out that these could be the same thing), a torture chamberette, a dining room with dribbly candles and a painting whose eyes moved, a secret passage, an organ that was so big that a hole had to be knocked in the parlour ceiling for it, a laboratory and a moat. The house fell down shortly after Arthur knocked down the last load-bearing wall in order to install an Iron Maidenette, and the Winkings subsequently lodged

Octarine. The eighth colour of the Disc spectrum. The basic colour of which other colours are merely pale shadows impinging on normal four-dimensional space. It is a sort of fluorescent greenish-yellow-purple. (*See also* LIGHT.)

Octarines. Gemstones which glow in a strong magical field. Otherwise they look like rather inferior diamonds. [S]

Octavo, the. The CREATOR's own grimoire. Reputedly left behind by the Creator – with characteristic absent-mindedness – shortly after completing his major work.

The Eight Spells are imprisoned on its pages.

For the whole of recorded time – except for a brief spell inside the LUGGAGE – it has been kept in a little room off the main LIBRARY, in the cellars of Unseen University. The walls are covered with occult symbols and protective lead pentagrams, and most of the floor is taken up with the Eightfold Seal of Stasis. The only furnishing is a lectern in the shape of a bird – or at least in the shape of a winged thing it is probably best not to examine too closely – and on the lectern, fastened to it by a heavy chain covered in eight padlocks (one key for each of the Heads of the Eight Orders of Wizardry), is a book, so full of magic that it has its own keen sentience.

It is a large, but not particularly impressive book. The rather tatty leather cover has a representation of BELSHAMHAROTH and could be described in a library catalogue as 'slightly foxed' although it would be more honest to admit it looks as though it has been badgered, wolved and possibly beared as well. Metal clasps hold it shut. They aren't decorated, they're just very heavy – like the chain, which doesn't so much attach the book to the lectern as tether it. They look like the work of someone who had a pretty definite aim in mind, and who has spent most of his life making training harnesses for elephants.

No one is allowed to stay in the room for more than 4 minutes and 32 seconds (a figure arrived at after 200 years of cautious experimentation).

Octiron. A strange, iridescent metal, almost as highly valued in the lands around the CIRCLE SEA as SAPIENT PEARWOOD and about as rare.

A needle of octiron will always point to the Hub of the Discworld, being acutely sensitive to the Disc's magical field; it will also miraculously darn socks.

Octiron radiates a dangerous amount of raw enchantment and is a metal so unstable that it can exist only in a universe saturated with raw magic.

Octogen. A gas that radiates dangerous amounts of raw magic.

Odium. A moving-picture house in Ankh-Morpork. Owned by Bezam PLANTER. Destroyed by fire. [MP]

Offler. Great Offler of the Bird-Haunted Mouth. Six-armed Crocodile God of Klatch, but also the default god of any place with a big river and warm climate. He has a flock of holy birds that bring him news of his worshippers and also keep his teeth clean. The teeth in his fanged snout cause him to speak with a marked lisp. [M, S]

Ogg, Gytha. 'Nanny Ogg' – most Ramtop witches of any note have some suitable grandmotherly honorific (Granny, Nanny, Gammer, Old Mother, etc.), regardless of actual marital status.

Age: uncertain, even to her. Probably in her seventies, which means she was still capable of bearing children in her early fifties (this is by no means unusual for a healthy LANCRE woman, especially a witch, and certainly for an Ogg). There is a large population of long-lived dwarfs on the mountainous fringes of the country, and the Oggs are a remarkably ancient family with traditional skills in magic and iron-working; it may be, as CASANUNDA has claimed, that she has some dwarf in her, although this is probably an expression of his hopes rather than any genetic expertise.

After an adventurous girlhood –

always chaste, often caught – Gytha Ogg was accepted by a Biddy Spective as her successor to the cottage in Lancre town, where she brought to the craft of witchery an honest, earthy outlook, a non-judgemental understanding of human nature, and the ability to crack walnuts with her knees.

Nanny Ogg's family arrangements are cosy but haphazard. She has been formally married three times, to Albert Ogg, Winston Ogg and Sobriety Ogg (witches are matrilinear and in any case a man would be expected to accept the family name when marrying into such an ancient lineage as the Oggs). All three have passed happily, if somewhat energetically, to their well-earned rest.

She has fifteen living children: Jason, Grame, Tracie, Shirl, Daff, Dreen, Nev, Trev, Kev, Wane, Sharleen, Darron, Karen, Reet and Shawn. Many of them, Shawn, for example, live and work around Lancre; others have sought their fortune in far-flung foreign parts. There are innumerable grandchildren and great-grandchildren. Only two grandchildren have appeared in the chronicles – Shane, a bold sailor lad, and Pewsey, the stickiest child in the world. Contrary to the rules of traditional witchcraft, Nanny Ogg now lives in quite a modern cottage in the centre of Lancre, with up-to-date conveniences like a modern wash copper and a tin bath a mere garden's walk away on a nail at the back of the privy. The cottage is between those of Shawn and Jason. She likes to have all her family around her in case of an emergency, such as when she needs a cup of tea or the floor washed.

Ogg, Jason. Eldest son of Gytha Ogg. Master blacksmith and farrier, and a member of the LANCRE Morris Men. His youngest son is called Pewsey.

With his hairy brow, cheese-grater chin and 15-stone body, Jason looks as though he was not born but constructed. In a shipyard. He is a man with an essentially slow and gentle nature that should have gone to a couple of bullocks, arms like tree trunks and legs like beer barrels stacked in twos.

The smith in Lancre is a very powerful smith indeed. The Lancre smiths have an ancient bargain – if they shoe anything brought to them, their reward is the *ability* to shoe anything. It is not clear who the pact is with, but it may have something to do with Lancre's proximity to the worlds of the ELVES, against whom iron is a sovereign defence. Or it may be because, every so often, *someone* comes at the appropriately named dead of night to have his horse re-shod. Whatever the reason, Jason can put a shoe on anything with feet.

They brought him an ant once, for a joke. He sat up all night with a magnifying glass and an anvil made out of the head of a pin.

Jason also knows the mystic secret of the Lancre Horseman's Word, used by smiths to calm the wildest stallion. It broadly consists of a whispered explanation into the animal's ear of what all those hammers and pliers will be used for if the horse doesn't stop kicking and present a docile hoof *right now*. [WS, WA, LL]

Ogg, Shawn. Gytha Ogg's youngest son:

a short, red-faced youth in his early twenties. He is guard and general odd-job man at LANCRE CASTLE, where he dreams of a glorious military career. Many days spent guarding Lancre Castle on a repetitive carbohydrate diet have given him an inner self-reliance and an ability to fart in tunes. [WS, LL]

Oggham. Ancient runic alphabet, still used by dwarfs throughout the RAMTOPS. There is some suggestion that this has something to do with the Ogg family – a suggestion which Nanny OGG is careful to foster.

Ohulan Cutash. A quite barbaric and uncivilized sprawl of a hundred or so houses about 15 miles from LANCRE and considered by Lancrastians to be a big city. It has one suburb. It's too small to have more than one, and this is just an inn and a handful of cottages for people who can't stand the pressure of urban life. There is a cobbled main square and on one side are the temples of the Disc's more demanding deities.

It has a tiny river dock, on the upper ANKH, with broad, flat-bottomed barges bobbing gently against the wharves. [ER]

Old High Ones, the. Only very obliquely referred to in the Discworld religions. Such piecemeal references as have been discovered suggest that there are eight 'entities' that oversee the universe, although 'oversee' is far too strong a word. There is no single word that really does explain their role, which seems to be to observe in a dynamic way, in order for the observed events to be able to happen. It might be simpler to say that the universe exists because they believe in it. They are not gods – from their point of view, gods are only a slightly more troublesome version of human beings.

They are far above the AUDITORS OF REALITY, who are their executive arm. The names of seven of them, if they have names, have not been revealed. The eighth is AZRAEL.

Old Man Trouble. One of a large number of 'anthropomorphic personifications' brought into existence by the low reality quotient of the Discworld universe, which means in essence that anything believed in strongly enough will eventually come into existence.

Old Man Trouble wears a long mac and a large, raggedy, broad-brimmed hat. All that can be seen between the two are his dreadful glowing eyes. He is a personification variously of Murphy's Law, the general intractability of the universe, and the darkness in the cellar. He is easily summoned by failing to have 1) rhythm or 2) music or even 3) your girl. In which case, if you hear a soft knocking at your door – don't open it.

Olerve the Bastard. King of STO LAT and father of KELI. A tall, heavily built man with a golden beard and the kind of stolid, patient face you'd confidently buy a used horse from. No sense of humour, but kings don't need them, since people will laugh anyway. [M]

Om. The Great God Om. He has a vast church in Kom, OMNIA. When he is first encountered, he is a small tortoise with one beady eye and a badly chipped shell. When at full strength, he is an enormous, shimmering, golden figure (the appearance of a god when manifest is directly proportional to the amount of belief they command). Om is omnipotent, omnipresent, and many other oms-, but only within the boundaries of the Omnian church. [SG]

Omnia. A dry country on the Klatchian coast between the deserts of KLATCH and the plains and jungles of HOWONDALAND. There are two million people in the Omnian empire. Its principal city is Kom.

The Citadel in Kom extends for miles – temples, churches, schools, dormitories, gardens and towers. It also has a lot of underground cellars and sewers, forgotten rooms, dead ends, spaces behind walls and natural caves. There are very few steps in the Citadel – the progress of the many processions demands long, gentle slopes. What steps there are are shallow enough to allow for the faltering steps of very old men.

One of the main thoroughfares leads to the Place of Lamentations – a square 200 yards across. On one side of the square is the Great Temple, its roof adorned with the golden horns of OM. The doors in the central temple are 100 feet tall, weigh 40 tons each and are said to be made of bronze, reinforced with Klatchian steel. They open only outwards. On them, in letters of gold set in lead, are the Commandments (512 so far).

Omnia and the Church of Om are more or less synonymous; there is no civil authority. The entire country is ruled by the priesthood.

Its army – the Divine Legion – wear polished fishmail and black and yellow cloaks on special occasions. Apart from national defence, which is sometimes undertaken in advance of any actual attack, their main duty for many years was to stamp heavily on heresy – which, despite having been stamped on heavily for millennia, still kept on taking root all over the place. (*See* QUISITION.) [SG]

One-Man-Bucket. Spirit guide of Mrs CAKE. A member (once) of a HOWONDALAND tribe who was killed when he was run over by a cart in Treacle Street,

Ankh-Morpork, while drunk. He is a ghost, with a reedy and petulant voice. Called One-Man-Bucket because of his tribe's tradition of naming a child after the first thing its mother saw after giving birth. The first thing his mother saw was a man pouring a bucket of water over two dogs causing a disturbance outside the tent. One-Man-Bucket's marginally older brother, who slid into the world a few seconds earlier, was not so fortunate in his name. [RM]

One Sun Mirror. A past emperor of the AGATEAN EMPIRE. He has two claims to fame: 1) He had the stone garden of Universal Peace and Simplicity laid out, and 2) His habit of cutting off his enemies' lips and legs and then promising them their freedom if they can run through the city playing a trumpet. [M]

Orang-Utan/Human Dictionary, the. A major project being undertaken by the LIBRARIAN of Unseen University, who is himself of the orang persuasion. Since he was also, once, a human being, he feels himself in a position to advance the understanding between the two species. This may be a problem since one of the species consists of mankind, but he is persevering.

A flavour of the work, which already runs for more than 500 closely written pages, may further illustrate the difficulties:

Ook: Oh, I do beg your pardon, I didn't realize there was a dominant male in this group.

Ook: I'll just go and sit over here very quietly, shall I?

Ook: You're out of your tree. This is *my* tree.

Ook: Yes.

Ook: No.

Ook: Banana.

Ook: It may be vital oxygenating biomass to you, but it's home to me.

Ook: Did you see a rain forest around here a moment ago?

Orinjcrates. Ephebian philosopher and author of *On the Nature of Plants*. [SG]

Orohai Peninsula. (On the Rim coast of KLATCH.) Home to the sponge-eating pygmies, who live in little coral houses. For further information, see General Sir Roderick Purdeigh's book: *My Life Among the Sponge-Eating Coral-House-Dwelling Pygmies*, in which he discusses at length the twin problems of daily indigestion and concussion. [COM]

Osric. Victor TUGELBEND's uncle. Victor thought that the HOLY WOOD statue of a golden knight resembled him. [MP]

Ossory. One of the Great Prophets of the Omnian church. The 193-chapter *Book of Ossory* was dictated to him by the Great God OM, it is said. It was certainly said by Ossory, and no one was going to argue with anyone who came out of the desert just after the mushroom season with his eyeballs spinning in different directions.

The Book contains the Directions, the Gateways, the Abjurations and the Precepts. Ossory's staff is a religious artefact. [SG]

Palm, Rosemary. ('Rosie', although not to her face.) Mrs Palm is a stout and refined lady, who lives with a lot of younger ladies in a house in the SHADES, and whose occupation is broadly understood. It has been said that she keeps a house of ill-repute but, on the contrary, a lot of people have spoken very highly of it.

A lonely man may while away many an hour playing dominoes and Chase My Neighbour Up the Passage with Mrs Palm and her girls with no fear that he will end up naked in an alley with all his money gone (unless of course his tastes run that way).

Mrs Palm is president of the SEAMSTRESSES' Guild.

Panter, Lemuel. A wizard, one of RINCEWIND's old tutors and a Member of the Order of Midnight. [LF]

Pantries. One universal manifestation of raw, natural magic throughout the universe is this: that any domestic food store, raided furtively in the middle of the night, always contains, no matter what its daytime inventory, half a jar of elderly mayonnaise, a piece of very old cheese, and a tomato with white mould growing on it. [M]

Paps of Scilla. An eight-peaked mountain range, visible on the route from ZEMPHIS to Ankh-Morpork. Many have speculated about the lady concerned. [ER]

Parrot. ERIC's pet. It spoke, but utilized a somewhat limited vocabulary based around one metasyntactic variable. It had one evil but intelligent red eye; most of the rest of it was pink and purple skin, studded with fag-ends of feathers, so that the net effect was of an oven-ready hairbrush. It was given to PONCE DA QUIRM. [E]

Pasha of Re'Durat. A past owner of the magical sword KRING. Re'Durat has never been identified, but is presumed to be in HERSHEBA. [COM]

Patrician, Office of. The Patrician is the ruler of Ankh-Morpork. There have been no monarchs in Ankh-Morpork for 300 years, since the death of the last and possibly nastiest (*see* LORENZO THE KIND). The only real qualification to rule Ankh-Morpork is the ability to stay alive for more than five minutes, because the great merchant families of Ankh have been ruling the city as kings or Patricians for the last twenty centuries and are as about to relinquish power as the average limpet is to let go of its rock. Past Patricians have included:

Hargarth, Frenzied Earl [GG]
Harmoni, Deranged Lord [MAA]
Nersch the Lunatic [GG]
Olaf QUIMBY II
Scapula, Laughing Lord [MAA]
Smince, Lord [GG]
Snapcase, Mad/Psychoneurotic Lord
 [GG, MAA]
Winder, Homicidal Lord [MAA]

The holder of the office throughout the Discworld chronicles is Lord Havelock Vetinari. (*See also* MONARCHY.)

Patrician, the (Lord Havelock Vetinari).

Age uncertain. Background unavailable. Reputedly trained at the ASSASSINS' GUILD school. Now supreme ruler of the city of Ankh-Morpork, to which he is totally devoted. Tall, thin, and generally to be seen wearing black.

He is the most recent of a line of

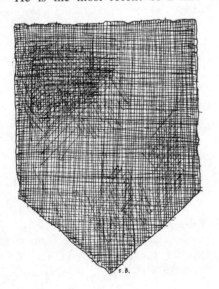

unelected heads (see above). As their names suggest, these were not wholly pleasant or well-balanced men and soon met their ends, as did a red-hot poker in the case of one particularly unpopular ruler. Lord Vetinari, on the other hand, is very, very sane. And still alive.

He appears to have survived by being equally distrusted and disliked by all interest groups in the city but also by carefully not being as unpopular as every interest group is to all the others.

A popular form of punishment and mass entertainment in the reign of Mad Lord Snapcase was the tearing to pieces of criminals by teams of wild horses. Lord Vetinari appeared to be like the man in the middle of the arena who had managed somehow to chain all the wild horses to one another and is groaning theatrically while watching them drag one another to their knees. The result, in political terms, is stability achieved by equal tension in all directions.

His genius lies in the realization that everyone craves stability even more than they hunger after justice or truth. Even revolutionary anarchists want stability, so that they have breathing space to fight their real enemies, i.e., those higher than themselves in the revolutionary anarchist council, and those heretics whose definition of revolutionary anarchy differs from their own by about half a sentence in paragraph 97 of the charter.

This policy is dimly perceived by the more intelligent Guild leaders in the city. Yet when an assassination attempt was last made (*Men At Arms*), the ASSASSINS' GUILD themselves were prominent in the search for the perpetrator. Annoying as the Patrician is, it is so easy to think of someone worse. Technically, Vetinari seems to have given in to every demand of every Guild for years, so the Guilds are driving themselves mad wondering why he is therefore still in charge.

It has been remarked that if the Patrician were thrown to a pack of wolves he would, after chatting to them for a few minutes, have them tearing one another to shreds. It is certainly the case that when he was thrown into one of his own rat-infested, scorpion-filled dungeons [GG] he organized the rats to eat

may be considered an excusable peccadillo or possibly an amusing character trait. He does have a small and very old terrier, called Wuffles, to which he is said to be quite attached.

Probably his greatest enemy is Captain (later Commander) VIMES of the City WATCH but, strangely, the person with

the scorpions and then to bring him food and reading matter. He'd also, years before, secreted a key to the dungeon behind a secret slab. As he wrote in his unpublished MS entitled *The Servant*, a sort of handbook for the politically ambitious: 'Never build a dungeon that you cannot get out of.'

He is entirely without vices in any normal sense of the word. If he had any, we can be sure some Guild or other would have made use of them by now.

It is true that he has banned street theatre and hangs mime artists upside down in a scorpion pit opposite a sign that says 'Learn The Words', but this

whom he gets on best – or least badly – is Corporal (later Captain) CARROT Ironfoundersson of the same Watch. They share the same obsessive interest in the city itself.

Lord Vetinari lives in what was once the royal family's Winter Palace in Morpork (the summer palace is a long way from the city, and the reason will easily be appreciated by anyone who has spent a summer near the river). He manages the city either from a wooden seat at the foot of the steps on which is the ancient golden throne of the city, or more usually from the Oblong Office, high in the palace.

This is where he gathers information. People tell him things, for all sorts of reasons. He has a bedroom. He presumably sleeps.

The Patrician has expressed a wish that, one day, he could retire and cultivate a garden. It will probably never happen. It is impossible to imagine him as a mere civilian. But if he did indeed take up horticulture, the roses would grow in lines, the garden would bloom on command – and the slugs would eat the caterpillars.

Patrician's Palace. The old Royal Winter Palace of the Kings of Ankh. The most famous room in the Palace is the Oblong Office, which is the personal sanctum of the current PATRICIAN. Although much of the Palace is given over to the Patrician's clerks, collating and updating the information gathered by his exquisitely organized spy system, it still contains the public rooms left over from the city's royal heritage – in particular the Throne Room, which houses the magnificent Golden Throne of the Kings of Ankh. This throne is not used by the current Patrician; he prefers to sit on a plain wooden chair at the foot of the steps leading to the throne. Also of note are the Palace dungeons, which include all the usual equipment, together with the scorpion pit.

It is, however, the Palace Grounds that are the crowning glory. These include a bird garden, a little zoo, a racehorse stable . . . and gardens laid out by Bloody Stupid JOHNSON. Of particular note are the ornamental trout lake, the fountain, lawn, maze, ornamental chiming sundial and the hoho.*

*A haha is a cunningly concealed dip in the land enabling one to enjoy the view without being nibbled by inconvenient cows – it is, in fact, a sort of negative fence. A hoho is merely a much deeper version.

The trout lake has room for one long thin trout, the fountain only operated once when it blew a small stone cherub right outside the city, and the maze, far from being big enough to get lost in, is so small that people get lost looking for it. All in all, the gardens represent Bloody Stupid's erratic genius in full flower.

Patricio. 23-stone Despot of QUIRM. He was the largest victim/client of the ASSASSINS' GUILD; they had to break for lunch. [P]

Peavie. Treasurer of the ALCHEMISTS' GUILD. A nervous man whose contribution to the development of moving pictures was the invention of banged grains. This may have done nothing for his nerves. [MP]

Peedbury, Iago. A farmer neighbour of Miss FLITWORTH. The first man to use a Combination Harvester. [RM]

Perdita. Agnes Nitt. Daughter of Thomas 'Threepenny' Nitt. A member of DIAMANDA's coven in LANCRE. A small fat seventeen-year-old with a naturally rosy complexion; the sort of girl who would love to be a Goth but was cut out by nature to be two Goths. Easily swayed by her more imaginative friends, Perdita wears black, has a black hat with a veil, and even a black lace hanky, all this conspiring to give the effect of a small, low-flying thunderstorm. According to Nanny OGG, who is seldom wrong in these matters, Agnes actually does have some useful magical talent. [LL]

Perdore, Brother. A member of the Nine Day Wonderers, a religious order in the RAMTOPS. He is an amiable old man, which is just as well given that his flexible parish contains so many witches. [LL]

Pestilence. Anthropomorphic personification. A member of the Four Horsemen of the APOCRALYPSE. He has a breathy, wet voice, which is practically contagious in itself. Pestilence's favourite drink is believed to be a small egg nog with a cherry in it. [LF]

Philosophy. EPHEBE is the home of philosophy, but other lands have also produced famous philosophers, most notably, of course, LY TIN WHEEDLE. There are almost as many systems of philosophy as there are philosophers. They include: Sumtin, Zen, Stoicism, Cynicism, Epicureanism, Stochaticism, Anamaxandritism, Epistemologism, Peripateticism, Synopticism.

Astro-philosophers of KRULL once succeeded in proving conclusively that all places are one place and that the distance between them is an illusion. This news was an embarrassment to all thinking philosophers because it did not explain, among other things, signposts. After years of wrangling the whole thing was then turned over to Ly Tin Wheedle who, after some thought, proclaimed that although it was indeed true that all places were one place, that place was very large.

Xenoists say that the world is basically complex and random. Ibidians say the world is basically simple and follows certain fundamental rules. DIDACTYLOS says basically it's a funny old world – and it doesn't contain enough to drink.

Pills, Dried Frog. The wizards of Unseen University are right at the forefront of modern medical thinking, and make up these pills for the current Bursar, who is mentally as stable as a tapdancer in a ballbearing factory.

Pine Dressers. A village high in the RAM-TOPS and 500 miles from the sea which nevertheless has managed to develop a thriving fish-gutting, smoking, and canning industry based on the very frequent rains of fish that occur in the area. The townsfolk see no reason to object to strange phenomena if they can make a decent kipper out of them.

Pivey, Mrs. Neighbour of Count and Countess NOTFAROUTOE. Known to be unsympathetic to things like moats and crypts in a next-door context. [RM]

Pizza. The first pizza was created on the Disc by the Klatchian mystic Ronron 'Revelation Joe' SHUWADHI, who claimed to have been given the recipe in a dream by the CREATOR of the Discworld Himself, who had apparently added that it was what He had intended, all along. Those desert travellers who have seen the original, which is reputedly miraculously preserved in the Forbidden City of EE, say that what the Creator had in mind then was a fairly small cheese and pepperoni affair with a few black olives, and things like mountains and seas got added out of last-minute enthusiasm, as so often happens.

After the Schism of the Turnwise Ones and the deaths of some 25,000 people in the ensuing jihad, the faithful were allowed to add one small bayleaf to the recipe.

Pizzas are a food that is highly adaptable to the multi-species community in

Ankh-Morpork, as attested by the Quatra-rodenti (for dwarfs) and Four Strata (for trolls).

Planter, Bezam. Owner of the ODIUM, a moving-picture pit in Ankh-Morpork. [MP]

Planter, Calliope. Daughter of Bezam PLANTER. A beefy young woman who played the organ at the ODIUM. [MP]

Plasterer, Brother. A member of the ELUCIDATED BRETHREN OF THE EBON NIGHT. [GG]

Plays.

*Blood-Soaked Tragedy of the Mad
  Monk of Quirm, The* [LL]
Dragon of the Plains, The [WS]
Gretalina and Mellias [WS]
King of Ankh, The [WS]
King Under the Mountain [WS]
King's Brides, The [WS]
Mage Wars, The [WS]
Mallo, the Tyrant of Klatch [WS]
Night of Kings, A (also called *The
  Lancre Play*) [WS]
Taming of the Vole, The [LL]
Troll's Tale, The [WS]
Tyrant, The [WS]
Wizard of Ankh, A [WS]
Wizard of Sorts, A, or *Please Yourself*
  [WS]

All these appear to have flowed from the quill of HWEL, the dwarf playwright attached to VITOLLER's Men.

Pleasant, Mrs. A fat, naturally jolly black lady who is a cook at the palace in GENUA (and this is just as well, in a period when failing to be fat and jolly while being a cook was punishable by death). A very superior cook, with the Genuan talent for making a gourmet meal out of things found under a damp rock. She is a close personal friend of Mrs GOGOL. [WA]

Plugger. A shoemaker with premises in New Cobblers, Ankh-Morpork. The first to take advertising space on C.M.O.T. DIBBLER's invention, the short-sleeved-singlet-made-of-cheap-cotton. [SM]

Plumber's Guild. (Guild of Plumbers and Dunnikindivers). Motto: NON ANTE SEPTEM DIES PROXIMA, SQVIRI.

Coat of arms: a shield, per pairle reversed. Top right, appaumée, argent on a field, gules. Top left, a bezant on a field, vert. Below them a coq, gules on a field, bouse.

The Guild House is in Pleaders Row, Ankh-Morpork.

Ankh-Morpork does not, currently, have a functioning sewerage system, and fresh water, once brought from distant hills by aqueduct, is now generally pumped from shallow wells. No one knows why this has not resulted in the city being a soup of diseases; it has been suggested that the centuries have bred a very high resistance among the population, and also that germs don't attack Ankh-Morpork citizens out of fellow feeling.

The Guild digs wells, plumbs houses and empties cesspits (the dunnykin, or dunnikin, divers – a small, select but lonely group of men who are always incredibly well-scrubbed and neatly dressed when off duty but never seem to attract many friends).

It is believed that the plumbers possess a specialized form of time travel which means they have no grasp of the concept of 'today', since 'immediately' to a plumber is identical with 'next week, maybe the week after'.

The president of the Guild is C.H. LAVATORY (Sir Charles Lavatory), of Mollymog Street. He in fact invented the device which bears his name (and is fast replacing the somewhat primitive invention of William de Privy). This marvellous device cleans and flushes beautifully, but not to anywhere particular. The people of Ankh-Morpork have a cat-like approach to sanitation and waste disposal: if you can't see it, it isn't there, and if it's next door then it's their problem.

The Guild has no training school as such, being a prime exponent of the apprentice system. Boys are taught to carry bags, tell a three/eights Gripley from a 0.3 Cosworth, and never, ever, to do today what you could do next week, maybe the week after.

Ponce da Quirm. A Discworld explorer from the famous da Quirm family. He sought for the Fountain of Youth for most of his life and in fact found it, dying shortly afterwards having failed to remember to boil the water before drinking it. [E]

Poons, Windle. 130-year-old deaf, toothless wizard.

In the closing years of his life Windle moved, and was moved, around in an iron-wheeled wheelchair; a wide and long construction, steered by means of a little front wheel and a long, cast-iron handle. Bits of baroque ironwork adorned its frame, which seemed to have been made of old drainpipes welded together. There were various dread levers of mysterious function and a huge oilskin hood. The front lever of this very heavy machine was adorned with a selection of trumpets, hooters and whistles.

At the time of his death Windle was the oldest wizard in the world – born in the year of the Significant Triangle, in the Century of the Three Lice. He died in the year of the Notional Serpent in the Century of the Fruitbat. He was an expert on ancient magical writings, although his expertise was somewhat suspect in his later years.

Windle was the first person to reach the end of his life after DEATH was (briefly) pensioned off, and he spent a short but on the whole enjoyable time as a zombie which he seemed to feel made up for the numbing boredom of the previous century or so. [MP, RM]

Pork Futures. Probably no other world in the multiverse has warehouses for things which only exist *in potentia*, but the pork futures warehouse in Ankh-Morpork is a product of the Olaf QUIMBY II rules about baseless metaphors (thoroughly enforced by the current PATRICIAN), the literal-mindedness of citizens who assume that everything must exist somewhere, and the general thinness of the fabric of reality around Ankh. The net result is that trading in pork futures – in pork that doesn't exist yet – led to the building of the warehouse to store it until it does. The extremely low temperatures are caused by the imbalance in the temporal energy flow. [MAA]

Postulate, Granny. A witch who went out borrowing one day and never came back.

Nanny OGG thinks she lived out the rest of her life as a bluetit. [LL]

Potent Voyager. Vessel constructed by DACTYLOS to take two chelonauts out over the Rim to determine the sex of the Great A'TUIN. A huge bronze space ship, without any motive power other than the ability to drop. [COM]

Prime. A modern, logical and efficient measure of magical strength propounded by the wizard Augustus Prime to replace the traditional thaum. The Prime was to be based on a very careful observation of the amount of magic it took to move one pound of lead one foot, and it was to be broken down into milli-, nano- and micro-Primes.

The system never really caught on, however, with old wizards traditionally saying to a student using the 'Prime' system – 'But what's that in old money?'

The Prime/Thaum business is very similar to Centigrade/Fahrenheit.

Everyone knows that freezing at 0 degrees and boiling at 100 degrees is logical, but it doesn't stop them believing in their hearts that 70 degrees should be a nice comfortable temperature.

Printing. Movable type has not yet been utilized in Ankh-Morpork and, surprisingly enough, the printing industry is basic in the extreme. Books are either copied by hand in the numerous copying shops around Gleam Street or, increasingly, engraved and printed one whole page at a time by the engravers in the alleys around the Street of Cunning Artificers.

The reason for this is the tremendous power Unseen University wields over the whole business, as the biggest customer for copying services in the city. The possibility of movable type is known to a few wizards – it certainly is to the current

LIBRARIAN – and thoroughly disapproved of. They wholeheartedly approve of books themselves, and for that very reason are violently against their multiplication.

Books, they say, aren't there to be read by just anyone. A large print run would seriously dilute the power of the words. And, they add, it is one thing for a magical book to be copied by the human hand in controlled circumstances, and quite another for it to be 'printed' by type that might then be broken up and used to print a book about household management, or squirrels. The metal might *remember* . . .

Movable type is widely used on the COUNTERWEIGHT CONTINENT but, as the wizards say, they are foreigners and don't know any better. (*See also* ENGRAVERS' GUILD.)

Prung, Bundo. Expelled from the THIEVES' GUILD for unnecessary enthusiasm and conduct unbecoming in a mugger. Subsequently fled the city after an alleyway encounter with Lance-constable ANGUA of the City WATCH. [MAA]

Ptaclusp. An architect and jobbing pyramid builder in DJELIBEYBI. Owner of Ptaclusp Associates, Necropolitan Builders to the Dynasties. He has twin sons – Ptaclusp IIa (interested in accounts/finance) and Ptaclusp IIb (an inveterate architect and designer). [P]

Pthagonal. An Ephebian philosopher, specializing in geometry. A glum-looking heavy drinker, because of his discovery of the irrational value of pi. [P]

Ptorne. A Djelibeybian farmer who was a plaintiff before TEPPIC in the Supreme Court. [P]

Ptraci. Favourite handmaiden (and

daughter) of King TEPPICYMON XXVII. Long, dark hair; small, pretty jaw; painted toenails. She uses scent like a battering ram. Not a great singer, despite the traditional requirement of handmaidens to be skilled in music; in fact she sounds like a flock of vultures who've just found a dead donkey. Ptraci became Queen of DJELIBEYBI when TEPPIC renounced the throne, whereupon the priests and courtiers found that sweet young handmaidens can be far tougher to deal with than amiable old pharaohs. [P]

Puzuma, ambiguous. The fastest animal on the Disc, the puzuma is extremely neurotic and moves so fast that it can actually achieve near light-speed in the Disc's magical field. This means that, if you can see one, it isn't there. Most male puzumas die young of acute ankle failure caused by running very fast after females which aren't there and, of course, achieving suicidal mass in accordance with relativistic theory. The rest of them die of Heisenberg's Uncertainty Principle, since it is impossible for them to know who they are and where they are at the same time, and the see-sawing loss of concentration this engenders means that the puzuma achieves a sense of identity only when it is at rest – usually about 50 feet into the rubble of what remains of the mountain it just ran into at near light-speed. The puzuma is rumoured to be about the size of a leopard with a rather unique black and white check coat, although those specimens discovered by the Disc's sages and philosophers have inclined them to declare that in its natural state the puzuma is flat, very thin, and dead. [P]

Pyjama, Hrolf. A dwarf enlisted into the Ankh-Morpork city militia by CARROT. [MAA]

Pyramids. Dams in the stream of time. Correctly shaped and oriented, with proper paracosmic measurements correctly plumbed in, the temporal potential of the great mass of stone can be diverted to accelerate or reverse time over a very small area, in the same way that a hydraulic ram can be induced to pump water against the flow.

The whole point of a correctly built pyramid is to achieve absolute null time in the central chamber so that a dying king, tucked up there, will indeed live for ever – or at least never actually die. The time that should have passed in the chamber is stored in the bulk of the pyramid and allowed to flare off once every twenty-four hours.

Many of the Klatchian countries have built pyramids at some stage in their history, but in Djelibeybi they became a national obsession. [P]

Quarney. The only shopkeeper in LAN-CRE. Mrs Quarney also helps him to run the store. [LL]

Quezovercoatl. The Feathered Boa. God of Human Sacrifices. Half-man, half-chicken, half-jaguar, half-serpent, half-scorpion and half-mad. Quezovercoatl is both a God of the Tezuman Empire and a demon. He is also six inches high. Or *was*. He got trampled to death. The Tezumen now worship a metal-bound chest with hundreds of little legs. [E]

Quimby II, Olaf. A PATRICIAN of Ankh-Morpork. He passed some legislation to put a stop to excessive exaggeration in descriptive writing, and to introduce some honesty into reporting. Thus, if a legend said of a hero that 'all men spoke of his prowess', any bard who valued his life would add hastily 'except for a couple of people in his home village who thought he was a liar and quite a lot of other people who had never really heard of him.' Poetic simile was strictly limited and any loose talk about a beloved having a face that launched a thousand ships would have to be backed by evidence that the object of desire did indeed look

like a bottle of champagne. Quimby was eventually killed by a disgruntled poet during an experiment conducted in the palace grounds to prove the disputed accuracy of the proverb 'The pen is mightier than the sword.' In his memory it was amended to include the phrase 'only if the sword is very small and the pen is very sharp'.

Quirke, 'Mayonnaise'. Captain of the Ankh-Morpork Day WATCH. Plumed helmet, and a breastplate you can see your face in. Called 'Mayonnaise' because he's thick, oily, and smells faintly of eggs.

Quirke's maxim is: 'It doesn't matter if you're right or wrong, so long as you're definite.' He is not actually a bad man, but only because he doesn't have the necessary imagination. He deals more in that sort of generalized low-grade unpleasantness which slightly tarnishes the soul of all who come into contact with it. [MAA]

Quirm. A pleasant little city in a wine-growing area overlooking the Rim Ocean. Wild geraniums fill its sloping, cobbled streets. It has a famous floral clock. And that really says it all about Quirm. It is a dull place. Most of its inhabitants have lived elsewhere during times of considerable excitement and have sworn mighty oaths that it won't happen here.

Quirm College for Young Ladies. School attended by DEATH's grand-daughter, SUSAN. It is surrounded by high, spike-topped walls whose aim is to protect its young inmates from the wicked world and whose effect is to cause them to have a keen curiosity about it.

The school uniform is a loose, navy-blue woollen smock that stretches from neck to just above the ankle, with a waistline somewhere around knee level (practical, healthy, and as attractive as a plank). The girls also have to wear their hair in two plaits; if they are dwarfs they may keep their iron helmets on but they have to plait their beards instead.

Riddled with a kind of genteel wrong-headedness though it is, the College is one of the very few establishments in the STO PLAINS where a girl can get other than the most simple vocational education. [SM]

Quisition. The sharp end of the religious system in OMNIA. It comprises the inquisitors – torturers who extract confessions and bodily parts from heretics – and the exquisitors, who just . . . arrange matters. By and large the inquisitors are simple, burly men who just have a job to do. It is they who will busy themselves about your person with knives and needles and hammers; it is the exquisitor who will talk to you afterwards. Some people who have survived both have said that half an hour with an inquisitor and his complete kit is preferable to a pleasant chat over a cup of tea with an exquisitor.

The Quisition can act without possibil-

ity of error. Suspicion is proof. How can it be anything else, it is argued? The Great God OM would not have seen fit to put the suspicion in the minds of his exquisitors unless it was right that it should be there. Some people have pointed out the essential flaw in this argument, but not very loudly and they are often running while they say it.

The Quisition's unwritten motto is: 'CVIVS TESTICVLOS HABES, HABEAS CARDIA ET CEREBELLVM', which, loosely translated, means that when you have people's full attention, you have their hearts and minds. [SG]

Quizzing device. A 3-ton, water-driven monstrosity based on a recently discovered design by LEONARD OF QUIRM. It is a games machine once used in the Mended DRUM but removed when Captain CARROT of the WATCH found it a useful way of picking up criminal intelligence. [SM]

Quoom, Ishmale. Inquisitor First Class Ishmale 'Pop' Quoom. A retired inquisitor in OMNIA. Handed in his knives and corkscrew-shaped things after fifty years. Remembered as an amiable, good-hearted sort, with plenty of time for everyone, and a man always ready to show apprentice torturers how to break every bone in the human body (including

188

the little ones in the fingers, which are quite hard to do). Breeds canaries in his spare time. [SG]

Quoth. A talking raven owned by C.V. CHEESEWALLER. Originally from the unkindness of ravens in the forever-crumbling, ivy-clad TOWER OF ART overlooking Unseen University, whose innate intelligence has been amplified by the magical radiation from the buildings below. Quoth is not his actual name; ravens have never felt the need for such things. [SM]

Ramkin, Lady Sybil Deirdre Olgivanna.
Ramkin Family motto: NON SVMET
NVLLVS PRO RESPONSO. Coat of arms: a
dragon vert, guardant passant, on a field,
gules. The whole encaged by bars, sable.

Lady Ramkin is the richest woman in
Ankh-Morpork.

Her estate is worth seven million
dollars a year. The Ramkin family own
about a tenth of Ankh and extensive
properties in Morpork, plus other considerable farm lands.

Although there are a few gaga old
uncles and some distant cousins so far
removed as to be confiscated, she is for
practical purposes the last survivor of
one of the oldest families in Ankh.

She is a toweringly big lady, with a
mass of chestnut hair (a wig – no one
who has much to do with dragons keeps
their own hair for long). The Ramkins
have never bred for beauty, they've bred
for healthy solidity and big bones, and
Lady Sybil is the shining result.

For almost all of her life she has apparently confined her own personal breeding to swamp dragons, which she keeps
in pens behind the house, and she is the
tower of strength behind the SUNSHINE
SANCTUARY FOR SICK DRAGONS. For

dragon handling, she wears huge and
fearsomely padded armour. She is the
author of several self-published volumes
on the diseases of the dragon, which is
a fruitful and probably endless field of
study.

Before her marriage to Captain VIMES
of the City WATCH she lived alone, apart
from thirty-seven dragons and a butler,
in the family's town house in Scoone
Avenue, Ankh, where she occupied

three rooms out of the available thirty-four. It was and is a rather pleasant old house with well-designed gardens, owing to one of Lady Ramkin's ancestors shooting 'Bloody Stupid' JOHNSON in the leg when the unfortunate man tried to walk up the drive one day.

Prior to her marriage both the house and the gardens were in a state of some disrepair, but a full staff is now employed and Lady Ramkin is once again surfacing in Ankh-Morpork society like a submarine in a boating lake. The house is easily identified from the road by the stone dragons on the gateposts. [GG, MAA]

Ramtops. A range of jagged peaks, upland lakes, dense forests and little river valleys so deep that the day light has no sooner reached the bottom than it is time to leave again. The Ramtop Mountains stretch from the frozen lands near the Hub all the way, via a lengthy archipelago, to the warm seas which flow into space over the Rim.

Raw magic crackles invisibly from peak to peak and earths itself in the mountains, because the range lies across the Disc's vast magical standing wave like an iron bar on a pair of subway rails. It is so saturated with magic that it is constantly discharging itself into the

Lady Ramkin's house

192

environment. In the Ramtops the leaves on the trees move even when there is no breeze; rocks go for a stroll of an evening. Even the land, at times, seems alive. It is not surprising that the Ramtops have given the world so many of its famous witches and wizards.

There is plenty of flat land in the Ramtops: the trouble is, it's nearly all flat in the vertical plane. There are little kingdoms all over the place. Every narrow valley, every ledge that something other than a goat could stand on, is a kingdom; LANCRE is one of the biggest.

On the Turnwise slopes, leading towards the STO PLAINS, are the rolling uplands known as the OCTARINE grass country from the distinctive colour imparted to its vegetation by the ambient local magic. From the highest points in the Lancre area – the High Tops – you can see all the way to the Rim Ocean. In the other direction, wrapped in eternal winter, they march all the way to the Hub.

The Ramtops have very definite weather. Winter in the Ramtops doesn't mess about; it's a gateway straight through to the primeval coldness that lived before the creation of the world. Winter in the Ramtops is several yards of snow, the forests a mere collection of shadowy green tunnels under the drifts. Winter means the coming of the lazy wind, which can't be bothered to blow around people and blows right through them instead. Ramtoppers have eighteen different words for snow (all of them, unfortunately, unprintable). No dweller in the Ramtops would dream of starting a winter without a log pile on three sides of the house – no one in the Ramtops lets their fire go out, as a matter of pride and, in the winter, survival.

And after the snow melts, there's the rain. Ramtop rain has a curiously penetrative quality that makes ordinary rain seem almost dry. It rains a lot in the spring. The weather is full of shrapnel rain and whiplash winds and permanent thunder storms.

The summer and autumn are hot, dry and pleasant. They are also quite brief. The Ramtops breed a phlegmatic, insular type of person.

Re-annual plants. Plants on the Disc, while including the categories known commonly as annuals (which are sown this year to come up later this year), biennials (sown this year to grow next year) and perennials (sown this year to grow until further notice), also include a few rare re-annuals which, because of an unusual four-dimensional twist in their genes, can be planted this year to come up last year. They can be grown only in excessively high magical fields, such as are found in the RAMTOPS.

Re-annual grapes produce wine much sought after by fortune tellers since they enable them to see the future. Although re-annual wine causes inebriation in the normal way, the action of the digestive system on its molecules causes an unusual reaction whose net effect is to thrust the ensuing hangover backwards in time, to a point some hours before the wine is drunk. A hangunder, in fact. These tend to be very bad, because people feel so dreadful with the effect of the alcohol they have not yet consumed that they drink a lot to get over it. Hence the saying: 'Have a hair of the dog that's going to bite you.'

Re-annual crop-growing is an art in itself. It does have some advantages, in that the grower can raise enough on the crop to afford to buy the seed and rent the field, but there are concomitant drawbacks. A farmer who neglects to sow his seed loses his crop, whereas anyone who forgets to sow seeds of a crop that was harvested twelve months before

risks disturbing the entire fabric of causality, not to mention acute embarrassment.

Reet. A lady of the streets rescued from
some robbers by CARROT. She was apparently a girlfriend of his for a while, but
the relationship foundered quite quickly
because Carrot's idea of an exciting time
was to walk to some distant part of the
city to view an interesting example of
iron bollard. [GG]

Reforgule (of Krull). A scientist who
theorized that the Disc revolves once in
every 800 days in order to distribute the
weight fairly upon its supportive pachy-
derms. [COM]

Remitt. An armourer in Ankh-Morpork.
Generally used by the Night WATCH when
their armour needs repairing. [MAA]

Rerpf. Proprietor of the Groaning Plat-
ter, down by the Brass Bridge, Ankh-
Morpork. A short, fat man, very richly
dressed. With beringed hands. He was a
founder member of the MERCHANTS'
GUILD. [COM]

Research witchcraft (or whichcraft). A
small but very valuable side of the
Craft. Eye of what kind of toad? Maw
of which sea-ravin'd shark? The Granny
WEATHERWAX view of whichcraft is that
it simply doesn't matter, but many
witches of an enquiring mind have, down
the centuries, experimented with thousands of different ingredients. One of the
results is the – presumably – penicillin-
encrusted mouldy bread poultice used by
Magrat in *Lords and Ladies*. The patient
was quite lucky. Stretching down the
ages must have been considerable
experimentation with the antibiotic
effects of mouldy cheese, mouldy apples,
mouldy sheep, and so on.

Retrophrenology. Phrenology, as everyone knows, is a way of reading someone's character, aptitude and abilities by
examining the bumps and hollows on
their head. Therefore – according to the
kind of logical thinking that charac-
terizes the Ankh-Morporkian mind – it
should be possible to mould someone's
character by giving them carefully
graded bumps in all the right places. You
can go into a shop and order an artistic
temperament with a tendency to intro-
spection and a side order of hysteria.
What you actually get is hit on the head
with a selection of different sized mal-
lets, but it creates employment and
keeps the money in circulation, and
that's the main thing. [MAA]

Rham-ap-efan. Admiral of the Djelibeybian navy. [SG]

Rhoxie, the. Palace of the Seriph of AL
KHALI. Famed in myth and legend for its
splendour. Said to have been built in one
night by a genie, and therefore known
colloquially as the Djinn Palace. [P]

Ribobe, Deccan. The last Keeper of the
Door in HOLY WOOD. He took over from
old Tento, who had taken over from
Meggelin – people known only from
their entries in the logbook kept by the
Keepers. He wore a frayed ceremonial
robe of dark red plush with gold frog-
ging. [MP]

Ridcully, Mustrum. Ridcully the Brown.
ARCHCHANCELLOR of Unseen University.
He became a seventh-level mage at the
incredibly young age of twenty-seven.
He then quit the University in order to
look after his family's estates deep in the
country.
He had not set foot in Unseen Univer-
sity for forty years when he was made
Archchancellor, and his surprising elev-

ation came only because the faculty wanted a bit of a breather after several rather hectic years in which Archchancellors (never a job with long-term prospects) were dying off so fast that they were getting buried with their inaugural dinner only half-eaten. What was needed was someone quiet and easy to manipulate. It was known that Ridcully was an inveterate countryman and it was assumed that a wizard so close to nature would fit the bill and, if he became a nuisance, could easily be disposed of.

Ridcully in the flesh therefore came as a breath of fresh air in a wind-chime factory.

He has a huge personality. He is quite capable of getting drunk and playing darts all night, but then he'll leave at five in the morning to swim, or at least clamber, in the frozen Ankh or to go duck hunting; at one time he had a pack of hunting dogs installed in the butler's pantry at UU.

He likes beer with his breakfast of kidneys and black pudding and especially likes those sausages, you know the ones, with a transparent skin through which can be seen the occasional green fleck which you can only hope is sage; he is a shameless AUTOCONDIMENTOR and makes his own version of the infamous wow-WOW SAUCE.

Intellectually, Ridcully maintains his position for two reasons. One is that he never, ever, changes his mind about anything. The other is that it takes him several minutes to understand any new idea put to him – this is an invaluable trait in a leader, because anything anyone is still trying to explain to you after two minutes is probably important and anything they give up after a mere minute or so is almost certainly something they shouldn't have been bothering you with in the first place.

Nevertheless, Ridcully isn't stupid; he

has quite a powerful intellect but it is powerful like a locomotive, and runs on rails and is therefore almost impossible to steer. He shouts at people and tries to jolly them along. He is brusque and rude to absolutely everyone and he never wastes time on small talk. It's always large talk or nothing.

A key to understanding him is that, like Granny WEATHERWAX, he sees himself as quite outside the rules which he nevertheless imposes on everyone else. He is quite incapable of understanding any reasonably intelligent joke and therefore frowns upon them; nevertheless he prides himself on his sense of humour, which is rudimentary, and he himself often tells jokes – long, dull ones, often with the punch line incorrectly remembered. And, while he is a stickler for his staff to be dressed in proper wizarding robes, he himself avoids wearing them on all but the most formal occasions, although he does of course retain the wizarding hat.

Mrs WHITLOW has made him up a sort of baggy trouser suit in garish blue and red, which he wears for his early morning jog with his pointy hat tied on to his head with string.

The hat is quite a work of art, and he made it himself. It has fishing flies stuck in it. A very small pistol crossbow is shoved in the hatband and a small bottle of Bentinck's Very Peculiar Old Brandy is stored in the pointy bit. The very tip unscrews to become a cup. It also has small cupboards in it. Four telescopic legs and a roll of oiled silk in the brim extend downwards to make a small but serviceable tent, with a patent spirit stove just above it and inner pockets containing three days' iron rations.

He is now about seventy. He weighs around 19 stone but it is well-distributed and he is large rather than fat. He has a big pink and orange face, sticky-out ears and a beard featuring a moustache that looks as though he's trying to swallow a cat.

About fifty or more years ago he had a romantic fling with young Esmerelda WEATHERWAX.

His brother is the Chief Priest of BLIND IO in Ankh-Morpork, and his uncle lives near LANCRE.

Depending on your point of view, Ridcully is either the best or the worst Archchancellor that UU has had for a hundred years. He is certainly the most long-lived, having survived dragons, monsters, rogue shopping trolleys and, most importantly, his fellow wizards. The unkillability of Mustrum Ridcully has had an amazing knock-on effect through University wizardry, because it has effectively slowed to a halt the practice of rising through the magical ranks by killing wizards of a superior grade.

Some of the fun goes out of this when the man at the top is not only very good at the game, but tends to creep up behind ambitious would-be murderers, shout at them very loudly, and then slam their head repeatedly in the door.

Riktor. 'Numbers' Riktor. Riktor the Tinkerer. A wizard at Unseen University. A man with a one-track mind; he was convinced that the universe could be entirely understood in terms of numbers and, indeed, *was* numbers. He invented the resograph (a 'thingness-writer'), a device for detecting and measuring disturbances in the fabric of reality. Also the Star Enumerator, Mouse Counter, Swamp Meter and Rev Counter for Use in Ecclesiastical Areas. [MP]

Rimbow. The eight-coloured, world-girdling rainbow that hovers in the mist-laden air over the RIMFALL. A double rainbow. Close to the lip of the Rimfall are the seven lesser colours, sparkling

and dancing in the spray of the dying seas. But they are pale in comparison to the wider band that floats beyond them, not deigning to share the same spectrum.

The Rimbow hangs in the mists just beyond the edge of the world, appearing only at morning and evening when the light of the Disc's little orbiting sun shines past the massive bulk of the Great A'TUIN and strikes the Disc's magical field at exactly the right angle.

Rimfall. The long waterfall at the vast circumference of the Discworld, where the seas of the Disc boil ceaselessly over the Edge into space.

People ask how the water gets back on to the Disc.

Arrangements are made.

Rimfisher. A small bird with a tuft of blue and green feathers, iridescent as jewels. It lives on the Rim, feeding off whatever raw fish plummet past its perch. [COM]

Rincewind. A wizard. At least, generally referred to as a wizard.

He is tall, thin and scrawny, with a raggedy beard that looks like the kind of beard worn by people who aren't cut out by Nature to be beard-wearers. He is a non-smoker (unusual in a wizard).

He traditionally wears a dark red, hooded, frayed plush robe on which a few mystic sigils are embroidered in tarnished sequins. The robe has been made darker by constant wear and irregular washings. Under his robe he wears britches and sandals. Around his neck is a chain bearing the bronze octagon which marks him as an alumnus of Unseen University (quite wrongly, it must be pointed out, since he has never passed any kind of magical exam). On his head is a battered pointy hat with a floppy brim, which has the word 'WIZZARD' embroidered on it in big, silver letters by someone whose needle-work is even worse than their spelling. There's a star on top. It has lost most of its sequins.

He was born under the sign of the Small Boring Group of Faint Stars – a sign associated with chess board makers, sellers of onions, manufacturers of plaster images of small religious significance and people allergic to pewter. His mother ran away before he was born, and the young Rincewind grew up in Morpork.

He does have an innate gift for languages, which enables him to shout 'Don't kill me!' and be understood in a hundred different countries. He is also good at practical geography, which means that he always knows exactly where it is he is running away from. He has a razor-sharp instinct for survival equalled only by an uncanny ability to end up in situations where every bit of it is required.

Rincewind's room number as a student at UU was 7a (wizards avoid the number eight). Later, during his spell as deputy Librarian (an ape's Number Two, as the Dean nastily remarked), he lived in a room close to the LIBRARY used mainly to store old furniture. It contained a large wardrobe (on top of which the LUGGAGE hibernated) and a banana crate which he used as a dressing table.

There are eight levels of wizardry on the Disc; after sixteen years, Rincewind failed to even achieve level one. It was in fact the opinion of some of his tutors that he was incapable of even achieving level zero, which most normal people are born at. It has been contended that when Rincewind dies the average occult ability of the human race will actually go up a fraction.

'To call his understanding of magical theory "abysmal" is to leave no suitable word to describe his grasp of its practice,' said one of his tutors. He is also not very good at precognition: he can scarcely see into the present.

Some of this is unfair. For a bet, the young Rincewind dared to open the pages of the last remaining copy of the CREATOR's own grimoire, the OCTAVO. A spell leapt out of the page and instantly burrowed deeply into his mind,

Unseen University alumnus medallion

whence even the combined talents of the Faculty of Medicine were unable to coax it. No one knew which spell it was, except that it was one of the Eight Great Spells that were intricately interwoven with the very fabric of time and space itself. Since then, no other spell dared stay in the same head. For that prank, he was expelled from UU.

Subsequently he has been an unwilling travel guide, has been through Hell, has visited most of the countries of the Disc, has travelled extensively in time as well as in space, has been present at the creation of the Discworld where he caused the origin of life by dropping an egg-and-cress sandwich into the sea, has defeated the greatest magic-user on the Disc while armed with nothing more than a half-brick in a sock,* and is believed to have been one of only nine people to have visited the country of DEATH while mortal.

His current whereabouts are unknown.

*There has been much discussion about this, but UU wizards do reluctantly concede that this is the historical state of affairs. Rincewind certainly challenged Coin with said sock, and as a result Coin ceased his troublesome reign (admittedly because being challenged by the most ineffective wizard in the world with such a primitive weapon amused him, caught his imagination and persuaded him to defy the power of his father). There are other ways to defeat someone than by bashing their head in with a brick (although this does remain the means of choice in many of Ankh-Morpork's shadier streets).

Rjinswand, Dr. This is the name assumed by RINCEWIND when he and TWOFLOWER appeared briefly on an aircraft in COM. He was then thirty-three, a bachelor, born in Sweden, raised in New Jersey, a specialist in the breakaway oxidation phenomena of certain nuclear reactors. It is believed that, while falling off a dragon in a field of high magical energy, he desperately wished to remain airborne – and was re-arranged in the nearest available dimension where this could be possible. [COM]

Rock. (*See* GALENA.) Rock is a perfectly good name for a silicaceous troll, but it has also become a term of abuse used by the more speciesist humans in Ankh-Morpork.

Rocksmacker, Minty. CARROT's childhood sweetheart. A dwarf. It was partly in order to get him out of her life that Carrot was originally sent to Ankh-Morpork. After all, as his parents pointed out, when he was 6′6″ she would still be only 4′2″. [GG]

Rodley, Lady Brenda. The Dowager Duchess of Quirm. A small, white-haired, wiry woman with a face like old saddle leather. She owns Treebite Brightscale (a swamp dragon) and is a friend of Sybil RAMKIN. She lives at the Dower House, Quirm Castle, QUIRM. [GG]

Rodley, Lord. Heir to the fabulous QUIRM estates. A rather stupid and fat young man who once danced with DEATH at a party. [M]

Rodney. Brother-in-law to Brother WATCHTOWER. It was his undeserved success (in the view of his brother-in-law) that was one of the motives behind the ELUCIDATED BRETHREN's search for a better social order, i.e., one where they got more of the cake. [GG]

Ron, Foul Ole. A member of the BEGGARS' GUILD. He is a Mutterer – he walks behind people muttering in his own private language until they give him money not to. His familiar phrases included 'Bug'r'em', 'Bugrit' and 'Millennium hand and shrimp'. People assume that Foul Ole Ron has no grasp on reality but this is not true. He holds very tightly indeed on to reality, but it is not the one shared by most of the rest of the world.

Foul Ole Ron is often but not always accompanied by his Smell, which has become so powerful over the years that it has developed a life of its own and often goes about its own occasions in the city without its theoretical owner. It is in fact rather more socially aware than Ron, and has been known to attend the opera while Ron is enjoying a meal of old boiled boots several streets away. [MAA]

Ronald the Third. A past king of LANCRE. He is believed to have been an extremely unpleasant monarch, and is remembered by posterity only in an obscure bit of rhyming slang. Roland the Third = . . . er . . . manure. [WA]

Rthur. A fresco painter in DJELIBEYBI. His small claim to fame is that the dead kings and queens in his paintings look identical, and beautiful. Perhaps this is why he has survived to paint so many. [P]

Ruby. A troll. She looks slightly like the statues cavemen used to carve of fertility goddesses thousands of years ago, but mostly she looks like a foothill. She is nearly 140 (not a great age for a troll, considering that in some respects they never actually die, but it is around the time a male troll decides to settle down and a female troll tends to think about the biological clock).

She and DETRITUS are romantically linked, and it is thought that it is her influence which caused him to apply to become the Ankh-Morpork City WATCH's first troll guard. Ruby is, at least intellectually, a modern troll and feels it would be demeaning to be married to someone who hits people all the time without wearing some kind of uniform. [MP, MAA]

Rust, Lord. A blue-eyed nobleman of Ankh. His ancestor was created a Baron after single-handedly killing thirty-seven Klatchians while armed with nothing more than a pin. [MAA]

Sal. Daughter of LIFTON, an innkeeper in SHEEPRIDGE. A small child, with a small child's way of speaking loudly whatever thought is occupying its mind at the time, such as 'You have a big nose.' Rescued from a fire by Bill DOOR (DEATH). [RM]

Salamanders. Magical creatures. They have no mouths, since they subsist entirely on the nourishing quality of the OCTARINE wavelength in the Discworld's sunlight, which they absorb through their skins. They absorb the rest of the sunlight as well, storing it in a special sac until it is excreted in the normal way. This allows them to be used as torches or, if surprised, as flashbulbs. A desert inhabited by salamanders is a veritable lighthouse at night. [COM]

Salami. The Ankh-Morporkian composer of 'Prelude to a Nocturne on a Theme by Bubbla'. [SM]

Sandman. A fairly recent anthropomorphic personification in the Ankh-Morpork area, where he travels nightly from house to house sending children to sleep by means of his magic sand. Unlike sandmen on other worlds, he doesn't bother to take it out of the sack first. [SM]

Sapient pearwood. A plant so magical that it has nearly died out on the Disc and survives in only one or two places outside the AGATEAN EMPIRE, where it is still quite common; it is a magical equivalent of rosebay willowherb, a plant that traditionally colonizes bomb sites and areas devastated by fire. Sapient pearwood, in a similar way, sprouts in areas that have seen vast expenditures of magic. It owes its origins to the MAGE WARS; this has left it ingrained with a bad temper. It is totally impervious to all forms of magic.

It is traditionally used to make wizards' staffs, and many of these still survive. But since no trees are now found within 500 miles of Unseen University, most modern staffs are made of oak or ash.

The LUGGAGE is made of it.

Sator Square. The famous square in Ankh-Morpork's rather upmarket mercantile district is the traditional home of the Sator market, held weekly at considerable inconvenience to the traffic of the city. The market charter dates right back to the days when what is now the Square was a mere patch of ground outside Unseen University; traders were encouraged to set up stalls there for the convenience of the wizards, since the alternative was shopping in what is now the SHADES, where the merchandise even then included assault and grievous bodily harm.

Saturday, Baron. One-time ruler of GENUA. Now a zombie. When alive, he was a wicked man, albeit tall and handsome. He was murdered by the DUC, and as a result of being dead seemed to develop a more reflective attitude to things. As a zombie, he had burning eyes, grey skin, a resonant voice and he smelled of river mud. He looked as though he had just walked through a room full of cobwebs.

The Baron, with the assistance of Mrs GOGOL and to some extent also of Granny WEATHERWAX, invaded the Samedi Nuit Mort Ball at Genua to wreak a long-awaited revenge on his murderer. [WA]

Saturday, Ella. Daughter of Baron SATURDAY and Mrs GOGOL. A very attractive girl, with skin as brown as a nut and hair so blond as to be almost white. Because she works as a skivvy she is known as Emberella, or Young Embers. [WA]

Scalbie. A seabird; a member of the crow family. It seldom flies, walking everywhere in a sort of lurching hop. Its distinctive call is similar to that of a malfunctioning digestive system.

The scalbie has very greasy feathers and looks like other birds do after an oil slick. Nothing eats scalbies, except other scalbies. Scalbies eat things that would make a vulture sick. Scalbies would *eat* vulture sick. [SG]

Scant, William. Official Hereditary Keeper of the Monuments in Ankh-Morpork. An old man, and one of a number of people in Ankh-Morpork still doing jobs no longer appropriate to its modern civic life. According to ancient tradition, his pay is one dollar a year and a new vest every Hogswatchday. (For details of the monuments, *see* JOHNSON, BLOODY STUPID.) [MAA]

Scharron, Red. A Discworld adventuress. [E]

Schleppel. A bogeyman, and a member of the FRESH START CLUB. A large, hairy creature with hands the size of wheelbarrows. He is also very, very shy, which is why he tends to be found under beds and behind doors. [RM]

Sconner, Benado. A wizard. He led the party who once planned to burn the LIBRARY. [S]

Scorbic, Mrs. The cook at LANCRE CASTLE. Huge pink arms, three chins and a whiskery face (the kind where the warts have whiskers, like a lot of little hills with woods on them). A power in her own kitchen. The kind of woman who thinks that cabbage isn't cooked until it is yellow, and who can't be having with this vitamin nonsense. She believes that the proper colour of meat is grey. [LL]

Scree. Son of Mica the Bridge Troll and Beryl. [TB]

Scrofula. A rather worried demon. Has been known to stand in for DEATH when Death is busy. However, since Death has on every other occasion shown a most commendable dedication to duty this must have been a unique occasion. [COM]

Scrope, William. A deer hunter, killed by a unicorn. He was a tall man, with a beard and one leg longer than the other (a common feature in LANCRE, and possibly a genetic adaptation to its lack of flat ground; a slightly smaller number of people have one leg shorter than the other). One of three brothers from the village of Slice, in Lancre. [LL]

three old men outside the tavern . . .

Scrote is notable only for its mayor, Late Jim Cloop. Jim Cloop became Mayor of Scrote about 150 years ago, but died in office very soon after. There was no time or money for another election so soon after the first; after a year the townsfolk realized that Jim's period in office had been marked by a time of

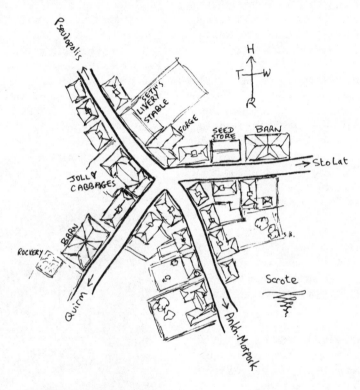

Scrote. Tiny agricultural town about a day's slow ride from Ankh-Morpork. The usual shape – a cross-roads around which is a seed merchant, a tavern, a livery stable. There are three old men sitting outside the tavern, and three young men lounging outside the livery stable saying what a hole this is and how they're going to up and leave as soon as they've got the money from the cabbage harvest, and don't you just know that in fifty years' time there'll be

general prosperity: he hadn't raised taxes, embezzled the road-repair fund or taken any bribe. They voted him in again. They have voted him in ever since.

Scum. A friend to Crash and the drummer in his musical band, first called Insanity. Considered to be without equal among drummers since he often entirely failed to make contact with the drums. [SM]

Scumble. A drink made, mainly, from apples and served in thimble-sized glasses. It tastes something like apples, something like autumn mornings, and quite a lot like the bottom of a log pile. You could clean spoons with it.

Many stories are told about scumble – how it is made out of the damp marshes according to ancient recipes handed down rather unsteadily from father to son, how the only apples that make good scumble are the Lancre Blackheart, the Golden Disagreeable and Green Billets . . .

It is not true about the rats, or the snake heads, or the lead shot. The one about the dead sheep is a complete fabrication as are all the variations of the one about the trouser button. The one about not letting it come into contact with metal is true. So is the one about the drowned soldier.

It is also dangerous to let water touch scumble. It is, all in all, safer not to let scumble touch lips.

Scurrick, Mrs. Widow of an Ankh-Morpork City Watchman, and the object of Captain VIMES's surreptitious charity. [MAA]

Seamstresses' Guild. Motto: NIL VOL-VPTI, SINE LVCRE (this is possibly a play on the similar motto of the ASSASSINS' GUILD, whose members also work strictly for money).

Coat of arms: aiguilles croisé over a lanterne, gules, on a field sable et etoilé.

One of the youngest Guilds in the city, despite the fact that its members practise the second-oldest profession in the world (the oldest profession is that of flint-knapper, a confusion which has caused many an embarrassed misunderstanding in quarries everywhere).

For it has to be said that the Guild is not there to support hard-working women who make what living they can through their skills with needle and thread. It is simply that 'seamstress' is considered a more polite term than otherwise might be used for young women whose affection is, not to put too fine a point on it, negotiable.

An Ankh-Morpork MERCHANTS' GUILD survey of tradespeople in the dock areas of Morpork found 987 women who gave their profession as 'seamstress', and two needles.

The Guild House in Sheer Street is, like the MUSICIANS' GUILD, purely an administrative centre; there is no Guild school as such, most training being on the job. The Guild's concerns are with professional standards, certain specialized areas of preventive medicine, and particularly with investment finance.

The current Guild president is Mrs Rosemary PALM.

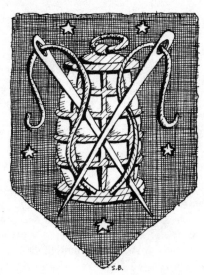

Selachii, Lady. A noblewoman of Ankh; the family are traditionally associated with the ASSASSINS' GUILD. [MAA]

Selachii, Lord Robert. A senior assassin. [SM]

Sendivoge. Secretary of the ASSASSINS' GUILD. [MP]

Sestina, Sister. Sister Sestina of QUIRM. She defied the wrath of the local king and walked unharmed across a bed of coals, and propounded a philosophy of sensible ethics on behalf of a goddess whose only real interest was in hairstyles. [SG]

Seven-league boots. A classic component of fairy stories that was the subject of brief experiment at Unseen University. It soon became clear, however, that an unacceptable amount of groinal strain was involved in wearing boots that periodically caused your feet to be 21 miles apart.

Shades, the. The original and ancient part of the city of Ankh-Morpork whose inhabitants are largely nocturnal and never enquire about one another's business, because curiosity crept up on the cat in a dark alley and gave it a quick burst of skull percussion with a length of lead pipe. It is an abode of discredited gods and unlicensed thieves, ladies of the night and pedlars in exotic goods, alchemists of the mind and strolling mummers; in short, the grease on civilization's axle and the unidentified sticky stuff on the sole of its boots.

It is an inner city area sorely in need of either government help or, for preference, a flame thrower. It can't be called squalid, because that would be stretching the word to breaking point. It is beyond squalor and out the other side, where by a sort of Einsteinian reversal it achieves a magnificent horribleness that it wears like an architectural award. It is noisy and sultry and smells like a cowshed floor.

The Shades is about ten minutes' slow stroll from Unseen University. If you drew a relief map of immorality, then even in Ankh-Morpork the Shades would be represented by a deep shaft.

In the MERCHANTS' GUILD publication, *Wellcome to Ankh-Morporke, Citie of One Thousand Surprises*, the Shades is described as: 'a folklorique network of old alleys and picturesque streets, wherre exitement and romans lurke arounde everry corner and much may be heard the traditional street cries of old time also the laughing visages of the denuizens as they goe about their business private.' (In other words, you have been warned.)

The Shades is also a pub in Skegness, England, which is probably very nice.

Sheepridge. A town in the RAMTOPS, and scene of the annual hiring fair on Hogswatch Eve. Very small – not much more than four sides to a cobbled square, including an ornamental clock tower, lined with shops that provide the service industry of the farming community. [M]

Shoe, Reg. A zombie. Founder of the FRESH START CLUB, whose premises are at 668 Elm Street, Ankh-Morpork. He still works at the mortuary in Elm Street, and he stays with Mrs CAKE. It doesn't matter what you say when talking to Reg Shoe, because Reg supplies your side of the conversation from somewhere inside his head.

Dead? Depressed? Feel like starting it all again? Then why not come along to the FRESH START CLUB Thursdays, 12 pm, 668 Elm Street EVERY BODY WELCOME

He has a pallid skin, and wears a 'Glad To Be Grey' badge. His clothes look as if they've been washed in razor blades and smell as though someone has not only died in them but is still in them. This is, of course, the case.

It is not known what Reg did when he was alive, but his tireless activities on behalf of the Dead – his Campaign for Dead Rights, his enthusiasm for the Fresh Start Club, his endless protest songs played on a guitar (he has to crawl around on the floor looking for his fingers afterwards) suggest that life for Reg began around the time of death. [RM, MAA]

Shops, Wandering. *Tabernae vagrantes.* No one knows why, but all the most truly mysterious and magical items are bought from shops that appear and, after a trading life even briefer than a double-glazing company's, vanish like smoke. They can turn up wherever there is a suitable stretch of blank wall, but once there they *have always been there*; dust and grime and a general worn look instantly dispel any doubts in the minds of people who may have walked down that same street every day for a year without noticing it.

There are three general theories to explain the phenomenon of wandering shops:

1. Many thousands of years ago there evolved somewhere in the multiverse a race whose single talent was to buy cheap and sell dear. Soon they controlled a vast galactic empire or, as they put it, Emporium, and the more advanced members of the species found a way to equip their very shops with unique propulsion units that could break the dark walls of space itself and open up vast new markets. Long after the worlds of the Emporium perished in the heat death of their particular universe (after one

defiant fire sale), the wandering star shops still ply their trade, eating their way through the pages of space-time like a worm through a three-volume novel.

2. They are the creation of a sympathetic Fate, charged with the role of supplying exactly the right thing at the right time.

3. They are simply a very clever way of getting around the various Sunday Closing Acts.

All these theories have two things in common: they explain the known facts and they are completely and utterly wrong. (*See also* SKILLET.) [LF]

Shuwadhi, Ronron. Ronron 'Revelation Joe' Shuwadhi. A Klatchian mystic and creator of the first PIZZA on the Disc. [M]

Sideways, Arnold. A beggar in Ankh-Morpork. He has no legs, and gets around on a small four-wheeled cart. His particular begging technique is to grab people by the knees and say, 'Have you got change for a penny?' – invariably profiting by the ensuing cerebral confusion. [SM]

Sidney, Dribbling. A member of the BEGGARS' GUILD. [MAA]

Silverfish, Thomas. President of the ALCHEMISTS' GUILD. He also dabbled briefly in the world of moving pictures. Despite being an alchemist, he is a very practical man who prides himself on being far more level-headed and down-to-earth than wizards. He believes that the function of the alchemist is to pursue those goals laid down by the wisdom of antiquity, and whose realization would make human existence so much more bearable – such as immortality and endless supplies of gold. The bane of his life is the Guild apprentices, who fritter away their time playing with lemons and bits of metal and lengths of wire. [MP, MAA]

Simnel, Ned. Blacksmith in the village near Miss FLITWORTH's farm. He is a young man with black, curly hair, and a face, shirt and apron all black with soot and dirt.

He is by inclination an engineer rather than a farrier, and built the only working Combination Harvester on the Disc. The goal of his life is to find a way of making machines work without the need for horses. However, so far he has watched a kettle lift its lid and boil over 147 times with no other thought in his head than 'that's a nuisance'. [RM]

Simon. An apprentice wizard, but with very good magical potential and an amazing grasp of magical theory.

He is a thin, gangling boy, with a xylophone chest – one of those tall lads apparently made out of knees, thumbs and elbows. He is also in dire need of a decent haircut, subject to hay fever (which gives him a red nose) and he also suffers from a stammer. Nevertheless, even as a first-year student he amazed his seniors by pushing back the narrow boundaries of ignorance to reveal the wide, rolling vistas of fresh ignorance beyond. [ER]

Simony, Sergeant. Sergeant in the Divine Legion in OMNIA and a follower of the Turtle Movement. Born in Istanzia. A muscular young man with the deadpan expression of the truly professional soldier. He was, according to BRUTHA, a good man with only one flaw in his nature: he wished to overthrow a corrupt religion that ruled by fire and the sword by even greater fiery sword applications.

Sergeant Simony was made head of the QUISITION by Brutha. [SG]

Sisters, the. Two snakes transmogrified by Lily WEATHERWAX into women. As women they are taller than Granny Weatherwax, slender as sticks and wear broad hats with veils and shimmery dresses. Although beautiful, they have no voices and can sit for hours without blinking. Last seen fighting Magrat GARLICK; it was their misfortune that, when cornered, Magrat fights like a mongoose. [WA]

Size 15. Legionary in the KLATCHIAN FOREIGN LEGION. (For an explanation of his name, *see* COTTON.) [SM]

Skater, Viscount. A nobleman of Ankh. [MAA]

Skazz. A student wizard at Unseen University. He looks about 7 stone and has a shoulder-length fringe of hair all around his head – it's only the tip of his nose poking out that tells the world which way he's facing. [SM]

Skiller. Landlord of the FIDDLER'S RIDDLE in OHULAN CUTASH. Too stupid to be really cruel, too lazy to be really mean. He and his thin wife sell only beer, which customers say he gets out of cats. [ER]

Skillet, Wang, Yrxle!yt, Bunglestiff, Cwmlad and Patel. A wandering shop, encountered by RINCEWIND, BETHAN and TWOFLOWER. The proprietor was believed to have given poor service to a sourcerer, and was thus condemned to run a shop for ever. (*See also* SHOPS, WANDERING.) [LF]

Skindle. The Skindles live just up the hill from Gytha OGG. Mr Skindle looks after Granny WEATHERWAX's goats when she is away from home. [LL]

Skipps, Lord Henry. Led the army that

defeated the trolls at the Battle of Pseudopolis. [MP]

Skrp. Large, grey, red-eyed rat. Lives in the PATRICIAN'S PALACE. [GG]

Slumber, Chas. Children's entertainer in Ankh-Morpork. [TOC]

Small Gods' Eve. Falls on the occasion of first midsummer. [COM]

Smith, Eskarina. (*See* ESK.)

Smith, Gordo. Blacksmith in BAD ASS. Not very tall (blacksmiths often aren't; it's amazing how many are short, wiry men). The father of ESK. Also father of Jaims, Cern and Gulta. [ER]

Smith, Howondaland. A balgrog hunter. No one knows what a balgrog is, perhaps because he has never actually caught one. During the great day of the Discworld moving picture industry, it was generally accepted as looking like Morry the troll painted green with wings stuck on. [MP]

Snell, Rebecca. Schoolfriend of SUSAN, one of whose earliest intimations of immortality was seeing a TOOTH FAIRY by Rebecca's bed. [SM]

Snoriscousin, Snori. Leader of Snori Snoriscousin and His Brass Idiots – a traditional dwarf band. [SM]

Sock, Gerhardt. A member of the Butchers' Guild, and a master butcher. [MAA]

Songs of the Disc. The nations of the Disc – at least, in those areas so far chronicled – are musically inclined, although their taste is not necessarily commendable. Songs are either traditional folk melodies (the Hedgehog song), cheap popular music of the blow-your-nose-ain't-it-so variety ('Carry Me Away From Old Ankh-Morpork'), or religious songs ('Claws of Iron Shall Rend the Ungodly' and, arguably, anything about gold sung by dwarfs). There are hints of a classic and baroque tradition in Ankh-Morpork, and presumably the opera house must have some raw material, but so far the hints allow no conclusions to be drawn.

Titles recorded are:
'Amber & Jasper' [MP]
'Ankh-Morpork Malady' [RM]
'Ankh-Morpork! Ankh-Morpork! So Good They Named it Ankh-Morpork!' [RM]
'Ball of Philodelphus, The' [E]
'Ballad of Amber and Jasper, The' [MP]
'Carry Me Away From Old Ankh-Morpork' [RM]
'Cavern Deep, Mountain High' [SM]
'Claws of Iron Shall Rend the Ungodly' [SG]
'Dingdong, Dingdong' [WA]
'Don't Tread On My New Blue Boots' [SM]
'Gathering Rhubarb' [SM]
'Give Me That Music With Rocks In' [SM]
'Gold' [MAA]
'Good Gracious, Miss Polly' [SM]
'He is Trampling the Unrighteous with Hooves of Hot Iron' [SG]
'Hedgehog Can Never Be Buggered At All, The' [WS]
'Hiho Song, The' [MP]
'I Fear I'm Going Back to Ankh-Morpork' [RM]
'Lo, the Infidels Flee the Wrath of Om' [SG]
'Pathway to Paradise' [SM]
'Sioni Bod Da' [SM]
'Something's Gotten Into My Beard' [SM]
'Sto Helit Lace' [SM]

'Streets of Ankh-Morpork, The' [RM]
'There's a Great Deal of Shaking
  Happening' [SM]
'Way of the Infidel is a Nest of Thorns,
  The' [SG]
'We Shall Overcome' [RM]
'Wizard's Staff Has a Knob on the End,
  A' [WS]

Soul Cake Days. The first Tuesday, Wednesday, Thursday after the first half-moon in Sektober.

A STO PLAINS/RAMTOPS festival roughly corresponding to the traditional European/North American festivals of Hallowe'en and Bonfire Night. Celebrated both by dwarfs (Bobbing for Trout, Toffee Rats on a Stick) and humans (Trickle-Treating, All-Comers Morris Dancing, and a rather mysterious custom involving the rolling of boiled eggs down the Tump in Ankh-Morpork). In short, a three-day feast and celebration whose origins are lost in the mists of alcohol.

Soul Cake Tuesday Duck, the. A species of magical fauna in the Easter Bunny/Reynard the Fox league, possibly associated with the fact that Soul Cake Tuesday is the opening of the duck-hunting season. The sighting of the first duck on Soul Cake Tuesday is considered very lucky, except, of course, for the duck.

Soup II. Mad King Soup II. Past king of LANCRE. His mistress was Mme CUPIDOR. [LL]

Sourcerer. A type of super-wizard; one who can create magic rather than simply utilize it. (*See also* MAGIC.)

Spells. A spell can be thought of as a kind of mental pill, containing all the ingredients necessary for achieving its purpose. They are short cuts, the results of tireless experimentation by wizards in the past.

A wizard wishing to change the shape of some living thing could, of course, start from first principles and carefully work out how to do it; but he will generally use Stacklady's Morphic Resonator, for example, simply because it is tried and tested.

A spell, once memorized, will remain in the wizard's head until it gets said or he dies, in which case it auto-casts itself, with unpredictable results.

A spell takes up quite a lot of mental space. For instance, RINCEWIND in possession of one of the Great Spells was unable to memorize any others at all. The fact that he had never been able to do so before this happened is beside the point.

Many deceased wizards are remembered by the spells they have added to Unseen University's grimoire. Spells named in the chronicles include:

Atavarr's Personal Gravitational Upset
  [COM]
Brother Hushmaster's Potent
  Asp-Spray [S]
Chant of the Trodden Spiral [LF]
Eringya's Surprising Bouquet [RM]
Fresnel's Wonderful Concentrator
  [COM]
Gindle's Effortless Elevator [MP]
Herpetty's Seismic Reorganizer [RM]
Infernal Combustion Enigma [COM]
Maligree's Wonderful Garden [S]
Megrim's Accelerator [S]
Pelepel's Temporal Compressor [S]
Quondum's Attractive Point [RM]

Raising of the Cone of Power [LL]
Rite of ASHKENTE
Spell of Binding [LF]
Stacklady's Morphic Resonator [LL]
Sumpjumper's Incendiary Surprise [RM]
Vestcake's Floating Curse [COM]

Spelter. Fifth-level wizard and former Bursar of Unseen University. A tall and wiry man, he looked as though he'd been a horse in previous lives and only just avoided it in this one. Killed for trying to prevent the LIBRARY's destruction during the brief reign of COIN. [S]

Sphinx, the. An unreal and therefore chronically bad-tempered creature, with the body of a lion, the bosom of a woman and the wings of an eagle. It lurks on the dimensional borders of DJELIBEYBI. [P]

Spigot, William. An old farm worker with skin like leather. He helps out with the harvest at Miss FLITWORTH's. He is also known for his folk singing and fiddle-playing. [RM]

Spircle. A low-value chameleon gemstone that can take on the hue of real gemstones when put in a bag with them. Spircles are mined from the mountains near BAD ASS. [ER]

Spold, Greyhald. A wizard of the Ancient and Truly Original Sages of the Unbroken Circle. In his day, he was the oldest wizard and determined to remain so. He tried, unsuccessfully, to find a place impregnable by DEATH, and built a dense and magically protected box that nothing whatsoever could penetrate. This included, as he became briefly aware, any air molecules (the last words he ever heard were DARK IN HERE, ISN'T IT . . . ?). [LF]

Spriggins. Mr Spriggins is the butler at LANCRE CASTLE. He has a bad memory, a nervous twitch and a rubber knee. [LL]

Spuds, Hoggy. An old army pal of Sergeant COLON. [MAA]

Staffs, wizards'. Wizards in foreign parts may think they can get away with a crystal ball and some magic scarves, but what an Unseen University wizard expects to find in his hand is six feet of good solid oak or ash – or even SAPIENT PEARWOOD, if he is lucky – as a repository and storehouse of personal magic, a walking aid and, if necessary, a weapon. As the current ARCHCHANCELLOR of UU has pointed out in his robust way, what cannot be stopped by the magic in a staff can often be brought short by a good poke in any available soft bits with a length of heavy timber.

Most staffs in use today are quite venerable, having been handed down from wizard to wizard for perhaps hundreds of years, and in very extreme cases – the staff possessed by Drum BILLET and subsequently by Eskarina Smith (*see* ESK), for example – can be so imbued with magic as to have lives of their own.

A wizard will treat his staff with respect, taking care to top up its power every day and then give it a good polish, paying particular attention to the knob on the end. The fact that there is a popular song about said knob is deeply puzzling to wizards. So what? they say, staffs have always had knobs on. What's funny about that? It's just the tool of our trade. It's nothing to joke about.

The knobs may be ornate jewellery, a complicated piece of sculpture, a music box or even a small polished container handy for some matches and a packet of fags. Sometimes, such artificial additions are not required because the staff grows its own knob, a growth rather like the 'knees' grown by the American swamp cypress. Because this gall is the wood's response to the magic within it, it can take many forms – the face of the wizard himself, or an object dear to him, or even stranger things . . .

Staffs made of metal are occasionally tried. They are efficient, but somehow the magic always seems to change for the worse.

Stamp, Miss. Teaches Maths at the QUIRM COLLEGE FOR YOUNG LADIES. [SM]

Standards, Ankh-Morporkian.
Obviously any civilization needs some way of standardizing weights and measures and time. In modern times, for example, an official unit of measurement is likely to be a length of metal bar kept at a precise temperature, or some reproducible count based on atomic decay or the speed of light.

The old Ankh-Morpork Bureau of Measures in the Barbican still performs this role for a large part of the Discworld, but less so for its common units of measurement (which in any case have been filed down, soldered on to, drilled and had bits of chewing gum stuck to them on too many occasions) than for its more esoteric ones, a legacy of the precise-minded Patrician Olaf QUIMBY.

Here, for example, may be found the *exact* Blunt Stick, a crude but effective measurement of the acceptability of just about anything; it is *this* Blunt Stick* that the test object may, or may not, be better than. Although the official Pie that it may even be as nice as is not maintained here, there is a standardized recipe readily available. Also, kept in a glass cabinet, are the original Two Short

*Originally a Sharp Stick was installed, but extensive tests found that few things were worse than a poke in the eye with it.

Planks and the stone used in the original Moss-Gathering trials.

Bureau officials still maintain a small programme of tests of, for instance, the degree of similarity of any two peas or the alcoholic tendencies of newts. It is vital, as the current PATRICIAN has noted, that something like this is found for people with minds like that to do, otherwise they might do *anything*.

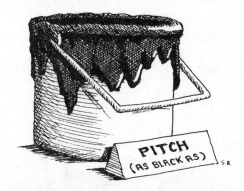

PITCH
(AS BLACK AS)

Standing Stone, the. Stands on the crest of the moor in the RAMTOPS. It is the same height as a tall man and is made of bluish tinted rock. It is considered to be intensely magical because, although there is only one of it, no one has ever been able to count it. If it sees anyone looking at it speculatively, it shuffles behind them and, in extreme cases, goes and hides in the peat bogs. It is also one of the numerous discharge points for the magic that accumulates in the Ramtops. [WS]

Stibbons, Ponder. Originally a fellow student wizard with Victor TUGELBEND at Unseen University. He graduated by getting Victor's rigged exam paper in error (which had one question – Name?). He became the Reader in Invisible Writings. Lazy by nature, Ponder really wanted to just spend the next hundred years in the University, eating big dinners and sleeping late. He is a plump

211

young man with a complexion the colour of something that lives under a stone.

However, as one of the few wizards at the University with his head screwed on in any fashion, he now seems quite against his will to be in the front line. He has discovered too late that he has the unfortunate defect of a logical mind and an incipient desire to understand the Universe.

Sto Helit, Duke of. Original motto: FABER EST QVISQVE FORTVNAE SVAE. Original coat of arms: a boar's head, sable, on a field, argent.

A man with a little moustache and a grin like a lizard. Not the nicest of people, since he was quite capable of killing all who stood between him and the throne of Sto Helit or even between him and the drinks cabinet. He murdered his way close to the throne of STO LAT and was only prevented from killing Princess KELI, the last barrier to his accession, by the actions of MORT. [M]

Sto Lat. A walled city kingdom, 20 miles Hubwards of Ankh-Morpork, clustered around a castle built on a rock outcrop that pokes up out of the STO PLAINS like a geological pimple. It is a huge stone from the distant RAMTOPS, which was left there by retreating glaciers.

Its younger citizens consider it to be boring and indeed its night life is not as colourful and full of incident as that of Ankh-Morpork, in the same way that a wastepaper basket cannot compete with a municipal tip. On fire. In the rain. [M]

Sto Plains. A rich country, full of silt and rolling cabbage fields, and neat little kingdoms whose boundaries wriggle like snakes as small, formal wars, marriage pacts, complex alliances and the occasional bit of sloppy cartography change the political shape of the land.

The black earth of the Sto Plains has been constructed over aeons by the periodic flooding of the great, slow ANKH, and every bit of it has at some time travelled along someone's alimentary canal. [M, S]

Street Theatre (prohibition of). Street theatre and mime artistry are banned in Ankh-Morpork under one of the strictest city ordinances (fire eaters and jugglers are considered acceptable, provided they are good at it and can pass the exam; in the case of jugglers, this consists of juggling six razor-sharp knives and a live cat. It is seldom necessary to take the exam a second time).

The unusually inflexible rule has led to the development of street theatre as a criminal activity, and those who feel inexorably drawn to looking like a dumb tit in white make-up or hectoring people while doing something dull with a diabolo live a desperate existence outside the law. Many of them have more mundane jobs as a cover, but they can be spotted by their tendency to unicycle when they think no one is looking.

If caught, they are imprisoned and tortured, usually by being put in a cell with one another (although scorpions also often feature). No one is certain why the PATRICIAN, who has a relaxed approach to assassins and thieves, has this particular quirk, but the citizens of Ankh-Morpork seem quite happy to accept it.

Strippers' Guild. Motto: NVMQVAM VESTIMVS.

Coat of arms: enlevé.

Officially the Guild of Ecdysiasts, Nautchers, Cancanières and Exponents of Exotic Dance. This small, all-female and mainly human guild is located in SoSo Street, SoSo. Its members are hard-working women, especially at lunchtimes; Ankh-Morpork is in many respects an unreconstructed society and removing one's clothes for money is considered perfectly acceptable, although doing it for nothing would be considered immoral.

Dwarfs have no grasp of the basic idea, since removing any item of clothing except in the direst emergency is quite foreign to them, and there are no dwarf members. Trolls, however, form a small but vital part of the membership, although the troll outlook on life, their habit of going around more or less naked in any case and their unusual grasp of the nature of time all mean that a troll stripper actually dons more clothes as the dance progresses, often causing a riot as the fourth overcoat goes on.

The Guild president for life – and, indeed, the entire committee – is Miss Dixie 'VaVa' Voom, now officially retired from the stage along with Edward the snake but still taking a very active part in the Guild's training programme. Her farewell performance in the Skunk Club, Brewer Street, resulted in three heart attacks, a riot and five separate fires; as she tells her trainees, 'It's not what you've got but what you do with it that counts.'

Stronginthearm, Abba. A dwarf enlisted into the Ankh-Morpork militia by CARROT. [MAA]

Stronginthearm, Bjorn. A dwarf. CARROT Ironfoundersson's great-uncle. [GG]

Sumtin. A philosophical system from KLATCH. ZEN is a sub-sect of Sumtin. [WA]

Sun, Place Where It Does Not Shine. This has been firmly located near Slice, LANCRE, where it is coincidentally between a rock and a hard place.

It is, as its name suggests, a deep dark hole under an overhang so that even heavy Discworld light cannot find its way into it. The people of Slice, considered crazed even by Lancre standards, occasionally lower one of their number to prospect for the items that turn up there – usually workmen's tools, musical instruments and unpopular jobs.

This geographical anomaly serves to illustrate the unusual role of metaphor and colourful language on the Discworld. As another example, the curio-biological museum in Unseen University contains, among even stranger things, The One That Has Bells On (preserved in formaldehyde) and the original Horse You Rode In On (stuffed).

Sunshine Sanctuary for Sick Dragons.
Located in Morphic Street, Ankh-Morpork. Outside is a small and hollow and pathetic *papier mâché* dragon, holding a collection box, chained very heavily to the wall and bearing the sign 'Don't Let My Flame Go Out'.

Scrawled over the big double gates is a big sign saying 'Here Be Dragns'. A brass plaque beside the gate reads: 'The Ankh-Morpork Sunshine Sanctuary for Sick Dragons'.

There is also yet another, smaller sign: 'Please Leave Donations of Coal by Side Door'.

The building is built with very, very

The Place Where the Sun Does Not Shine

thick walls and a very, very lightweight roof, a method of construction found elsewhere only in firework factories.

The Sanctuary is a home for lost or strayed or abandoned swamp dragons. There tend to be more of the latter every day. There is occasionally a vogue for keeping young swamp dragons as pets, or even as cigarette lighters, but the charm wears off as the creatures grow and their essential dragonishness manifests itself in corroded carpets and big burn marks on the walls. Many are simply abandoned; if they are lucky they end up at the Sanctuary.

The charity is run by Rosie DEVANT-MOLEI, with the very regular help of Lady Sybil RAMKIN. Much of the actual work is done by a group of betrousered upper-class young women described by that class warrior Captain VIMES as 'the INTER-CHANGEABLE EMMAS'.

Supreme Grand Master. Leader of the Unique and Supreme Lodge of the ELUCIDATED BRETHREN OF THE EBON NIGHT. (*See also* WONSE, LUPINE.) [GG]

Susan. Susan Sto Helit. Daughter of MORT and YSABELL, and grand-daughter of DEATH, from whom she has inherited a number of traits (this should be impossible, since Ysabell was adopted, but *see* GENETICS).

A self-possessed and frankly unlovable young woman. As a pupil at the QUIRM COLLEGE FOR YOUNG LADIES, she is good at those sports that involve swinging some sort of stick (hockey, lacrosse, rounders) and she is academically brilliant at the things she likes doing. But brilliant, though, like a diamond – all edges and chilliness. It is noteworthy that the only other pupils she even vaguely considers friends are a dwarf and a troll, both in some way 'outcasts' from normal school society. She has the ability to make herself so inconspicuous as to be invisible to non-magical minds (a definite family attribute).

She is attractive, in a skinny way. Her hair puts people in mind of a dandelion clock on the point of telling the time: it is pure white, apart from a black streak, and its preferred shape is a sort of Medusa's-snakes style. On her face is a birthmark, which shows up only when she blushes, or when she is angry. It takes the form of three pale lines across her cheek (Discworld students will recall that her father was once slapped across the face by Death, leaving just such a mark).

When she is covering for her grandfather she wears a black lace dress of the sort worn by healthy yet necronerdic young women who want to look consumptive. [SM]

Swires. A gnome. Lives in a mushroom with a red-and-white spotted cap and little doors and windows. He is six inches high, picks his nose and looks like someone who smells like someone who lives in a mushroom. [LF]

Tailor. A weaver in LANCRE. Member of the Lancre Morris Men. [LL]

Tear of Offler. The biggest diamond in the world, weighing 850 carats. Used to be kept in the innermost sanctuary of the Lost Jewelled Temple of Doom of OFFLER the Crocodile God in darkest HOWONDALAND. All Offlian temples have a Tear of greater or lesser size, and they are stolen on a regular basis. This particular one was picked up after the Harvest Dance at SHEEPRIDGE and given to his daughter by William SPIGOT, who reasoned that any gem that big had to be glass. [RM]

Teppic. (Pteppic). Son of King TEPPICYMON XXVII and 1398th monarch of DJELIBEYBI.

His father shocked the country's priesthood by sending his son away to be trained at the Assassins' School in Ankh-Morpork, since he had heard that it gave a very good education; the priesthood were very much against any kind of secular education for someone who would one day be a god.

After many adventures Teppic returned to his own country and acceded to the throne and then abdicated in favour of the handmaiden PTRACI. [P]

Teppicymon XXVII. 1397th monarch of DJELIBEYBI. TEPPIC's father. Also known as Pootle (by his grandmother). A pleasant and intelligent man who was therefore entirely unsuited to be king of that sombre kingdom. He died in an accident when he thought he could fly. [P]

Terton. A lengthman on the CIRCUMFENCE. Lived in a hut built on wooden piles driven into the sea bed. He collected salvage for KRULL along the 45th length of their Circumfence. As a result of his encounter with the LUGGAGE, he developed hydrophobia and went to live in the Great NEF. [COM]

Tethis. A sea troll. Another lengthman for KRULL. He originally came from the water world of Bathys, but was first encountered in a driftwood shanty on a crag on the Rim of the world. Through the shanty passed a rope leading to the 10,000-mile-long net which runs along the CIRCUMFENCE to catch the salvage arriving at the Rim.

Tethis was a rather squat (although his

height altered with the tides) but not entirely ugly old troll composed of water and little else. He was a pleasant translucent blue colour, with cold, fishy breath and a voice that made people think of submarine chasms and things lurking in coral reefs.

He briefly left the Disc with TWO-FLOWER and RINCEWIND and has not been heard of since. The POTENT VOYAGER, the ship on which they reluctantly travelled, eventually landed in a lake near Skund. Presumably he is still there. [COM]

Tez. Tez the Terrible. A student wizard at Unseen University. [SM]

Tezuman Empire (Kingdom of Tezuma). Kingdom in the jungle valleys of central KLATCH. The people are renowned for being the most suicidally gloomy, irritable and pessimistic you could ever hope to avoid meeting.

The Tezumen invented the wheel, but didn't put it to its right use. As a result, their chariots, which are pulled by llamas, have two people running along each side, holding up the axles. The wheel itself is used as headgear and jewellery.

Nor have the Tezumen discovered paper, or even wax tablets. Their pictographic language is chiselled into blocks of granite, allowing the more depressed members of the tribe to beat themselves to death with their own suicide notes.

The country is known for its organic market gardens, exquisite craftsmanship in obsidian, feathers and jade, and its mass sacrifices in honour of QUEZOVER-COATL. Their music sounds like someone clearing a particularly difficult nostril. [E]

Thargum I. Red-bearded past king of LANCRE. When he was killed (poisoned by the father of VERENCE I) they stuck his head on a pole and carried it around the village to show that he was dead, an exercise that everyone thought was very convincing. Then they had a big bonfire and everyone in the palace got drunk for a week. No one remembers now whether Thargum was particularly good or bad. Lancre people are traditionalists and aren't choosy about their monarchs, but the greatest sin an incumbent of the throne can commit is not acting like a proper king. [WS]

Thaum. The basic and traditional unit of magical strength. It has been universally established as the amount of magic needed to create one small white pigeon or three normal-sized billiard balls (a smaller measure for purposes of calculation is the millithaum). A thaumometer is used to measure the density of a magical field. It is a dark blue glass cube, with a dial on the front and a button on the side.

In Unseen University's High Energy Magic building the thaum has been successfully demonstrated to be made up of resons (lit: 'thing-ies') or reality fragments. Current research indicates that each reson is itself made up of a combination of at least five 'flavours', known as 'up', 'down', 'sideways', 'sex appeal' and 'peppermint'.

(*See also* PRIME.)

Thaumaturgists. Many spells require things like mould from a corpse dead of crushing, or the semen of a living tiger, or the root of a plant that gives an ultrasonic scream when it is uprooted. Who is sent to get them? Right.

Thaumaturgists receive no magical schooling. They can just about be trusted to wash out an alembic. They are the lowest rung of the hierarchy of magical practitioners – apart from witches, of course. That's the wizards' view. [ER]

Thieves' Guild. Motto: ACVTVS ID VERBERAT ('Whip it quick').

Coat of arms: a shield with alternate bars of sable and argent. On it a bourse, coupé.

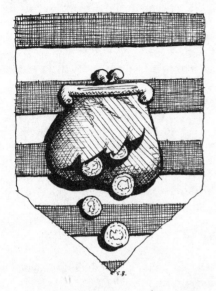

Originally known as the Guild of Thieves, and then the Guild of Thieves, Cutpurses, Housebreakers and Allied Trades and latterly the Guild of Thieves, Burglars and Allied Trades, pursecutting having fallen out of favour.

Despite its pretensions to ghastly brigandage and claims to venerable antiquity – based on a perceived descent from the ancient gangs that roamed the city – the Guild is a young and very respectable body which in a practical sense represents the major law enforcement agency in Ankh-Morpork.

The Guild is given an annual quota which represents a socially acceptable level of thefts and muggings, and in return sees to it in very definite and final ways that unofficial crime is not only stamped out but also knifed, garrotted, dismembered and left around the city in an assortment of paper bags. In keeping the lid on unofficial crime they have turned out to be far more efficient than the WATCH, who could only cut crime by working harder – the Guild, on the other hand, have only to work less. All of this works so effectively that when, in the Year of the Engaging Sloth, the Guild declared a General Strike, the level of crime actually doubled.

This formal system, introduced by Lord VETINARI, is held to be a cheap and enlightened arrangement (except by those malcontents who are actually mugged or robbed and refuse to see it as their social duty). It enables the thieves to plan a decent career structure, entrance examinations and codes of conduct similar to those adopted by the city's other professions – which, the gap not being very wide in any case, they have rapidly come to resemble. The Guild have also introduced a complex system of annual budgeting, licensing, chits and allowances to see that (a) the members can make a reasonable living, and (b) no citizen is robbed or assaulted more than an agreed number of times. Many farsighted citizens in fact arrange to get an acceptable minimum amount of theft, assault, etc., over at the beginning of the year, often in the privacy of their own homes, and are therefore able to walk the streets quite safely for the rest of the year. A number of small firms operate under the auspices of the Guild, offering attentive and personal service to this end.

It is probably unnecessary to point out that the system is less advantageous to the thieves than at first seems to be the case. Firstly, an awful lot of energy is expended on internal Guild politics. Secondly, almost all the crime in the city is controlled by the Guild Council. Thirdly, if there is any trouble Lord Vetinari now knows where they all live.

Thighbiter, Jethrod. Author of *The*

Ankh-Morpork Succesſion, the definitive history of the Ankh-Morpork monarchy. [MAA]

Thogsdaughter, Gloria. A schoolfriend of SUSAN. A dwarf. She has a beard a foot long, which is plaited and tied in ribbons in the school colours. [SM]

Thrum. A member of the LANCRE Morris Men team. Not a participant in the events of *Lords and Ladies*, however, having been injured during an attempt at the notorious Stick and Bucket Dance. [LL]

Thundergust, Grabpot. Proprietor of a cosmetics mill in Hobfast Street, Ankh-Morpork. His products are labelled 'The Halls of Elven Perfume & Rouge Co.' A fine example of the dwarfish tendency to project a tough, hard-drinking outer image while quietly getting on with making corsetry or whatever. [WS, MAA]

Thursley, Eric. A self-styled demonologist, of Midden Lane, Pseudopolis. He is nearly fourteen when RINCEWIND encounters him: slim, quite short, dark-haired, with glasses. His face would be a lot better if his acne cleared up, and his general aura would improve with more frequent washing. [E]

Time. The idea that time is something that passes uniformly at every point in the universe has long been discredited but humans persist in believing that it is so at a local level; yet most people have encountered days that pass very quickly or hours that trudge past (random time variations, like lumps or bubbles in custard) and have been to places where time flows faster/slower than at home.

Time is one of the Discworld's most secretive anthropomorphic personifications. It is hazarded that Time is female (she waits for no man) but she has never been seen, having always gone somewhere else just a moment before.

Tinker. A tinker in LANCRE. A member of the Lancre Morris Men. [LL]

T'malia, Lady. A tutor at the ASSASSINS' GUILD. She lectures in Political Expediency on Octeday afternoons and is one of the few women to have achieved high office in the Guild.

The jewellery of one hand alone carries enough poison to inhume a small town. She is stunningly beautiful, but with the calculated beauty that is achieved by a team of skilled artists, manicurists, plasterers, corsetiers and dressmakers, and three hours' solid work every morning. [P]

Toby. A goblin dog, previously owned by Chas SLUMBER. [TOC]

Tockley, Lucy. (*See* DIAMANDA.)

Tomjon. Adopted son of Olwen and Mrs VITOLLER; half brother to the FOOL. Tomjon's real mother was the Queen of Lancre, his real father the Fool's father (a fact known only to the LANCRE witches and, one assumes, his mother).

He was given three gifts by Granny WEATHERWAX, Nanny OGG and Magrat GARLICK: To make friends well, To always remember the words and To be whoever he thinks he is. With the benefit of these three gifts he carved out a career as a very successful actor. It was so successful and personally fulfilling that he later turned down the crown of Lancre on the grounds that he could wear a different crown on stage every night. [WS]

Tooth Fairies. There are a number of

these, all anthropomorphic personifications; the idea seems to have been imported from the COUNTERWEIGHT CONTINENT. The one encountered in *Soul Music* is a young woman who looks a bit like a milkmaid. She has a sort of well-scrubbed beefiness about her, and resembles a nurse of the sort who assist doctors whose patients occasionally get a bit confused and declare they're a bedspread. She has a pair of pliers in a pocket in her dress; like the other tooth fairies, she is obliged to take an additional tooth out if she doesn't have the right change. [SM]

Tower of Art. The oldest building on the Disc. Older than Unseen University in whose grounds it stands, older than the city which formed about it like a scree around a mountain. Maybe even older than geography. There was a time when the continents were different . . . perhaps the tower was washed up on the waves of rock, from somewhere else. Maybe it was even there before the Disc itself. It is useless to speculate. It was certainly the original university.

It is 800 feet tall and totally without windows. Time, weather and indifferent repairs have given it a gnarled appearance, like a tree that has seen too many thunderstorms. It is topped by a forest of little turrets and crenellations. Its crumbling stones support thriving miniature forests high above the city's rooftops. Entire species of beetles and small mammals have evolved up there and, aided by the emanations of magic from the University, have evolved very strangely indeed.

The small door in its base leads to the foot of the famous spiral staircase of 8,888 steps. The interior smells of antiquity, with a slight suspicion of raven droppings. The tower is not now used for anything – the internal floors have rotted away so that all that is left inside is the staircase. From the top a wizard might see the edge of the Disc (after spending ten minutes or so coughing horribly, of course).

T'Phon, Great. One of the four giant elephants who support the Discworld. [COM]

Traitor, Miss. Teaches Logic at the QUIRM COLLEGE FOR YOUNG LADIES. [SM]

Treacle Mine Road, Ankh-Morpork. A major road separating the SHADES from the largely dwarfish community in the Cable Street–Easy Street area. Named after the treacle mines once found in the area, now abandoned.

It has always been assumed that the treacle (note to Americans and other rare and strange creatures: a thickly sweet syrupy substance) is the remains of thickets of sugar cane crushed by mud at about the same time as coal measures were being laid down. It was – and still is, in some parts of the Disc – mined either as a solid, which has to be cleaned and refined and cast in slabs ('pig treacle' or 'hokey-pokey') and, very rarely, as a liquid. In the area around GENUA, liquid treacle lakes near the surface have absorbed enough moisture to ferment naturally, giving rise to occasional springs of rum as the results burst forth under pressure.

Lest it be thought this is far fetched, treacle mines have been reported in a number of places in England (in Binsey, near Oxford, and Bisham, near Marlow).

Treatle. A wizard. Once Vice-Chancellor (a post now in abeyance) of Unseen University and a mage of the Ancient and Truly Original Brothers of the Silver Star. He has bushy eyebrows and a nicotine-stained patriarchal beard; these, combined with his nice green waterproof tobacco pouch, curly boots and spangled robe, make Treatle a wizard's wizard. Generally considered as self-centred as a tornado. He is also regarded as being stupid in the particular way that very clever people can be stupid. [ER]

Troglodyte Wanderer. A rather sad and bewildered ghost who haunted LANCRE CASTLE because it was built on his burial mound and he hadn't got the faintest idea where he was. [WS]

Troll's Head, the. A tavern in the SHADES, Ankh-Morpork. Not a nice place. The Mended DRUM is also not a nice place, but it is a lot nicer than the Troll's Head, which isn't nice at all. It still has, nailed on a pole over the door, the original genuine troll head. Here may be found the kind of people too nasty even to be tolerated in the Mended Drum. Think about *that*.

Trolls. Trolls are a (usually) silicareous but humanoid life-form, largely found in the RAMTOPS but increasingly migrating to Ankh-Morpork and other cities of the STO PLAINS. They are traditionally a strong, hardy and incredibly long-lived race. And proverbially, and quite unfairly, considered to be as thick as two short thick wooden things.

In the cold air of the mountains trolls are in fact quite bright, almost cunning; only in the lowlands are they a byword for stupidity. In fact the slowness of thought is induced by the effect of heat on the silicon troll brain. If sufficiently deep frozen, a troll is astonishingly intelligent.

It is widely believed that trolls turn to stone in daylight. In fact they are stone all the time. But many trolls have brains that are so close to the heat tolerance level for operation that even the slight heating effect of early-morning light is sufficient to cause them to shut down.

Conception and birth roughly parallel the same occupations among humans, but trolls do not die except by accident or design. Left to themselves, trolls get bigger and slower and tend to settle in one place and think, very slowly and deliberately, about Things. They become more and more rock-like, a process that may take thousands of years. At some point they stop thinking, possibly because they have reached a kind of conclusion, but by then their thoughts are so slow that they are taking place against a geological timescale.

Even so, there is nothing subtle about trolls. While they cannot digest a human being, they have traditionally been very reluctant to accept this fact. And hitting another troll over the head with a rock is about equivalent to two humans exchanging the time of day. Troll courtship consists of a male troll, after consulting the intended's father, hitting her as hard as he can. This is in order to demonstrate the strength necessary to support a growing family. In deference to trollish femininity, he will normally select a pretty rock to do this with.

Their relationship with rural humans is generally on the rob-the-henhouse, jump-out-and-stomp, one-to-one basis. Between trolls and dwarfs, however, possibly because they tend to occupy the same landscape, there is a chronic state of low-grade warfare. The reason is possibly that dwarfs, who are miners and masons, sometimes use as their raw material trolls who have settled down for the long think. It is a tolerant troll indeed who can contemplate with equanimity his grandfather functioning as someone else's fireplace. Like the very best feuds, however, it really continues because it has always continued and its origins are lost in the dawn of time.

Or the sunset of time. Trolls believe that they move through time *backwards*. You can see the past, they say, therefore it must be in front of you. The future is invisible and therefore behind you.

Trolls have a socio-political system based on the concept of the troll with the biggest rock. Trolls have some difficulty in adjusting to city conditions, because what is a quiet discussion to them is a riot to humans. Unlike dwarfs, who have a far more established civic culture, they don't fit easily into human houses or eat the same food. They tend to get the messy jobs. But recent experience in the great melting pot of Ankh-Morpork indicates that, with a little understanding on both sides, trolls and dwarfs can put aside their differences and settle down to trade, commerce, theft, usury*, tax avoidance and other human pastimes.

Although the term 'troll' is strictly speaking reserved for silicon-based bipeds of the I've-got-dis-big-club-wid-a-nail-in-it persuasion, there are also other life forms of sufficiently troll-like characteristics to be considered as trolls. Sea trolls are animate sea water. The ICE GIANTS of the Hub must also be considered as a kind of troll, as must the artificially created GOLEMS.

It would be perverse of Nature to allow only the evolution of humanoid trolls and, while Nature is indeed perverse, there are other non-sapient (allowing for the moment that humanoid

*Theft from bears.

trolls are sapient) creatures that come under the broad stone umbrella of trolldom, although these are rare. There are troll dogs, and something roughly equivalent to a horse is used in the deep fastnesses of the mountains. There are also, surprisingly enough, troll ducks. They sink a lot.

There are not a great many troll names and traditionally they are all rock-associated in some way, although these days modern young female trolls think nothing of calling themselves Pearl. Trolls of the Disc include:

Amber [MP]
Bauxite [MAA]
BERYL [LF, TB]
Bluejohn [MAA]
BLUESTONE, Lias
BRECCIA [MP]
CARBONACEOUS [LL]
CHERT [TB]
CHRYSOPRASE (also Krysoprase, Chrystophrase)
Clay [SM]
COALFACE [MAA]
Crag [SM]
DETRITUS
GALENA (Rock)
Hardcore [SM]
Jasper [LF]
Jasper (no relation, but featuring in the song 'Amber & Jasper') [MP]
Kwartz [LF]
Magma [MP]
MICA [TB]
MORRAINE [MP]
Old Grandad [LF]
Pyrites [TB]
RUBY [MP]
SCREE [TB]
TETHIS

Trousers of Time, the. There is probably a law, or at least a pretty strict guideline, that says that every book with the word 'Chaos', 'Time' or 'Fractal' in the title must, on some page, include an illustration of the Trousers of Time, viz.:

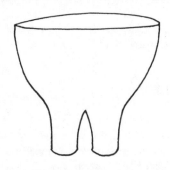

The trousers are used to demonstrate for very slow people the bifurcating nature of Time – how, for example, one simple choice can cause the universe to branch off into two separate realities (This One, and the One You Should Have Been In Where the Bus Wasn't About To Hit You).

On the Discworld, where metaphor can become interchangeable with reality, the Trousers of Time may actually exist. Where they are, and who will eventually wear them, and whether this has anything to do with the phrase 'Time Flies', may one day be revealed. Or not.

Trymon, Ymper. A wizard. Second in command to the ARCHCHANCELLOR. Became Head of the Order of the Silver Star on the death of Galder WEATHER-WAX, but had quite a short reign. A tall, nervous young man, whose personal habits are recalled only to the extent that he fussed about his hair and used all manner of magical spells and potions to get it to grow properly. He did not smoke – quite against the fashion among wizards at the time – and found solace instead in organizational charts that showed lots of squares with arrows pointing to lots of other squares. He was the sort of man who could use the word 'personnel' and mean it. [LF]

Tshup Aklathep. The Infernal Star Toad with a Million Young. Tortures its victims to death by holding them down and showing them pictures of its children until their brains implode. Probably an escapee from the DUNGEON DIMENSIONS who maintains a precarious existence on this plane. [MP]

Tsort. A desert kingdom on the continent of KLATCH. A neighbour of DJELIBEYBI and an historical enemy of EPHEBE. Tsort is known for the silent marshes of the Tsort river and the GREAT PYRAMIDS, although it has to be pointed out that pyramid building belonged to a much earlier phase of the country's history and – no doubt because of the example of nearby Djelibeybi – modern Tsorteans scorn the things. The ancient city of Tsort was put to the torch by, it is thought, the armies of Ephebe under LAVAEOLUS. The people of Tsort worship all manner of gods, some of which seem to have been built of all the bits the creators of other gods had left over. Tsortean food relies heavily on garlic.

Tsort, river. The chocolate brown, slow-moving waters of the river Tsort bisect the desert Rimwards of AL KHALI. Famed in myth and lies, it insinuates its way through the brown landscapes like a long, damp descriptive passage punctuated with sandbanks. And every sandbank is covered with sunbaked logs, most of which have teeth. [S]

Tubul. One of the four giant elephants that support the Discworld. [COM]

Tugelbend, Victor. A student wizard at Unseen University, and possibly the laziest person in the history of the world. Originally, Victor chose to remain a student as a means of avoiding the realities of life and of securing an inheritance.

(An uncle left him an annuity to allow him to study as a wizard but, being no fool, stipulated in his will that the annuity would cease if Victor ever got less than 80 in the examinations, the pass mark being 88. Victor therefore devoted tremendous effort to studying, in order to ensure that in every exam he achieved exactly 84; on one occasion he successfully appealed when a mistake in the marking awarded him 91 points.)

Despite his aversion to anything that appeared to resemble work, Victor was the most athletically inclined student in UU. He has a thin moustache and smiles a lot, in a faintly puzzled way, which gives the impression that he is more intelligent than he really is. He seems to amble everywhere, even when running.

He went on to make a short career in moving pictures, using the stage name Victor Maraschino. His current whereabouts are unknown, except that he is certain to be doing something he likes and devoting tremendous physical and mental effort to the pursuit of laziness. [MP]

Tumult, Gammer. A witch who taught Granny WEATHERWAX. But Granny also claims to have been taught by Nanny Gripes. Given the impatient nature of Esme Weatherwax, the truth of the matter is that she probably pumped *all* the local witches for as much instruction as they could give her. [ER]

Turnipseed, Adrian. (*See* DRONGO, BIG MAD.) [SM]

Turtle Movement. A secret society in OMNIA which believes that the Disc is flat and is carried through space on the backs of four elephants and a giant turtle. Their secret recognition saying is 'The Turtle Moves'. Their secret sign is a left-hand fist with the right hand, palm extended, brought down on it. Most of the senior officials of the Omnian church are members of the 'movement', but since they all wear hoods and are sworn to absolute secrecy each thinks he is the only one. [SG]

Turtle, the Great. (*See* A'TUIN, GREAT.)

Twoflower. The Disc's first tourist. Originally, he was a small, bald and skinny man, but he soon put on weight if not hair under the influence of Ankh-Morpork's robust cuisine. He had false teeth and wore glasses, which led many

of the Disc's inhabitants to assume that he had four eyes (both of these innovations were subsequently very popular in Ankh-Morpork).

He came from BES PELARGIC, the major seaport of the AGATEAN EMPIRE on the COUNTERWEIGHT CONTINENT, where he used to work at a desk job.

Twoflower was oddly dressed in knee-length breeches and a shirt in a violent and vivid conflict of colours. Central to his personal philosophy was the very strong belief that no harm could come to him because he was a visitor. A likeable, friendly and innocent man, his travels around the continent were marked by mayhem and sudden death. The fact that he was the original owner of the LUGGAGE has much to do with this. [COM, LF]

Tyrant, the. The elected ruler of EPHEBE. The current ruler is a little fat man with skinny legs, which gives the impression that an egg is hatching upside down. [SG]

Ungulant, S.T. Ungulant the Anchorite. Sevrian Thaddeus Ungulant – hence 'St'. A saint, possibly of the Omnian church but probably just a generic saint. He lives on a cartwheel nailed to the top of a slim pole in the desert between EPHEBE and OM.

S.T. Ungulant is a very thin man with long hair and beard and skin almost blackened by the desert sun. He wears a loincloth, and he has an imaginary friend called Angus. He is in fact almost completely and utterly mad, due to the sun and a continuous diet of the strange desert mushrooms. But the tiny core of reason left within him is aware that being completely insane is the only way to survive the desert existence. Besides, it means that he can enjoy the nebulous sumptuous meals and insubstantial carnal delights put before him by the small gods that swarm in the desert. His belief in all of them is possibly the only thing that keeps him alive. [SG]

Unseen University. Motto: NVNC ID VIDES, NVNC NE VIDES.

Coat of arms: a livre des sortilèges, attaché en cuivre, sur un chapeau pointu, on a field, azure.

There is a UU scarf, basically burgundy and midnight blue with some tasteless thin yellow and purple stripes. The stripes are extremely symbolic, although not of anything very specific. The University likes to pretend that their eye-watering clash is an attempt to portray OCTARINE,* but in reality it graphically illustrates the importance of not letting someone like the current Bursar choose a colour scheme after eating half a bottle of dried frog pills. The stripes have been retained anyway, because of Tradition.

UU is the Disc's premier college of magic, whose campus is the occult, if no longer the actual, centre of Ankh-Morpork.

The University was founded in AM 1282 (the city count at the time) by Alberto MALICH, but Ankh-Morpork dating is always suspect; suffice to say that it was some 2,000 years before the present. The aim was to force some sort of regulation on wizardry, which at that time

---

*Although octarine is the most important colour as far as wizards are concerned, it is not one that lends itself well to paint pigmentation. It quickly fades in sunlight and, in extreme cases, walks away.

was quite chaotic, and to permit the existence of an institution that would allow one wizard to meet another without immediately endeavouring to blow his head off with magical fire, as was then the case.

Like all really old universities, it is hard to tell where the University begins and the city ends, and in any case the size of UU can only be determined by reference to the kind of physics that you have to be a drunken physicist to understand.

In a purely mundane sense the main buildings occupy a large part of the river frontage between the ANKH and SATOR SQUARE, with various outbuildings stretching out as far as Esoteric Street. But a mere floor plan would be quite misleading; UU has rooms and floors where logic says they simply could not exist. It has been a home of magic for so long that this is now part of the architectural inventory, like cement.

There are two ways of getting admitted to UU: achieve some great work of benefit to magic, such as the recovery of an ancient and powerful relic or the invention of a totally new spell, or be sponsored by a senior and respected wizard, after a suitable period of apprenticeship. The eighth son of an eighth son has a right to demand and receive a place.

Er . . .

All right, three ways – actual *entry* can be achieved by anyone of either sex willing to scrub and cook and make beds.

Er . . .

Four ways, in fact – possibly the most famous entrance to UU is via the alleyway between the observatory and the Backs, where a few loose bricks in the wall can be removed to make an informal ladder that has been used by students for hundreds of years. Whatever its original name, the alley has been known for years as Scholars' Entry, which in the hands of those inclined to the obvious is always good for a snigger.

With one exception (during the Archchancellorship of CUTANGLE), UU has never admitted women. Usually this is said to be on the grounds of plumbing problems, but probably the real reason is an unspoken dread that women, if allowed to mess around with wizardry, would probably be embarrassingly good at it. And less likely to do what they're told.

There is theoretically no age limit on students, since obviously it is better to have anyone with magical talent under the aegis of the University than . . . er . . . not under it. The normal age of entrants is around sixteen, although in earlier days it was a lot younger and undergraduates as young as four were enrolled. These days, however, few people at UU undertake magical practice clutching a woolly lamb.

WEALTH

UU is immensely wealthy, in a nebulous and threadbare kind of way. It owns large sections of Ankh-Morpork, particularly around Sator Square and also in the SHADES, which grew up as a service centre for the new university (a safe distance downstream). However, most of the rents are fixed and tend to be of the half-a-groat-every-Hogswatchnight variety, and the leases are either no longer decipherable or have long since mouldered away.

Generally speaking, the University survives from day to day by voluntary donations, usually in kind. (If you were a greengrocer, living a few streets away from what you perceive as a group of fat and slightly deranged old men sitting on enough raw magic to blow a hole right through Reality and out the other side, then wouldn't you see they got the occasional cartload of potatoes?)

TOWN AND GOWN: UNSEEN UNIVERSITY AND ANKH-MORPORK

As the University is well aware, Ankh-Morpork owes its entire existence to the presence of Unseen. The Shades were the core of the original city but, as the city began to develop its own momentum, the urban sprawl soon encompassed the villages now known as Dolly Sisters and Nap Hill.

Not unnaturally, the early ARCH-CHANCELLOR resented any suggestion of control by the growing civil power and there were various trials of strength in the first few centuries, which usually ended with someone being turned into some kind of amphibian. Eventually an understanding was reached: UU would be left in peace to manage its affairs on the transtemporal level, and citizens would be allowed to go to bed the same shape as they were when they woke up that morning, whatever shape that had been.

Strictly speaking, the laws of Ankh-Morpork do not apply within the walls of the University even now, but this is nothing remarkable since they seldom apply outside the walls either. Wizards misbehaving in the city might be locked up by the WATCH for the night, but will then be handed over to the Archchancellors' Court upon payment of a small fine.

A list of offences under the rules of the Court, and their attendant punishments, includes:

Acceptable Waggishness   50p
High Spirits   60p
Being a Young Rip   75p
Having a Fling   75p
Sowing Wild Oats   33p per oat
Being found Drunk   80p
Being found Rascally Drunk   90p
Being found Objectionably Sober $1.00

Of course, where there is law there has to be crime, and where there is a court there must be policemen.

So it is at UU. Although these days they are really little more than porters, the University does have its 'policemen', known as the Bledlows (origin unknown) or 'lobsters'. They tend to be heavy-set, elderly men with nevertheless a good turn of speed and the sort of head that is made to wear a bowler hat. They are of limited yet highly focused intellect; their whole being is founded on the certain belief that all students are guilty of everything.

They are generally ex-soldiers or watchmen and their traditional cry is 'I know who you are!'

UNIVERSITY ORGANIZATION

Despite appearances, UU is not simply a college of magic. There are faculties of medicine, minor religions and lore (history), for example. But these are very small and, in any case, University rules require that faculty members must have trained initially as wizards.

UU government is headed by the Archchancellor, who also chairs the College Council, or Hebdomadal Board (from the Latatian *hebes* – sluggish or stupid, and *domo* – to tame or conquer. Hence the purpose of the College Council is to conquer stupidity. It is, say critics, beginning this activity by making a very careful and personal study of the enemy – really getting under its skin, as it were).

The Council traditionally consisted of the heads of the eight orders of wizardry. However, since the events chronicled at the end of *The Light Fantastic* (when the University lost all eight heads but gained some incredibly lifelike statues, most of them now decorating the wall overlooking Sator Square), the ex-officio membership of the heads of orders has ceased and the Council is now directly appointed by the Archchancellor.

The eight orders, each in theory headed by an eighth-level wizard, are:

The Ancient and Truly Original Sages
of the Unbroken Circle
The Hoodwinkers
Mrs Widgery's Lodgers
The Ancient and Truly Original
Brothers of the Silver Star
The Venerable Council of Seers
The Sages of the Unknown Shadow
The Order of Midnight
The Last Order, also known as The
Other Order

A new student may apply to join any one of these orders, which combine the functions of 'houses' in English public schools with something of the 'fraternities' in American colleges. Despite their names, most of them are not at all ancient – there have always *been* orders, but their names have been lost or mislaid or muddled by wars and time. The current crop are the result of a deliberate 're-creation' of the orders less than a century ago. Apart, that is, from Mrs Widgery's Lodgers, which is as old as the University; in the very early days of UU the TOWER OF ART (then the only building on campus) was not big enough to hold all the students and they were boarded at the house of Mrs Widgery, on the site of what is now New Hall.

Once accepted, the student may study for any one of the University's degrees:

Bachelor of Thaumatology (B.Thau.)
Bachelor of Magic (B.Mgc)
Bachelor of Sortilège (B.S.)
Bachelor of Magianism (B.Mn.)
Bachelor of Divination (B.D.)
Bachelor of Civil Lore (B.C.L.)
Bachelor of Applied Theurgy
  (B.Ap.Th.)
Bachelor of Impractical Necromancy
  (B.Im.N.)
Bachelor of Fluencing (B.F.)*
Bachelor of Amulets & Talismen
  (B.Am.Ta.)
Bachelor of Cabbalistic Rites
  (B.C.R.)
Bachelor of Hyperphysical
  Chiromancy (B.H.Ch.)
Bachelor of Esoteric Occultism
  (B.Es.O.)
Bachelor of Eldritch Lacemaking
  (B.El.L.)†

Master of Thaumatology (M.Thau.)
Master of Magic (M.M.)
Master of Sortilège (M.S.)
Master of Magianism (M.Mn.)
Master of Divination (M.D.)
Master of Civil Lore (M.C.L.)

Doctor of Thaumatology (D.Thau.)
Doctor of Magic (D.M.)

*A very popular degree and comparatively easy to obtain; a bit like sociology. Most wizards manage to get a B.F. after their name, to the quiet amusement of the citizenry in general.
†This one is a bit of a puzzler.

Doctor of Sortilège (D.S.)
Doctor of Magianism (D.Mn.)
Doctor of Gramarye (D.G.)
Doctor of Divination (D.D.)
Doctor of Civil Lore (D.C.L.)
Doctor of Magical Philosophy
  (D.M.Phil.)
Doctor of Morbid Spellbinding
  (D.M.S.)
Doctor of Condensed Metaphysics
  (D.C.M.)
Doctor of Wizardry (D.W.)

In addition to the above, the University

Unseen University Doctor's gown
and sash

also tolerates guest lecturers on 'fringe' aspects of magic (at least, fringe from the point of view of established wizardry) such as shamanism, witchcraft, voodoo and plumbing.

Progression through the eight levels of wizardry is determined in part by the acquisition of degree qualifications and, particularly towards the top of the tree where the number of available places become few and far between (there are only eight eighth-level wizards, at least officially), by a policy of 'dead men's pointy boots', no questions being asked about the manner of their emptying.

(We suppose at this point that it must be admitted, with extreme reluctance, that the formal level is not necessarily an indication of a wizard's actual power. Like the whole structure of UU, the levels and degree system is there to *control* the power of wizardry rather than further it. It has to be pointed out, for example, that by the University's own rules the wizard RINCEWIND, having defeated a sorcerer (in *Sourcery*), is therefore at the very least an eighth-level wizard. No one at UU seems to have worked this out, and it is just as well for their temper that this remains the case.)

Many of the faculties also support a sponsored Professorship, which, although carrying a sturdy stipend, also carries with it the stigma of actually being expected to teach the students. The current Professorships are:

Patricius Professor of Magic
Magus Professor of Wizardry
Invisus Professor of Condensed
  Metaphysics
Octavus Professor of Civil Lore
Haudmeritus Professor of Divination
Superbus Professor of Astrology
Infandus Professor of Morbid
  Spellbinding
Fluxus Professor of Sortilège

STAFF

Identified members of the University's staff include:

Archchancellor
Bursar
Chair of Indefinite Studies
Dean of College
Dean of Liberal Studies
Dean of Pentacles
Lecturer in Applied Astrology
Lecturer in Recent Runes
Librarian
Professor of Astrology
Reader in Esoteric Studies (also known as 'the Reader in the Lavatory')
Reader in Invisible Writings
Senior Wrangler

Again, the fact is that a University that has existed for two thousand years, and is as rambling as UU, develops all sorts of quirks. There are professors in distant parts of the building engaged in their own pursuits and hardly ever seen; there are lecturers who don't lecture, and research students who are older than most of the faculty. Mustrum RIDCULLY, Archchancellor at the time of writing, is resigned to the fact that there are plenty of wizards in outlying areas of UU who don't even know who he is. Once in UU, a wizard need never leave. Tenure is automatic. There is always a spare study somewhere, always room in the Great Hall. It is, in short, academic heaven – and a perfect way to ensure that the most potentially dangerous men on the Disc spend their time squabbling amongst themselves and, of course, eating big dinners.

TERMS

The University year is split into eight terms, each of which is approximately one week long in order to minimize the amount of time that the faculty needs to spend in any room with the student body.

The students, however, continue to live in the University throughout much of the calendar year, undertaking their own research and generally absorbing magic from the fabric of the building and adding to its storehouse of knowledge. (The theory runs thusly: it is very well known that students arriving fresh at any university know all there is to know about absolutely everything. But when they leave, after many years of study, they're usually only too ready to admit that there is a lot they don't know. Raw knowledge must therefore have been passing from the students into the University, where it accumulates.)

The University terms follow the Great or true astronomical Disc year, despite the fact that most of the world lives by the 'agricultural' year (see CALENDARS). All really old and important universities have terms linked to some temporal scheme now quite opaque to the mass of the population, to show them what they're missing by being so stupid.

The UU terms are: Octinity; Rotation; Backspindle; Hogswatch; Evelyn; Micklemote; Candlerent (Candlerent is rent from a house which continually deteriorates – this presumably has something to do with the Shades, where many of the buildings have deteriorated to the point at which flat ground would be urban improvement); Soul Cakes.

CEREMONIES AND FESTIVALS

The Convivium.

The UU degree ceremony. The University's Archchancellor, Council, eighth-level wizards, doctors and masters process through the city from the University to the opera house, led by (traditionally) the Commander of the City Watch or, in those recent years when there has been no Commander, by a man carrying a cushion on which is a small pot of mustard and a quill pen (because of Tradition). The procession is extremely colourful and popular and has put at least one nautical observer in mind of an entire fleet of galleons running in front of the wind.

In the opera house new graduates are awarded their degrees in the presence of the PATRICIAN. After the ceremony, the procession proceeds rather more quickly back to the University for a large meal.

Until two hundred years ago the Convivium was held within the University grounds; it appears to have been moved outside as an exercise in impressing the masses; a very similar exercise, in fact, to the Moscow May Day parades in the great days of Soviet power. Look at us, the wizards seem to be saying as they proceed with robes astream – we've all got big staffs, and *they've* all got knobs on the end. We don't want to have to use them.

Gaudy Night.
When graduate wizards attend a grand banquet in the Great Hall, with each wizard making a greater effort than usual to outdo his fellows in the splendour of his robes. The winner is carried shoulder-high out of the University and thrown on to the Ankh.

Boy Archchancellor.
This ceremony occurs around the turn of the year, at Hogswatch. A first-year student is selected to be Archchancellor for a whole day, from dawn until dusk. For that period he can exert the full power of the Archchancellorship and there are many tales of japes played on senior members of the College Council (hence the expression 'a wizard wheeze'). For this reason the student selected for this honour is usually the most unpopular boy in the University,

and his life expectancy the following day is brief.

Head of the River.
Like all riverside universities, Unseen is keen to promote its water sports. Because of the nature of the Ankh, rowing is tricky except in times of serious flood, and races consist of teams of eight student wizards chasing each other on foot up the Ankh while carrying a racing skiff (a similar practice, for different reasons, is found in the Alice Springs Regatta in Australia, which takes place on the dry river bed).

The race itself is known as the Bumps, because of the nature of the surface of the Ankh. The competing crews race from the University boathouses to the Brass Bridge. The winning crew is then awarded a 'brown' (pairs of brown pointy boots to replace the ones destroyed by close contact with the Ankh during the race), and becomes Head of the River, an earthy reference to the state of the members' boots and clothing.

May Morning.
Every Mayday morning at dawn, the UU choir sing an anthem from the top of the Tower of Art, while the faculty and students (or as many of them as are awake at dawn) stand in the University gardens and listen. Since the Tower is 800 feet high, the listeners cannot hear the singing but, since the anthem takes five minutes to sing, they all applaud five minutes after dawn.

On a number of occasions the choir itself has failed to get up in time but the 'listeners' still clap anyway. To sneer at this is to misunderstand the Value of Tradition. If you don't understand this, you are nothing but a foreigner.

The Wizards' Excuse Me.
Quite a new function, held on the last day of Backspindle term. It has been said

that wizards don't have balls, but the Excuse Me belies this. It is a large dance to which the cream of Ankh-Morpork society (or, as they say, at least the stuff which is floating on the top) is invited. There are two bands and, most importantly, a buffet with eighteen different kinds of meat and, of course, cheese cubes and pineapple lumps on a stick.

The Excuse Me is particularly favoured by the current LIBRARIAN, as a result of which sales of hair oil soar in the preceding week. He is the only person in Ankh-Morpork who can achieve a parting down his entire body.

Rag Week.
The entire Backspindle term. Wise citizens know enough to be on their guard around this time. The Week has all the normal perils of student humour with the additional seasoning of magic; these are viewed by the University authorities with the amused acceptance that is generally employed vis à vis student activities when baton rounds and tear gas have been found ineffective.

Citizens may encounter, for example, the Short Street Climb, in which wizards armed with crampons and pitons and ropes 'climb', in all seriousness, the length of the street. Many lose their grip and plunge helplessly through the door of the Mended DRUM where, in an attempt to revive themselves, much alcohol is consumed.

Another regular feature is the 'borrowing' of certain civic items and taking them to the Mended Drum, where much alcohol is consumed. Such items typically include street signs, potted plants and, on one occasion, the Brass Bridge.

An event often featured in the Week, but liable to break out at any other time, is 'tobogganing'. Traditionally this took place inside the Tower of Art, when students on tea trays – after consuming much alcohol – would slide down the 8,888 steps on the spiral staircase, with many death-defying plunges over the missing ones. By the time they were half-way down, in any case, centrifugal force was pinning them to the walls, and wizards often shot from the doorway at the bottom with enough speed to skim them across the Ankh.

These days Rag Week is more normally held inside the University buildings themselves, where the many curving staircases and polished corridors offer endless opportunity for impressively sudden death.

Beating the Bounds.
('Also known as 'Plunkers'.) At dawn on 22 Grune the entire faculty, led by the choir and with the student body trailing behind, walk the ancient boundaries of the University (approximately the Backs, the Maul, Esoteric Street and the river frontage). They walk through or if necessary climb over any buildings that have since been built on the line of progress, while ceremonially striking any members of the public with live ferrets (in memory of Archchancellor Buckleby). Any red-headed men encountered are seized by several strong young wizards and given 'a plunking'; this tradition has, most unusually – and subsequent to an incident that left three wizards hanging precariously from a nearby gutter – been amended to read 'any red-haired men except of course for Captain CARROT Ironfoundersson of the Watch'. After the progress, the entire membership of the University heads back to the Great Hall for a huge breakfast at which duck must be served.

Scrawn Money.
('Archchancellor Scrawn's Bequest'.) One of the oldest ceremonies in the University calendar, held in Sator Square. All

tenants of University property are required to attend, whereupon they are given two pennies, a pair of long socks and a loaf of bread baked the previous morning. They then file into the University where they are allowed to watch the wizards having lunch.

The Poor Scholars.

When UU was first established a class of students was accepted without the benefit of financial backing or formal seconding by a University graduate. These were the 'Poor Scholars', young men with magical potential. It was felt that it would be in the interests of all concerned if the young men were educated in the ways of UU (in the words of Alberto Malich, the founder: 'We'd better keep the bright young buggers where we can see 'em').

They were not given rooms in the Tower of Art, and many had to live in lean-tos constructed against the walls. Once a month, in recognition of these stoics' determination not to be put off from their studies, the faculty would appear at the upper windows of the Tower and throw food to the 'Poor Scholars'. It was a popular event among the staff because it was quite possible to achieve a knockout blow with a well-gnawed cutlet from 200 feet.

This tradition lives on, even though the University is now physically much bigger and takes no 'Poor Scholars'. Once a year, the entire student body forgathers in Sator Square, where the faculty pelts them with stale bread rolls. Thrown with some force.

'Sity and Guilds.

When the Guilds began to set up their own academic establishments there was a lot of rivalry between their various students, and lone UU students would frequently be set on by gangs from colleges. Ankh-Morpork has a relaxed atti-

Top of the Tower of Art

tude to sudden death, and many faculty members prefer dead students as being easier to teach, but the more pragmatic Guild Presidents, and the then current Archchancellor, decided that enough was enough because all those bodies around the place made it hard to open doors, and so on.

They decided to channel the rivalry into an annual sporting contest, to be called the 'Sity and Guilds Match (although A. J. Loop, in the *Ankh-Morpork Almanack and Book of Dayes*, claims that this was merely a slightly modernized form of a much older and rather sinister contest known as the Ankh-Morpork Poor Boys' Fun, which involved teams of up to five hundred; certainly the old Laws and Ordinances of Ankh-Morpork contain several pro- hibitions mentioning the term).

The principle was to kick or carry a football from the outskirts of the Shades (the oldest part of the city) to the Tower of Art (the oldest building on the Disc). The game involved teams of fifty stu- dents from each of the principal Guilds, plus UU. Goals were scored by kicking the ball through the door (or, more often, the window) of landmarks along the way, many of them having names like the Mended Drum, Bunch of Grapes, etc. The scoring team had then to be bought drinks by the other teams. After a few years, the Archchancellor ruled that only one goal could be scored in each pub since the match had, three years running, gone on for a month.

UU records suggest that students from the University have not participated recently, but street football with various rules is still an Ankh-Morpork tradition. (In troll areas of the city the troll version of football is still occasionally played, although out of deference to modern sensibilities the 'football' of choice is no longer a human head, and a dwarf is sub- stituted.)

UNSEEN UNIVERSITY: A GUIDED TOUR

The University's main gates open on to Sator Square. They are big and plated with solid OCTIRON. There is no door- knocker, and at sunset each day the gates are locked by magic (in actual fact by MODO, the University's dwarf gardener, but it pays to advertise).

Take a moment to inspect the interest- ing frontage, which is an amazing juxta- position of architectural styles, although it may be that the word 'confectionery' is more appropriate. From various niches the statues of former Archchancellors, of which UU has a more than adequate supply, stare down over the city.

We may at this point draw the atten- tion of gentlemen in the party to the statue of Archchancellor Bewdley, just over to the window to the right of the gates. If they are in a position to do so (i.e., alive), Archchancellors like to influence the style of their commemorat- ive statues; Archchancellor Bewdley always disliked Ankh-Morpork intensely and I think you will agree, when you notice the position of his hands, that this is abundantly clear posthumously.

Note that the various architectural styles suggest that the roof and upper floor of the University were constructed several hundred years before the other storeys.

Now the massive gates open rather jerkily to admit us to the main octangle of the University's campus.

We enter a wide courtyard surrounded by lawns and dominated by some ancient chestnut trees. There are benches under the trees. Around the octangle is a great rambling building or buildings, looking not so much an architectural design as a lot of buttresses, arches, towers, bridges, domes, cupolas, etc., huddling together for warmth. Wizards like *quantity*. Visi- tors are asked particularly to note the cunning and disconcertingly alert gar- goyles, a range of beaks, manes, wings, claws and pigeon droppings. Avoid feed- ing them if possible. They are at least as intelligent as trolls, by the way. You are being watched.

Behind us now is the University Clock Tower, with its ancient cracked bell (rumoured to be of octiron rather than bronze), Old Tom. The clapper dropped out shortly after it was cast, but the bell still tolls out some tremendously son- orous silences every hour.

Crossing the octangle, we proceed up a broad flight of steps to an impressive pair of doors, again made of octiron. Note the heavy locks, curly hinges and brass studs on the door itself and the intricate carvings on the archway. Passing through this entrance, we notice the University's keys on their huge iron ring. Not all of them are metal, not all are visible; some look very strange indeed, as if they are not entirely in this world.

We will go straight to the Great Hall. Around its walls hang or stand portraits or statues of past Archchancellors – full-bearded and pointy-hatted, clutching ornamental scrolls or holding mysterious symbolic bits of astrological equipment. They stare down at us with ferocious self-importance or, possibly, chronic constipation. In many cases they are unfinished, the subject having prematurely expired during the sitting.

However, it is worth seeking out the

niche containing not the likeness but the actual body of Archchancellor 'Trouter' Hopkins, whose will stipulated that upon his death the University should continue his own work and pickle his body in alcohol. It sits beautifully preserved in its niche gazing happily at the festivities below, and is occasionally purloined by students and left around the University in a variety of humorous poses (sitting at the High Table with a bib on, wearing a night-cap in the Bursar's bed, etc.).

The floor is decorated with a worrying pattern of black and white tiles, and covered with long tables and benches. There is a big fireplace at the turnwise end and a big clock at the other. A third wall is largely occupied by the Mighty Organ. This magnificent instrument,

recently restored, was the work of Bloody Stupid JOHNSON, famed wherever buildings are constructed back to front.

Genius knows no limitations. Leonardo da Vinci would design lock gates and new ways of soldering lead just as happily as he would paint pictures. In the same way, the reverse genius of people like Johnson also likes to dabble a bit. As he said, 'It's only air going through pipes, it can't be that difficult.'

And, indeed, the resulting construction must be one of the most versatile instruments known to pre-electronic mankind, with its three giant keyboards and range of additional controls seldom before encountered, including the one that floods all the pipes with poisonous gas to kill the mice. Dextrous use of resin, strips of metal, rubber tubing and special pipes allows a whole range of surprising effects, permitting composers to explore whole new areas of music-making (one has only to cite Bubbla's 'Variations On a Man Taking His Foot Out of a Pile of Mud', say, or Fondel's 'Double Top Overture', on the first playing of which the audience were mystified that they could hear nothing but were being stunned by falling bats).

No one is now allowed to use the *Terraemotus pedal*, which opens up the 128-foot pipe known as Earthquake. On the first occasion when it was used the sixteen students doing the pumping were sucked into the machinery, the population of a quarter of the city experienced acute bowel discomfort, and the building moved a quarter of an inch sideways.

To supplement the light from the small high windows, with their gentle patina of antique grease, the Great Hall is lit by a massive, heavy, black, tallow-encrusted chandelier which hangs from the Hall's dark, owl-haunted rafters like a threatening overdraft. It can hold one thousand candles.

The Great Hall is the scene of all major magical activities in the University, and it also hosts the four main meals of the day. The senior members of the faculty used to sit at the High Table which was indeed high, since it could float several yards up in the air, and landed only between courses. It now remains grounded as a result of what is referred to only as the Incident at Dinner.

Also in the main building are the Uncommon Room, with its roaring log fire, summer or winter, the University's small chapel and modest sanatorium (wizards tend to be either in rude health or dead), and of course the classrooms designed on the funnel principle, with their benches sloping precipitously over the central teaching areas.

Also worthy of note, for visitors who are interested in this subject, is the senior wizards' lavatory, which has real running water, interesting tiles and two big silver mirrors placed on opposite walls.

In the cellars are a maze of cold-rooms, still-rooms, kitchens, sculleries, bakeries and taprooms that together form the driving engine of the University. It will be noted that while most of the University is in a permanent state of happy decay, the kitchens are quite modern and also in a permanent state of bustle. An army, it has been said, marches on its stomach; wizards sit holding theirs. Also in the cellars is the curiobiological museum, probably best not visited after a meal, particularly since it is situated next to the pickle pantry.

Passing through the main building we come to the University Gardens. Dominating these, as it dominates the entire city, is the Tower of Art, 800 feet tall, and the subject of a separate tour. To our left is the main Observatory, with its broad mosaic floor inlaid with the sixty-four signs of the Disc ZODIAC,* and the gym, a large room lined with lead and rowan wood, where neophytes can work at High Magic without seriously unbalancing the universe. In that building is also the University squash court.

To our immediate right is the LIBRARY; access to this glass domed building is via the inside of the University but is only with the permission of the Librarian.

There is, incidentally, a second observatory in the deepest cellars. It is lined with lead, and it is used for viewing . . . the *other* stars.

Further to our right is the tiny-windowed High Energy Magic Building, the only building on the campus less than a thousand years old. The senior wizards have never bothered much about what the younger, skinnier and more bespectacled wizards get up to in there, treating their endless requests for funding for thaumic particle accelerators and radiation shielding as one treats pleas for more pocket money, and listening with amusement to their breathless accounts of the search for ever more elementary particles of magic itself. They are, though, nervous of the fact that the students there seem to be engrossed in their work and, in fact, apparently enjoy it. This is always a dangerous thing in a student.

The grounds, with their rose beds and ancient velvet lawns, their neat patterns of gravel paths and hedges, stretch right down to the river, where some of the University's boats are moored to the jetties. A small bridge leads over the Ankh to WIZARDS' PLEASAUNCE.

The grounds, which incorporate the Archchancellor's garden and verandah,

*At the time of the floor being re-laid, that is. This is done every few decades, during which time many of the constellations will have changed or been renamed.

are protected by walls twenty feet high, lined with spikes. To our left are the ornamental drain covers, bearing a likeness of Archchancellor William Badger, not a popular man.

And now we should just make our way into this mossy courtyard, criss-crossed with washing lines. Yes, that is what wizards wear *under* their robes . . . what did you expect?

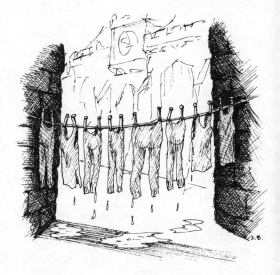

And now here is the University's back door, made of normal wood and with a knocker shaped like a dragon's head.

If you would just follow me through this door, which is used by most of the University's 'normal' visitors, we should find ourselves back in the streets of Ankh-Morpork.

Ah . . . it would seem that the party now includes an extra person, and he smells very strongly of embalming fluid and alcohol . . . those students, eh?

Urglefloggah. A demon. Spawn of the Pit and Loathly Guardian of the Dread Portal. He is over 30,000 years old, has various mouths and has more tentacles

Valkyries. Anthropomorphic personifications, appearing as women dressed in chain mail, with shiny 46D-cup breastplates and helmets with horns on. They are normally associated with BLIND IO and other gods of the thick-necked, celestial rugby-playing persuasion, and their function is to carry off the souls of warriors who have died in battle. These apparently go to some huge hall somewhere and carouse for ever. ('Carouse' belongs to the same vocabulary as 'quaff'; there's a strong suggestion that bread rolls are thrown and a lot of good food ends up on the floor. 'Carouse' offers no possibility of a vegetarian option.) [SM]

Van Pew, Urdo. President of the Guild of Thieves, Burglars and Allied Trades. [GG]

Varneshi. Ox-cart driver in the RAMTOPS. A trader in metals. The only regular contact CARROT's adoptive father had with the outside world, and therefore responsible for some of his old-fashioned views. [GG]

Vassenego, Duke. A demon. One of the oldest demons – if he didn't actually invent original sin, at least he made one of the first copies. He generally takes the form of an old, rather sad lawyer, with an eagle somewhere in his ancestry. [E]

Va Va Voom, Miss. A feather dancer at the Skunk Club, Ankh-Morpork. [SM]

Venturii, Lord. A nobleman in Ankh. [MAA]

Verence I. A past king of LANCRE. Coat of arms: a shield bisected vertically; on the right side an ours, d'or on a field, sable; on the left an ours, sable on a field, or. Seen in the chronicles only as a ghost. Verence I, whose death at the age of forty only marginally slowed him down, was a big, well-muscled man with a moustache and flowing hair. His enviable physical condition meant that he was one of the very few ghosts ever able to manipulate physical objects. [WS]

Verence II. Current King of Lancre. Used to be the court FOOL. An apparently short man, with runny eyes and ears that stick out a bit, he is the most amiable monarch in the history of

LANCRE. He is a great believer in the usefulness of knowledge derived from books. [WA, LL]

Vermine. A small, black-and-white relative of the lemming, found in the cold Hublandish regions, particularly the RAMTOPS. Its pelt is rare and highly valued, especially by the vermine itself; the selfish little bastard will do anything rather than let go of it. The fur is used primarily for trimming robes, especially those of wizards.

It is a more careful relative of the lemming; it only throws itself over small pebbles. The point is that dead animals don't breed and over the millennia more and more vermine are descendants of those vermine who, when faced with a cliff edge, squeal the rodent equivalent of 'Blow that for a Game of Soldiers'. Vermine now abseil down the cliffs and build small boats to cross lakes. When their rush leads them to the seashore they sit around avoiding one another's gaze for a while and then leave early to get home before the rush. [S, WS, RM]

Vernissage. A hat maker in Slice, in the RAMTOPS. [WA]

Vestigial virgins. Found in the temples of a number of Discworld religions, most particularly in those belonging to OM. A vestigial virgin is more easily pictured than described. There is a certain good-natured rumpledness about her, a suggestion that whatever the body has done the mind has remained more or less uninfluenced by it.

Vetinari, Lord. (*See* PATRICIAN, THE.)

Vimes, Samuel, Commander. Captain of the Ankh-Morpork City WATCH. Badge No.177. An upright and honest man whose appointment to the Night Watch

– regarded by all sensible people as a completely useless appendage to the running of the city – may have been the cause of his drinking problem. But it has also been suggested that he is in fact naturally more sober than other people (to put it technically, he is slightly KNURD).

A state of acute sobriety is not one in which a man would like to view the society of Ankh-Morpork and he naturally sought to ameliorate this with a drink or five, and got the number wrong.

It is known that he was born in the SHADES and would have joined the Watch shortly after leaving school had he ever gone to school. Vimes never got the hang of ambition and worked his way sideways rather than up, and his promotion to Captain was simply the result of the sheer unthinkability of promoting any other watchman.

By his own account he is a skinny, unshaven collection of bad habits marinated in alcohol. He is morose, cynical and ridiculously – and to his own embarrassment – soft-hearted in certain circumstances. He is almost certainly one of Nature's policemen; it has been said of him that his soul burns to arrest the Creator of the universe for getting it wrong.

He loathes kings, and hates undead and assassins. He is also unashamedly speciesist – he deeply dislikes trolls and dwarfs, but in an almost proprietorial way, so that he has risked his life and badge to defend them merely so that he can continue to dislike them. He hates the city in the same way; it's his to hate.

Married to Lady Sybil RAMKIN, he was promoted to Commander, and knighted against his will, by the PATRICIAN. [GG, MAA]

Vimes, 'Old Stoneface'. Commander of the City WATCH who beheaded – because no one else would do it – the last King of Ankh-Morpork, LORENZO THE KIND. It is thought that he may well have been a relative of Sam VIMES. This possibility, we suspect, is one secretly cherished by Vimes. [MAA]

Vincent the Invulnerable. Committed suicide by walking into the Mended DRUM and announcing that he was called Vincent the Invulnerable. [SM]

of a rich, golden brown and powerful voice. He wears a ragged jerkin, holey tights and a moth-eaten hat. [WS, LL]

Volfssonssonssonsson, Volf. Volf the Lucky. A youngish Vasung warrior from the Hublands. Since he is never seen alive, and even when dead is a man of many parts, the name is probably misplaced. [SM]

The Dysk Theatre

Vitoller, Mrs. Wife of Olwyn VITOLLER, the actor. An intelligent-looking woman with bottomless reserves of patience and organizational ability. And nimble fingers. [WS]

Vitoller, Olwyn. Manager of a band of strolling players. Large and fat, with an impressive moustache and a nose that might hide successfully in a bowl of strawberries. Aged sixty, he is the owner

Vorbis, Deacon. Head of the QUISITION in Kom, OMNIA. An exquisitor (like an inquisitor, only a lot more so). Well over 6 feet tall, with a mild, aquiline face and a body seemingly just skin stretched over bone. He looks like a normally proportioned person modelled in clay by a child and then rolled out.

His ancestors came from one of the desert tribes; he had dark eyes – not just dark of pupil, but almost black of eyeball. This made it very hard to tell where he was looking, because he was apparently wearing sunglasses under his skin.

Vorbis was bald, as were many of the Church of OM's senior members, but Vorbis was bald by design. He shaved all over. He gleamed. He wore a plain grey hooded robe, under which he wore a singlet with nails sewn into it, and carried a steel-shod staff.

He never raised his voice from a level monotone – a voice like a strip of dull steel. He didn't menace. He didn't threaten. He just gave everyone the feeling that his personal space radiated several yards from his body, so that superiors fifty years his senior felt it necessary to apologize about interrupting whatever it was he might be thinking about. Had he not stayed in the Quisition, he could easily have been an archpriest or even an Iam. But he didn't worry about that kind of trivia.

His goal was to become the Superior Iam of the Church, an ambition he achieved for the space of ten minutes. Possibly the most terrifying thing about him was that he was quite genuinely not ambitious for himself. He believed that he was what the Church needed. [SG]

Vortin. Troll dentist and owner of a diamond warehouse in Ankh-Morpork. [SM]

Vul nut. A re-annual plant. Ghlen Livid is made from the fermented vul nut drink they freeze-distil in the AGATEAN EMPIRE. Vul nut wine is particularly exceptional in that it can mature as many as eight years prior to its seed actually being sown. Vul nut wine is reputed to give certain drinkers an insight into the future which is, from the nut's point of view, the past. [COM]

Vyrt. Brother-in-law to King TEPPICYMON XXVII. An assassin; his probable influence resulted in TEPPIC being sent out of DJELIBEYBI to be educated. [P]

Wa, Cripple. A beggar who frequents the Pearl Dock, Ankh-Morpork. Well renowned for his floating crap game, which occasionally, owing to its closeness to the dock, results in the floating, or at least the gentle bobbing, of participants unmannerly enough to win; he is skilled at switching dice and once diced with DEATH. In person. He has had twenty-three people murdered, but does not consider that this in itself means he is a bad person. [COM, M]

Waggon, Lady Deirdre. Author of a book on etiquette. Very necessary in Ankh-Morpork. In a society that includes professional assassins and thieves, the seating arrangements at dinner can take some very careful working out. [MAA]

Wahoonie. A vegetable that grows only in certain parts of HOWONDALAND, where it typically grows to twenty feet in length, is covered in spikes the colour of earwax, and smells like an anteater that's eaten a very bad ant. Its flavour is prized by connoisseurs and makes everyone else want to be sick. It is banned in many of the cities of the STO PLAINS. Ankh-Morpork is affectionately known as the Great Wahoonie, in the same way that New York is the Big Apple. [MP]

Wallspur. Prophet of the Omnian religion. [SG]

War. Large, jolly anthropomorphic personification, a bit like your old sports teacher in red armour. One of the Four Horsemen. [LF]

Watch, the Ankh-Morpork City. Motto: FABRICATI DIEM, PVNC.

Strength (according to pre-republican records): one commander, five captains, ten sergeants of varying seniority, and a total of forty corporals, lance-corporals, constables and lance-constables, plus a 'city militia' of varying size, depending on need, made up of civilians.

Together these individuals form the Ankh-Morpork police force. It consisted originally of four loosely linked organizations: the Night Watch, the Day Ward (which had more or less the same functions, but the jurisdiction was exchanged at dawn and dusk), the Palace Guard and the Cable Street Particulars.

The Particulars are believed to have been quite an élite force and combined the roles of secret service and government (i.e., whoever was in the palace) office of investigation. They are now quite forgotten and their office building was long ago abandoned; it is currently a dwarf delicatessen. The Palace Guard were (and are) little more than tough men in armour whose job was (and is) to safeguard the life of whoever pays their wages. The Watches were gate guards, kickers of drunks, pursuers of common thieves, traffic controllers, market superintendents and in general the doers of all the tedious jobs of day-to-day city housekeeping.

Taken together they made quite an important body, but the elevation of the THIEVES' GUILD by Lord VETINARI was the final blow to an institution that was already ceasing to have any real function in the city owing to the growth of the Guilds.

For Ankh-Morpork is, in its way, a very democratic place. As it changed from medieval city to the semi-industrialized, multi-species society it is today, there were natural growing pains resulting in a breakdown of law and order and increasing friction between many more-or-less honest citizens and the Watch. This came to a head one day when a Commander of the Watch, faced with a large and angry meeting which was complaining that, what with all this theft and murder and robbery, no one was making as much money as they ought to, warned the throng 'notte to take the law into their owne handes'.

Legend says that the crowd worked this out silently for a minute or two and then, as one man or woman, rose up and threw the Commander into the river, with a chant of 'If it's not in our hands, whose hands is it in?' After that the existing Guilds began to police themselves and the Watch became increasingly irrel-

The Hubward Gate, Ankh-Morpork

evant. Lord Vetinari's decision to put crime itself under Guild control knocked away the last support.

In a city which runs on power politics, one man's view of morality and a legal system that is made up on the fly out of pragmatic decisions pasted together with spit, there was no room for people who go around asking awkward questions and arresting people for no more reason than that they were guilty of something. So the city prospered while the Watches dwindled away, like a useless appendix, into a handful of unemployables whom no one in their right mind could ever take seriously.

The last thing anyone wanted them to do was to get it into their heads to fight crime, and there is some evidence that Lord Vetinari took pains to ensure that the Watch consisted of sad drunks, incompetents and petty criminals too unreliable even to find employment in a Guild.

In the case of the Day Watch (as the old Day Ward has become known) this policy seemed to work extremely well, to the extent that they were pretty much like any other city gang. The Night Watch, such as it was, was too incompetent even to manage criminality. Much of this changed when it was joined by CARROT, who triggered a certain phenomenon: when you throw men down hard enough, they bounce.

By a kind of holy stupidity – they believed that, since they were being paid a handful of dollars per month by the city, they therefore had some kind of duty towards it – the Night Watch saved the city from a serious dragon attack.

The effect on their own morale was astonishing, and Vetinari was subsequently unable to prevent the Watch from taking on fresh recruits. His insistence that the recruits consist of representatives of ethnic minorities was probably – considering the kind of ethnic minorities Ankh-Morpork boasts, such as dwarfs and trolls and undead – another attempt to keep it under control. However, fused into something approaching an efficient police force by the suspiciously king-like charisma of Carrot and the cynicism of Captain VIMES, they played a prominent role in an attempt upon the life of the PATRICIAN (in thwarting it, that is).

This resulted in Captain Vimes being given the resurrected post of Commander of Police, Carrot being promoted to Captain, and a further swelling of the Watch's ranks. Carrot's idea, during a very tense period in the city, of conscripting the leading rioters and more intractable criminals into the ranks of the Watch and the capable paws of Acting-constable DETRITUS ('I cannot believe it what my eyes they seein'. You one horrible watchman. Get down an' give me . . . lots!') was a stroke of genius worthy of Lord Vetinari himself.

Following the dragon incident, which resulted *en passant* in the destruction of the old Watch House in Treacle Mine Road, the Night Watch had been given, by Lady RAMKIN, new premises in Pseudopolis Yard and this is now the official Watch headquarters. There are a number of derelict Watch Houses in other parts of the city and a strong suggestion, in *Men At Arms*, that these would shortly be reopened.

Watch officers' equipment includes a chain-mail shirt, an iron and copper helmet and an iron breastplate. They also wear leather knee breeches and, in wet weather, a leather rain cape. Footwear is sandals in the summer and cheap boots in the winter. It must be pointed out, though, that this is only approximately a uniform. The armour in particular is whatever antiques from the Armoury happen to fit.

At various times they may carry an oak truncheon, an emergency 7-foot pike or halberd, a crossbow, a short sword and, in the traditional night watchman role, an hourglass and a bell. Other weapons known to have been used by watchmen, on the 'first thing I could get my hands on' basis, include a siege bow intended to destroy city walls, a small dragon used as a handgun, and another (smaller) watchman.

Traditionally they carried a simple copper badge of office. In recognition of their efforts in defence of the city (and quite possibly to make sure Captain Carrot continued to devote his energies to the building-up of the Watch, rather than entertaining any ambitions towards ruling the entire city) the Patrician commissioned a splendid new badge, to replace the old copper disc – this has been scorned by Commander Vimes, who retains his old one.

They are known as 'coppers'. Not because of their copper badges, according to Captain Carrot, but from the old word *cappere*, to capture.

Watchtower, Brother. A member of the ELUCIDATED BRETHREN OF THE EBON NIGHT. A bulky man. [GG]

Weasel, the. A small, cunning and brown-clad swordsman. He and BRAVD the Hublander encountered RINCEWIND and TWOFLOWER, and robbed Twoflower of his watch. [COM]

Weatherwax family. Magical aptitude appears to be genetic, and the Weatherwax family (found around the RAMTOPS, particularly in LANCRE) has provided at least two witches of extreme power and one Archchancellor of Unseen University. Unlike the Oggs (a family which traditionally throws up witches but has no recorded wizards) the Weatherwaxes are not gregarious, even amongst themselves.

Weatherwax, Alison. A Weatherwax of whom little is known but who should be included out of completeness and because of the mystery attached to the name.

The registering of births and deaths is not legally compulsory in LANCRE but is invariably done out of social pressure. Even the deaths of former residents a long way off are generally recorded whenever the news turns up, for completeness. It is certain that the birth of an Alison Weatherwax was recorded some 125 years before the present, and equally certain that no death has ever been recorded. This makes it just possible that Granny Weatherwax's own grandmother is still alive, somewhere.

Weatherwax, Esmerelda ('Granny Weatherwax').

In the opinion of many, not least herself, the greatest witch on the Discworld.

Granny Weatherwax is the daughter of Violet Weatherwax, and was initially trained in witchcraft by Nanny Gripes, and subsequently other witches who taught her all they knew, after which she taught herself and was a remarkably apt pupil. Witches rarely acknowledge anything so definite or binding as a law but it is generally accepted that, although witch skills tend to run in families, a witch should be trained by someone who is not a relative and witchcraft certainly should not be passed from mother to daughter.

She is nominally the village witch of BAD ASS in the kingdom of LANCRE, although for practical purposes she regards the whole kingdom – and, indeed, anywhere else she happens to be – as her rightful domain. She lives in the woods outside the village in a traditional, much-repaired witch's cottage, with bee-hives and a patch of what might be medicinal plants called the Herbs (the patch is very thick, tends to move when there is no wind, and passers-by swear that the small flowers it occasionally produces turn to watch them). (*See also* GRANNY'S COTTAGE.)

She owns a broomstick, originally borrowed by an urban witch called Hilta GOATFOUNDER but technically not the same one because it has been entirely replaced over the years by spare parts. Despite the best efforts of dwarf engineers everywhere, it cannot be started without a considerable amount of running up and down with it in gear.

Granny Weatherwax's personal history is obscure, a fact which clearly suits her. It is known that she remained at home when her elder sister, Lily, left Lancre in dubious circumstances, and there is some suggestion of cruelty in the family. She nursed her mother until she died.

Beyond that, the picture is of a formidable character with every necessary attribute for the classical 'bad witch' – a quick temper, a competitive, selfish and ambitious nature, a sharp tongue, an unshakeable conviction of her own moral probity, and some considerable mental and occult powers. In fact, Granny Weatherwax's practical history puts her on the 'good' side of the ledger, in the same way that a cold shower and brisk run are good – they might sting a bit at the time but you'll feel all the better for it later.

Weatherwax, Galder. Supreme Grand Conjurer of the Order of the Silver Star, Lord Imperial of the Sacred Staff, Eighth-Level Ipsissimus and 304th ARCH-CHANCELLOR of Unseen University. An elderly, powerful and impressive-looking man, even dressed as we first saw him in a red night-shirt with hand-embroidered mystic runes (from which bony legs protrude), long cap with a bobble, Wee Willie Winkie candlestick and fluffy pom-pom slippers. He smoked a pipe the size of a small incinerator and was a distant relative of Esme Weatherwax – a cousin, it is believed. [LF]

Weatherwax, Lily. Elder sister of Esmerelda 'Granny' Weatherwax.

A fairy godmother. She was banished from the family home by her mother when she was just thirteen, after which she has had a speckled and profitable career as a witch and lady of fortune. Discworld society, while not generally offering much in the way of opportunity and careers to women, is all the more accessible to a woman of keen intelligence and flexible morality. Three husbands were acquired in the course of her progress; she has buried all three, and at least two of them were already dead.

Give or take the odd laughter-line and wrinkle, she is Granny Weatherwax to the life, although she looks younger than her younger sister. Moralists would say that this is because sin is easier than virtue, but moralists always say this sort of thing and some sin is quite difficult and requires specialized equipment.

She ran the city kingdom of GENUA with a sugary kind of cruelty, and she is an expert at mirror magic, so that she can observe the world through anything that can hold a reflection. This, in a contest with her sister, turned out to be her undoing – Lily had become so good at thinking of the world in terms of reflections that she had lost sight of the real one. She is still referred to in the present tense because, if she has in fact died, there has certainly been no body found.

While (*see* MAGIC) there is no Discworld concept of 'black' magic, the use of magic to steer the lives of other people for your own benefit is regarded in the same way (certainly it is by Granny Weatherwax, except of course on those occasions when it is she who is doing it). Lily is probably a good example of a Discworld 'wicked witch' – the criterion here being less what it is that you do and far more what you had in mind when you did it. [WA]

Weaver. A thatcher in LANCRE. Married to Eva. He is a member of the Lancre Morris Men. [LL]

Weezen. A hunter from Slice, who once

shot a hare in the leg when Granny WEATHERWAX was 'borrowing' it. [LL]

Wheedown, Blert. Author of a guitar primer and a highly skilled maker of guitars. [SM]

Wheels, Gabby. An elderly farm worker who helps with the harvest on Miss FLITWORTH's farm. He hardly ever speaks, and is called, because of that famous sense of humour for which country people are so well known, 'Gabby'. [RM]

Whemper, Goodie. The witch who trained Magrat GARLICK. A great collector of books about MAGIC (she had about twelve, a considerable number for a witch). She was a research witch (*see* RESEARCH WITCHCRAFT) and she died in an accident while testing whether a broomstick could survive having its bristles pulled out one by one in mid-air. The answer, apparently, was 'no'.

Mention of her name is always followed by 'may she rest in peace'. Witches do not follow any religion, but that is no reason, they say, to deny anyone some peaceful rest. [WS, LL]

Whiteface, Dr. Head of the FOOLS' GUILD. He is a white-faced clown – deadpan white make-up, thin mouth painted into a wide grin and delicate black eyebrows. He wears a pointy hat and shiny white clothes. In short, he's the clown all the other clowns are afraid of. Clowns are very possessive about their make-up but remarkably careless of their names (there are vast armies of Joeys and Boffos, for example) and it is very likely that 'Dr Whiteface' is the generic name for the head clown. [MAA]

Whitlow, Mrs. Housekeeper at Unseen University and commander of its below-stairs servant army. She is a very fat woman (restrained by whalebone) with a ginger wig. Her flat in the University is a vision of pink frills. There was presumably a Mr Whitlow once upon a time. She is the subject of some mild undirected fantasies among senior members of the faculty, especially after her behaviour during the craze for Music With Rocks In. [ER, MP, RM]

Wilkins, Mr. He once called Granny WEATHERWAX a domineering old busybody. She made him think he was a frog and there was a lot of trouble until Jason OGG dug a pond for him. [WA]

Willikins. One of VITOLLER's strolling players, who specializes in female roles. Willikins is also the name of Lady RAMKIN's butler. [WS, MAA]

Whiteface, Doctor s.B.

Winkings, Arthur and Doreen. (*See* NOT-FAROUTOE, COUNT AND COUNTESS.)

Wisdom. Wisdom comes from experience. Experience is often a result of lack of wisdom. Wisdom is also a lot wiser the further away it is; any old thing written down by some bald man with lots of Zs and Xs in his name is bound, under this rule, to sound a whole lot wiser than the same thing written down by the man next door.

This applies especially if the putative wise man lives up above the snowline somewhere. No one says: if he's so wise, why isn't he on the beach?

Wistley, Shaker. Boot-fetishist in Creel Springs, near LANCRE. [WA]

Witches and Witchcraft. (*See* WITCHES OF THE DISC, witches by individual name, and extensive entries under MAGIC.)

Witches of the Disc, known. These include:
ANNAPLE, NANNY
Beedle, Granny [M]
Brevis, Gammer [WA]
DEMURRAGE, ALISS
Dismass, Gammer (also known as Old Mother Dismass) [WS, WA]
Filter, Goodie [WS]
GARLICK, MAGRAT
GOATFINDER, HILTA
GOGOL, MRS
Gripes, Nanny [LL]
Grodley, Sister [WS]
HAMSTRING, GOODIE
Heggety, Goody [LL]
Hollow, Desiderata (Mother) [WA]
Hopgood, Millie [WA]
Hopliss, Granny [WA]
Nutley, Gammer [M]
OGG, NANNY
Peavey, Gammer Mabel [WA]
Plumb, Nanny [LL]
Postalute, Granny [LL]
Simmons, Gertie [WA]
Singe, Mrs [WA]

Skibbly, Old Deliria [WA]
Spective, Biddy (known to have been
    the 'trainer' of Nanny Ogg, although in
    many of her more fetching ways
    Nanny Ogg could be said to have taught
    herself) [LL]
Tumult, Gammer [ER]
WEATHERWAX, GRANNY
WEATHERWAX, LILY
WHEMPER, GOODIE
Whitlow, Granny [LF]

Witch's cottage. Although the basic unit
of witchcraft is the witch, the basic *continuous* unit is the cottage. The cottage
may have different incumbents over the
years, but people seeking cow cures and
other items will go to it as much as to
the witch.

A witch's cottage is a very specific
architectural item, to the extent that
'Middle Period Witch' is a recognizable
style. The chimney twists like a cork-
screw. The roof is thatch so old that
small trees flourish in it, the floors are
switchbacks, which creak at night like a
tea clipper in a gale. If at least two walls
aren't shored up with baulks of timber
then it's not a true witch's cottage, but
merely the home of some daft old bat
who reads tea leaves and talks to her cat.

Despite some popular misinformation,
there have been few cottages made out
of gingerbread, a singularly impractical
building material outside those areas
where the high ambient magic can com-
pensate for the tendency of the walls to
go stale and soggy.

Chicken legs (or duck, in swampy
areas) are a popular addition.

The home of Granny WEATHERWAX is
so typical of the type that the more
detailed information found under
GRANNY'S COTTAGE can be taken to apply
to the homes of most witches.

Withel, Stren. In his time, the second-
greatest thief in Ankh-Morpork. A cruel
swordsman and a disgruntled contender
for the title of nastiest man in the world.
He has one eye, and a scar-crossed face,
and he dresses in black (he was thrown
out of the ASSASSINS' GUILD for enjoying
himself too much). [COM]

Withel, Theda. A milkmaid who became
a famous actress in moving pictures. She
was called Ginger by her friends, but
adopted – or at least had adopted on her
behalf – the screen name of Delores de
Syn. She was around 5'2" tall and,
although she was not beautiful, the
magic of moving pictures could give you
real trouble in believing this. The word
'vivacious' springs to mind. Current
whereabouts and occupation unknown,
but they probably do not involve any
kind of livestock. [MP]

Wizards of the Disc, known. Apart from
those named solely as inventors of par-
ticular spells (*see* SPELLS), the wizards of
the Disc include:
Ajandurah [COM]
Arch-Astronomer of Krull [COM]
BILLET, DRUM
Billias, Skarmer [S]
Carding, Marmaric [S]
CATBURY
Changebasket, Skrelt [LF]
Churn, Ezrolith [E]
CUTANGLE
CUTWELL, IGNEOUS
Derment, Gravie [S]
Framer, 'Cucumber' [MP]
Garhartra [COM]
Granpone the White [ER]
GREICHA THE FIRST
Hakardly, Ovin [S]
Henchanse the Unsatysfactory [ER]
Hocksole, 'Scratcher' [RM]
Jeophal the Spry [ER]
MALACHITE, TUBUL DE
Maligree [S]

Marchesa [COM]
Panter, Lemuel [LF]
POONS, WINDLE
PRIME, AUGUSTUS
RIDCULLY, MUSTRUM
RIKTOR
Sconner, Benado [S]
Spelter [S]
SPOLD, GREYHOLD ('Tudgy') [LF]
STIBBONS, PONDER
Teatar, Prissal ('Merry Prankster')
  [RM]
TREATLE

TRYMON, YMPER
Vard, Rhunlet [LF]
Vestcake [COM]
Wayzygoose, Virrid [S]
Wert, Jiglad [LF]
YMITURY, ARCHMAGE OF
(*See also* ARCHCHANCELLORS.)

Wizards' Pleasaunce. A small, newt-haunted meadow in a horseshoe bend in the ANKH near Unseen University. On summer evenings, if the wind is blowing

Granny Weatherwax's cottage

towards the river, it is a nice area for a stroll. Traditionally, wizards are allowed to bathe naked in the river from there. None in recent history has taken advantage of this privilege. [S]

Wonse, Lupine. Former Secretary to Lord VETINARI. Wonse was one of life's subordinates, who rose from his childhood in the SHADES. He was neat, and always gave the impression of just being completed. Even his hair was so smoothed-down and oiled that it looked as though it had been painted on. As the Supreme Grand Master of the ELUCIDATED BRETHREN OF THE EBON NIGHT, he was responsible for the summoning of a great dragon to try and usurp the PATRICIAN. He achieved an accidental death while in WATCH custody owing to the literal-mindedness of the then Lanceconstable CARROT, who threw the book at him. [GG]

de Worde, William. A professional scribe. Ankh-Morpork has a number of these, who will write letters home for you, or draft a petition to the PATRICIAN. William, youngest son of the current Lord de Worde, is less than typical of the great mass of scribes because of two personal inventions.

One is the Standard Letter. Movable type has not yet been invented in Ankh-Morpork (*see* PRINTING); most printing of things like playbiils and posters is done by wood block engravers. It occurred to William ('Thynges Written Downe') de Worde to make use of this facility, because so many of the letters he had to write were so similar.

Take dwarfs, for example. Dwarfs are always coming to seek work in the city, and the first thing they do is send a letter home saying how well they are doing. This is such a predictable occurrence, even if the dwarf in question is so far down on his luck that he is forced to eat his helmet, that de Worde had his regular engraver produce a supply of stock letters which needed only a few spaces filled in to be perfectly acceptable.

Fond dwarf parents all over the mountains now treasure letters that look something like this:

Dear *Mume & Dad*,
    Well, I arrivede here all ryte and I am staying at *109 Cockbill Street The Shades Ankh-Morpk*. Everythnyg is fine. I have got a goode job working for *Mr CMOT Dibbler, Merchant Venturer* and will be makinge lots of monie really soone now. I am rememberinge alle your gode advyce and am notte drinkynge in bars or mixsing with Trolls. Well thats about itte muft goe now, loking forwade to seeing you and *Emelia* agane, your loving son,
        Tomas Brokenbrow

. . . who was actually swaying while he dictated it.

William de Worde's other concept is his 'letter of thynges that have happened'.

The basic idea wasn't new. Many nobles, foreign dignitaries and expatriate Ankh-Morporkians employ scribes to send them regular letters to keep them up to date with city affairs. But, again, William realized that all he needed do was write one letter with suitable spaces to allow for things like 'To my Noble Lord the . . . ', trace it backwards on pieces of boxwood provided for him by the engraver and then pay the said engraver twenty dollars to carefully remove the wood that wasn't letters and make twenty impressions on sheets of paper.

It meant that he could corner the market. Among many others, the Duke of STO HELIT sent him ten dollars a month to do it. The Dowager Duchess of Quirm also sent him ten dollars a month. So did King VERENCE II of Lancre. So did the Seriph of AL KHALI, although in this case the payment was half a shipload of dates, twice a year.

It could well be that the future holds great things for young de Worde . . .

Worrier, Lappet-faced (also known as the Wowhawk, i.e., similar to a goshawk but less forcible). A hawk. Small and short-sighted. It prefers to walk everywhere, and it faints at the sight of blood. It would take several Worriers to kill even a small sick pigeon, and they would probably do it by boring it to death. Peculiar to LANCRE, where it is the hawk that queens are allowed to fly. [LL]

Wow-Wow Sauce. A mixture of mature SCUMBLE, pickled cucumbers, capers, mustard, mangoes, figs, grated WAHOONIE, anchovy essence, asafoetida, sulphur and saltpetre. Much admired by Mustrum RIDCULLY, current ARCHCHANCELLOR of Unseen University.

Wow-Wow Sauce is one of those entities which, like chess, has an existence that spans worlds and dimensions. On Earth it was pioneered by Dr William Kitchiner (1775–1827), although without the grated wahoonie and several of the more explosive ingredients.

The only condiment more dangerous than Wow-Wow Sauce is the rare Three Mile Island salad dressing.

WOW-WOW SAUCE
The Off-Discworld Version
Unlike Mustrum Ridcully's more explosive creation, this is not very hot and can safely be eaten near a naked flame.

Butter or, for non-wizards, the substitute of choice, a lump about the size of an egg
plain flour, 1 tablespoon
beef stock, ½ pint
English mustard, 1 teaspoon
white wine vinegar, 1 dessertspoon
port, 1 tablespoon
mushroom concentrate, 1 tablespoon
freeze-dried parsley, 1 heaped tablespoon

pickled walnuts, chopped, 4
salt, freshly ground black pepper, to taste

Melt the butter or butter substitute in a saucepan. Stir in the flour and work in the beef stock. Stir continuously on a moderate heat until you have a smooth, thick sauce.

Stir in the made-up mustard, the wine vinegar, the port and the mushroom concentrate. Add a sprinkling of salt and freshly ground black pepper, and continue to cook the mixture for about 10 minutes.

Add the parsley and the walnuts; warm them through, and serve.

This sauce, when added to roast beef, will earn a vote of thanks from the ghost of the steer. We are unable to comment on its keeping qualities – the question has never arisen.

There are a number of recipes for Wow-Wow Sauce. Its apparent inventor, Dr Kitchiner, used pickled cucumbers and capers in preference to the walnuts – we felt they obscured some of the delicate flavours. But feel free to experiment. Worcestershire Sauce has been suggested as a substitute for the mushroom concentrate and port, but some of the delicacy of the flavour might again be lost. Big changes in the taste of the sauce can be made by quite small variations in the proportions of the vinegar and the mustard – generally, the higher the proportion of wine vinegar the sharper and more piquant the sauce (a tarter version can be made by increasing the wine vinegar to a tablespoonful and reducing the mustard to half a teaspoon).

Dr Kitchiner, incidentally, would have been welcome at Unseen University. He was in the habit of travelling with his own invention, the 'portable magazine of taste'; this consisted of twenty-eight bottles of favoured condiments, such as essence of celery, pickled cucumbers and, of course, the sauce.

For those brave souls who, in the age of the microwave dinner, wish to get the whole thing right we offer this recipe for mushroom concentrate (there are many others):

Put about six large button mushrooms into a bowl and sprinkle on some salt. Leave them for about three hours and then mash them. Cover the bowl and leave overnight. Drain off the liquid into a saucepan (energetically straining off the mushroom pulp through a sieve will extract more of the liquid). Boil, stirring all the while, until the volume is reduced by about a half. This should produce about a tablespoon of the essence for your sauce.

Wuffles. Lord VETINARI's pet dog. A small, toothless and exceedingly elderly wire-haired terrier with a bristly stub of a tail, who smells bad and wheezes at people. He also has halitosis. [S]

Wxrthltl-jwlpklz. Demon summoned by Granny WEATHERWAX, Nanny OGG and Magrat GARLICK. [WS]

Wyrmberg, the. A mountain that rises almost one half of a mile over the green valley where it stands. It is huge, grey and upside-down. At its base it is a mere score of yards across. Then it ascends through a clinging cloud, curving gracefully outward like an upturned trumpet until it is truncated by a plateau fully a quarter of a mile across.

There is a tiny forest up there, its greenery cascading over the lip. There are buildings and a lake. There is even a small river, tumbling over the edge in a waterfall so wind-whipped that it reaches the ground as rain. There are also a

number of cave mouths, a few yards below the plateau. They have a crudely carved, regular look about them. The Wyrmberg hangs over the clouds like a giant's dovecote.

The rock contains many corridors and rooms. In its hollow heart is a great cavern where the DRAGONS – the Wyrms – roost. Sunbeams from the myriad entrances around the walls criss-cross the dusty gloom like amber rods in which a million golden insects have been preserved. In the upturned acres of the cavern roof are thousands of walking rings, which have taken a score of masons a score of years to hammer home the pitons for. These rings are used with hook boots to walk across the ceiling. There are also eighty-eight major rings clustered near the apex of the dome – huge as rainbows, rusty as blood. Below are the distant rocks of the cavern floor, discoloured by centuries of dragon droppings.

The dragons themselves are clearly *Draco nobilis*, who have a permanent existence here because of the extremely high level of residual magic in the vicinity (surviving in much the same way as certain deep sea creatures survived in the presence of a warm-water vent in the sea bed). [COM]

Xeno. An Ephebian philosopher and author of *Reflections*. Small, fat and florid, with a short beard. [P, SG]

Xxxx. A fabled hidden continent, somewhere near the Rim. It reputedly contains a lost colony of wizards who wear corks around their pointy hats and live on nothing but prawns. There, it is said, the light is still wild and fresh as it rolls in from space, and the wizards surf on the boiling interface between night and day.

It is believed that Xxxx has been the subject of at least two expeditions from Ankh-Morpork; the first, several thousand years ago, was led by a sourcerer and the second, some five hundred years before the present, has never been heard of since. The few stories that filtered back, telling of giant leaping rats, ducks with fur, no wings and four feet, and huge flightless chickens, suggest that the place may be entirely mythical . . . [RM]

Tezuman temple

259

Yen Buddhists. The richest religious sect in the universe. They hold that the accumulation of money is a great evil and a burden to the soul. They therefore, regardless of personal hazard, see it as their unpleasant duty to acquire as much as possible in order to reduce the risk to innocent people. Many major religions, after all, stress that poverty is a stand-by ticket to salvation. [WA]

Ymitury, Archmage of. A powerful wizard, parted from his staff, his belt of moon jewels and his life, by the WEASEL and BRAVD the Hublander. Ymitury does not feature in the records of Unseen University, and in any case any wizard who could be tricked out of his staff by a couple of wandering mercenaries probably did not deserve to have it in the first place; it is likely he was some sort of charlatan or possibly even a foreigner. [COM]

Ymor. The greatest thief in Ankh-Morpork, and one of the last independent gang leaders to merge with the THIEVES' GUILD. His headquarters were in the leaning tower at the junction of Rime Street and Frost Alley. [COM]

Ynci the Short-Tempered. Apparently a past queen of LANCRE A beefy young woman sporting a winged, spiked helmet and a mass of black hair plaited into dreadlocks with blood as a setting lotion. She was heavily made up in the woad-and-blood-and-spirals school of barbarian cosmetics. She wore a 42D-cup breastplate and shoulder plates with spikes. She had knee pads with spikes on, spikes on her sandals and a rather short skirt in the fashionable tartan and blood motif. She carried a double-headed battle-axe. Her war pony was called Spike.

In the strictest sense, she never existed. She was invented by King LULLY I of Lancre because he thought the kingdom needed a bit of romantic history. But she has an official portrait in LANCRE CASTLE's Long Gallery, some armour in its armoury (in fact made by one of the OGG family at the King's instruction), and she features prominently (because of that breastplate) in Birdwhistle's *Legendes and Antiquities of the Ramtops*; there is therefore rather more evidence of her existence than most people leave behind them; in these circumstances actual reality is more or less irrelevant. [LL]

Yob Soddoth. An outer-dimensional monster, recognizable from his distinctive cry: 'Yerwhatyerwhatyerwhat'. [MP]

You Bastard. A camel. The greatest mathematician in the world. The origin of his name lies in the fact that camels believe that they really are called whatever it is people say to them most often. [P]

You Vicious Brute. A camel. Created the Theory of Transient Integrals, and spent most of his life carrying a man who could count to twenty only because he wore sandals. [P]

Yoyo, de. The de Yoyos are a noble family with a seat near Pseudopolis. Their fortunes have risen and fallen regularly. Perhaps this is why they have produced many explorers and adventurers, who have discovered obscure areas of the Disc hitherto known only to natives, peasants and other people whose opinions are too insignificant to count. The head of the family is titled the Compte de Yoyo; the current head, Guy de Yoyo, is a lecturer at the ASSASSINS' GUILD (Modern Languages and Music). He is certainly a great traveller; he was a guest at the famous Samedi Nuit Mort Ball in GENUA. [WA]

Ysabell. DEATH's adopted daughter. When first introduced, she was a sixteen-year-old young woman with silver hair, silver eyes and a slight suggestion of too many chocolates. Not, of course, a blood relation to the Grim Reaper – no real explanation has been given as to why he saved her as a baby when her parents were killed in the Great NEF.

It says a lot for Ysabell's basic mental stability that she remained even halfway sane in Death's house, where no time passes and black is considered the appropriate colour for almost everything. She certainly developed an obsessive interest in tragic heroines and also a fixation for the colour pink.

She married MORT and became Duchess of Sto Helit. [LF, M, GG]

Zacharos. A blacksmith used by URN and Sergeant SIMONY to help build the Disc's first 'tank'. [SG]

Zemphis. Walled town on the ANKH. It lies at the junction of three trade routes (apart from the river itself), and is built around one enormous square, which is a cross between a permanent exotic traffic jam and a tent village. [ER]

Zen. A sub-sect of the Klatchian philosophical system of SUMTIN, noted for its simple austerity and the offer of personal tranquillity and wholeness achieved through meditation and breathing techniques; an interesting aspect is the asking of apparently nonsensical questions in order to widen the doors of perception. Learning how to beat six heavily armed opponents with your bare hands while occasionally doing unnecessary backward somersaults does not, strangely enough, appear to be in the introductory teachings. [WS]

Zephilite, Brother. Brother Zephilite of KLATCH left his vast estates and his family and spent his life ministering to the sick and poor on behalf of the invisible god F'rum. He did many good works, was kind to animals, was renowned for his piety, simple wisdom and generosity, and all in all certainly magnified the name of a god generally considered unable, should he have a backside, to find it with both hands, should he have hands. It is a sad fact that gods often don't deserve their believers. [S]

Zodiac. There are sixty-four signs in the Disc zodiac. These have included:

Celestial Parsnip, the
Cow of Heaven, the
Flying Moose, the
Gahoolie the Vase of Tulips
Knotted String, the
Mubbo the Hyena
Okjock the Salesman
Perhaps Gate, the
Small Boring Group of Faint Stars, the
Two Fat Cousins, the
Wezen the Double-Headed Kangaroo

It would be more correct to say that there are *always* sixty-four signs in the Discworld zodiac *but* also that these are subject to change. Stars immediately ahead of the Turtle's line of flight change their position only very gradually, as do the ones aft. The ones at right angles, however, may easily alter their relative positions in the lifetime of the average person, so there is a constant need for an updating of the Zodiac. This is done for the STO PLAINS by Unseen University, but communications with distant continents (who in any case have their own

The Knotted String

interpretations of the apparent shapes in the sky) are so slow that by the time any constellation is known Disc-wide it has already gone past. This does at least mean that astrology on the Disc is a dynamic thing and not a repository for some rather unimaginative mythology, but it does rather reduce the science to something on the lines of 'Look! There! No, *there*! Where I'm pointing! *There!* Doesn't that look like a crab to you? Oh, too late, you've missed it.'

Zoon, Amschat B'hal. A liar (*see* ZOONS). Bearded and tanned and dressed like a gypsy; he has a lot of gold teeth and hands heavy with rings. He runs and owns a barge which trades up and down the ANKH. He lives on the barge with his three wives and three children. [ER]

Zoons. 'You can always trust a Zoon,' they say. They are an absolutely honest race; the average Zoon can no more tell a lie than breathe underwater. There is no physical reason for this fact. It simply seems that most Zoons cannot grasp the idea that something may be described as other than what it is. This is a drawback in a trading race, so once the Zoons discovered the essential role played by mendacity, the tribal elders began to encourage likely young Zoons to bend the truth ever further on a competitive basis.

They introduced the office of tribal Liar, which is subject to much competition. (The Zoons' most famous liar was Rolande Pork, with 'My Grandfather Is Seventeen Feet Tall'.) The Liar represents the tribe in all its doings with the outside world. [ER]

Zorgo. A retrophrenologist in Knuckle Passage, Ankh-Morpork. [MAA]

Zweiblumen, Jack. Name applied to TWOFLOWER when, because of a brief dimensional crossover, he found himself on an aircraft instead of a dragon. He wore britches which ended just above his knees and a vest of brightly striped material, plus a little straw hat with a feather in it. For an explanation of the phenomenon, *see* RJINSWAND. [COM]

A BRIEF HISTORY OF DISCWORLD

In late 1983 Colin Smythe Ltd, a small press publisher, published *The Colour of Magic*. It sold quite well and impressed Corgi Books sufficiently for them to publish the paperback in January 1985.

But they nearly *didn't* publish it. They *liked* it; they just weren't sure where its market was. In the end they went ahead with quite a large initial print run of 25,000. They had to reprint very soon afterwards.

The book was published without hype and without any special publicity. And it started to sell simply by word of mouth. Roger Peyton of Andromeda Books, one of the country's leading sf and fantasy bookstores, recalls: 'When the Corgi rep showed me the cover and blurb for *The Colour of Magic* I had a gut feeling that this would be big and I asked if there was any chance of a signing session. The rep said, "How many books will you take, then?" and I said, "We'll take a hundred minimum." The staff said that I was mad, that earlier Pratchett books had been remaindered*, but I said, "I'm the boss . . . do it . . ."'

'In the first year, it was our number 2 best seller of the year, and Terry stayed in our top four for the next two years. He only started to move out of that position when his books became so widely available that fans no longer needed to come to specialist shops to get them.'

And Terry Pratchett recalls his first signing session there or, more accurately, standing before the cashier of a filling station on the way home practising his signature until he could bring it back to something resembling the one on his Access card.

* *Strata* and *The Dark Side of the Sun*, which in later editions have been selling buoyantly for years. Strange are the ways of bookselling.

A year later a second book, *The Light Fantastic*, was published by Smythe. Its sales were so good that he realized that he had on his hands something a small publisher does not necessarily welcome – a bestselling author. There was, both recall, some amicable discussion, and Terry Pratchett moved to Gollancz, who became his hardcover publisher; Colin Smythe became his agent.

The books came out in a sequence that has settled down to two a year. The fourth in the series, *Mort*, went to No. 2 in the national bestseller lists. Every other book since then has made it into the lists, in hardcover or paperback or, usually, both.

Pratchett still remained, though, a best-known unknown author. All across the country parents were curious to see what it was their children found so amusing; in offices people would tell bemused colleagues: 'Look, there's this world on the back of a giant turtle, and Death rides a white horse called Binky and – look, I'll loan you this copy, all right?'

Then the books began to be reviewed, usually very favourably. And bookshops found that they were hard to keep in stock. And librarians started to write to the author – he treasures comments like, 'What is so marvellous is that you get people into the library so that we can introduce them to real books.'

It is hard to distil the secret of Discworld. The books are funny. The early ones are *simply* funny, containing everything from subtle wordplay to unashamed antique jokes, the written equivalent of custard pies. As the series progresses, the stories become more complex. The humour is still there, but so are many other things. There is no central character in the series, although Death – a sort of Bergmanesque figure who is totally bemused by the antics of the human race, and who is oddly comforting – appears in every book and stars* in several.

The world itself is absurd. It is flat and round and rests on the back of four elephants, which are themselves carried through space on the back of a giant turtle. It just happens also to be firmly rooted in our planetary mythology. It is a subset of one of the great world myths, found in Australia before Cook, and North America before Columbus and in Bantu legend. The human race appears predisposed to believe that the world is flat and rides on a turtle.

In fact the actual mechanics of the world seldom feature in the books. After the first two or three they are about people, even if those people are not always human, or even two-legged. Or even alive.

---

* Terry Pratchett's own term; he often talks about his books as if they are films.

There are certain themes. There is a certain quiet optimism. If there is a struggle, the good win – but not easily and often at some cost. There is a strong dislike of coercion of people, either by other people or gods or some concept of Fate or Destiny. There's a very frequent theme which says that what people happen to be *doing* does not define what they actually *are*. In the memorable words of Granny Weatherwax, one of Pratchett's most well-observed characters and the one who most probably speaks his mind: 'Where people stand is not as important as which way they face.'

These are simple enough messages, and they echo the folk and fairy tales at which Pratchett often takes a fresh and sideways look.

But people won't tell you about this. They'll tell you about the Luggage, a box on hundreds of little legs which will follow its adopted owner anywhere. Or they'll enthuse about the Librarian of Unseen University, who is both an orang-utan and one of the most popular characters despite a vocabulary consisting of 'ook' (librarians have been known to wear 'Librarians Rule Ook' badges and write to Terry Pratchett congratulating him on having raised the status of the profession).

And nearly all of them will talk at length about Death. He gets fan mail. It is easy to see why. The Death of Discworld is not some rotting Gothic figure (despite *Mort* winning an award from the Dracula Society as Best Gothic Novel of the Year – at an annual dinner which included, with marvellous Discworld appropriateness, a Vegetarian Option). He is at once tragic and funny. While Terry Pratchett declares himself to be an atheist of the old-fashioned, angry-with-God-for-not-existing kind, the fact that his deceased characters often have conversations with Death and sometimes take an active part in the rest of the plot suggests a secret belief that death is, indeed, only a milestone – although, as they would say on the Discworld, one that is dropped on you from a very great height.

One critic declared that the success of the series was due to 'a snug mindfit of opinion between writer and reader'. It was meant nastily, but shorn of its spiteful spin it is probably a key comment. Whatever he is as a novelist or a writer, Pratchett is a superb storyteller and showman – he lures you inside, moves you along, and gently shows you the way, at the other end, to that most interesting of sights: the egress. While it is true that he writes primarily because he wants to, and to please himself, it is clear that he knows his audience. He knows when to move the soft-hearted almost to tears, and when to step sideways and introduce the clowns (although, come to think of it, Discworld clowns would probably cause further tears). He is a master of the double laugh – the first laugh is at the joke, the second one, a few seconds later, is at the *other* joke which is revealed as the first one sinks in.

So far the Discworld is almost entirely a written thing, but it is evolving. There have been a couple of graphic novels based on the first two books (and one of *Mort* is on the way), and the books are being taped. There has been a Radio 5 dramatization of *Guards! Guards!*, and before that some readings of the books (in the great days of 'Woman's Hour'; since the name Terry is more or less unisex the perceived strong feminist slant of *Equal Rites* meant that he got mail which, despite his beard and baldness, assumed he was female). A computer game is being written. So (at the time of writing) is an album of Discworld music. The books are a great attraction to amateur dramatics groups.

And there have been film offers. As Terry Pratchett says, there are *always* film offers, either from people with sense and no money, or money and American citizenship. But too many of the approaches suggest that they don't really understand what the books are about, and maybe never could, and just want to acquire rights because they've heard it's a property. He gets things on the lines of 'Wow, we'd love to do *Mort*, it's fantastic, it's high concept, but we think Americans will have a problem with Death so we'll leave him out, OK?' He tends to resist them – 'a man can only eat so many lunches at the Groucho Club' – partly because of the implied suggestion that a book only becomes real when it is filmed. There is a strong suggestion in his conversation, and in the gruelling signing tours he seems to think are part of the authorial after-sales service, that he really respects the one-on-one link between writer and reader, that feeling that all the truly successful cult books engender – that *you* are the only reader, that it's really only being fully appreciated by *you*. When you can get a million people all thinking that, you're working some kind of magic.

The Discworld books are full of allusions, parodies and what Pratchett calls 'resonances'. He has created a whole spurious physics to explain why this is. He gets a lot of letters on the subject of 'narrative causality' – the suggestion that some things happen because of the sheer pressure of the Story itself. Urban myths, according to the theory of narrative causality, are not always just good stories that get constantly repeated as happening 'to a friend of a friend'; they are little coils of free narrative which latch on to human history and get themselves repeated, time and again. As he tells it, he made it up and it is not true.

But he looks uneasy when he says this, as if he suspects that it might not be the case.

All the Stage's a World . . .

Almost as frequent as requests to buy the film rights to a Discworld book are requests to *stage* Discworld. The author shows far more enthusiasm for these, because quite often the things happen, there's no money sloshing around to make everything difficult, and people don't insist on taking him out to lunch.

Oxford's Studio Theatre Club was the first.

We had a theatre that would seat ninety people. We had a stage about the size of a pocket handkerchief with the wings of Tinkerbell. Put on a Discworld play? Simple . . .

A flat, circular world borne through space on the backs of four enormous elephants who themselves stand on the carapace of a cosmically large turtle? Nothing to it. A 7-foot skeleton with glowing blue eyes? *No* problem. A 60-foot fire-breathing dragon? A cinch. (And, in fact, it was – it is strange but true that *huge* unstageable effects are always easy to stage. Give any technician experienced in the ways of the amateur stage a choice between devising the destruction of a city by a volcano or getting a simple throat mike to work reliably, and I know which one he'd choose . . .)

The Studio Theatre Club had already staged my adaptations of other works: two by the Monty Python team and two of Tom Sharpe's books. We were looking for something new when someone said 'Try Terry Pratchett – you'll like him.'

Wyrd Sisters sold out.

So did *Mort* the year after.

So did *Guards! Guards!* the year after that. In fact, 'sold out' is too modest a word; we had under-estimated the pulling-power of Discworld. 'Oversold very quickly' is nearer the mark. 'Embarrassingly full up so that by the time the local newspaper mentioned it was on we'd had to close the booking office' is about right.

The cast were all happy enough to read whichever book we were staging, and to read others in the canon too. The books stand on their own, but some knowledge of the wider Discworld ethos helps when adapting the stories, and helps the actors with their characterizations. It's almost imposs-ible to play a Discworld main character properly unless you've read the books in which they appear. An adapter, too, needs to have read all the books. Fortunately, this is no hardship.

Terry writes very good dialogue. Not all authors do. But Terry, like Dickens, writes stuff which you can lift straight into your play. His dialogue is a world away from the 'As you know, your father, the king –' plots-R-us school of narration. It is seldom used to directly propel the plot; it is far more often used to quietly shape character and background and, incidentally, make people laugh.

I invite experienced Discworld readers to think of the 'She gave me a bun' dialogue between the Sergeant and Duke Felmet in *Wyrd Sisters*, the 'secret password' scene with Brother Fingers in *Guards! Guards!*, and the conversation between Mort and Abbott Lobsang in *Mort*. These were all show stoppers – the Elucidated Brethren scenes in *Guards! Guards!* were a gift to the actors and the highlights of the play.

Whatever special effects you can manage to conjure up on top of that are bonuses.

Since the Studio Theatre Club started the trend in 1991, the UK has seen a number of productions of *Mort* – one done by three people! Enquiries about staging the books have come from as far afield as California, New Zealand and Australia (as well as Croydon, New Malden and Purley).

So how did our productions actually go? We enjoyed them. Our audiences seemed to enjoy them (after all, some of them were prepared, year after year, to travel down to Abingdon in Oxfordshire from as far afield as Darlington, Newcastle-upon-Tyne, Nottingham, Basingstoke and . . . well, Oxford). Terry seemed to enjoy them, too. He said that many of our members looked as though they had been recruited straight off the streets of Ankh-Morpork. He said that several of them were born to play the 'rude mechanicals' in Vitoller's troupe in *Wyrd Sisters*. He said that in his mind's eye the famous Night Watch of Ankh-Morpork *are* the players of the Studio Club Theatre.

I'm sure these were meant to be compliments.

The Seriously Cunning Artificer

In 1980 Bernard Pearson was drummed out of the local constabulary for operating a pottery kiln in the cells of his police station, thus rather neatly giving extra meaning to the term 'jug', and running a craft shop in the local village in police time. He was reduced to living in a caravan and was working away in his pottery when a female voice asked, 'Do you do pottery lessons?' Bernard turned, looked, fell in love and lied, 'Yes,' he said. He then maintained the fiction of a pottery class by press-ganging his drinking cronies into turning up on Wednesday nights to pretend to learn pottery so that Bernard could build up to asking the girl out.

Bernard married Isobel in 1981 and they set up Clarecraft (their workshop was in Clare, Suffolk).

They were the first to start making dragons and fantasy figures. So ahead of their time were they that they were once evicted from a craft fair in a church hall in Norfolk – local fundamentalists thought their witch, wizard and dragon figures were 'creatures of Satan'.

Then came the watershed in their career. In 1990, someone handed Bernard a novel by Terry Pratchett and asked whether he thought he could make some of the characters. Isobel did a lot of research, ploughing through the books and noting every reference to each character's appearance and personality. Bernard and Isobel took along the first Rincewind and Twoflower to a meeting with Terry Pratchett in a café in Covent Garden where, to the accompaniment of a nearby brass band, they were presented for inspection. Bernard recalls that Terry Pratchett seemed to like them, and could only be persuaded to give them back the prototype Librarian when they promised him an ice cream. With a chocolate flake.

The first 'production' model goes off to Terry Pratchett. Sometimes things falter at this stage . . .

The whole process, though, is amicable. If a figure can be proven wrong 'according to the book' it is changed – because if it *is* wrong, then it's just another fantasy figure. And the people who buy the figures tend to be the *keen* readers, who notice details.

Marketing, in the early days, was an interesting experience. It began when the books were just breaking out into the mainstream. Shops hadn't heard of Discworld but took a trial order anyway. One shopkeeper, in a town where delicate figurines are a more usual item, phoned up to say reproachfully 'Now my shop's full of *Hell's Angels*.'

He meant young people.

Other Projects

At the time of writing there are two further Discworld spin-offs – the computer game and the 'concept album'. It won't be the first computer game, although it will probably be the first to sell in any quantity. *The Colour of Magic* game, written by Fergus O'Neill of Delta Four for such cutting-edge machines as the ZX Spectrum, was published in the mid-1980s. Alas, the company involved did not have C.M.O.T. Dibbler's marketing skills, although there are a few thousand copies out there somewhere.

Since then various other companies have tried to get through the Pratchett iron will on the subject but, mindful of the way the first attempt disappeared into the void, he refused to release rights unless he could be certain the game would be published by someone with a track record or, as he put it, 'at least someone I've heard of'.

Out of something akin to superstition, he isn't too keen to talk in much detail about either project until they've actually happened.

Discworld, designed by Gregg Barnett and the team at TWG Ltd, will be launched by Psygnosis for (initially) the PC towards the end of 1994.

There are encouraging signs – the company asked for a proof copy of the Ankh-Morpork Map because, although they were not intending to follow it on a street-by-street basis, they wanted to make sure that two distant parts of the city in the books weren't cheek by jowl in the game. Terry says: 'It's a long way from being finished but it does look as though they're trying for a proper Discworld feel. They'd even based their Librarian on Josh Kirby's cover drawing for *Sourcery* until I pointed out that, skilled though he is, Josh at that time in his career was under-achieving in the orang-utan drawing department and had drawn a chimp.'

From the Discworld, a sort of Discworld theme album, should already be out when this Companion is on sale. It is a mainly instrumental collection written by Dave Greenslade, a long-time friend probably best known for the *Pentateuch* double-album in the early eighties and these days, says Terry, 'the man they call on when they want a new TV theme'.

'It's a shot in the dark. He wanted to do it. I said fine, why not? It's his project, though – I felt enough of an idiot making the suggestions I *did* make, because most of the time I hadn't got the faintest idea of the terminology or what was possible. It was an education watching the tracks being put together. What can I say? I hope it works for people . . . '

The Language Barrier: *'It's All Klatchian To Me.'*

The Discworld books are translated into eighteen languages, including Japanese and Hebrew. They present astonishing pitfalls for the translator.

The problems are not (just) the puns, of which there are rather fewer than people imagine. In any case, puns are translatable; they might not be *directly* translatable, but the Discworld translators have to be adept at filleting an English pun from the text and replacing it with one that works in German or Spanish.

What can loom in front of a translator like the proverbial radio on the edge of the bathtub of the future are the resonances and references.

Take Hogswatchnight, the Discworld winter festival. It's partly a pun on 'hogswash', but also takes in 'Hogmanay' and the old Christian 'Watch Night' service on 31 December. Even if people don't directly spot this, it subconsciously inherits the *feel* of a midwinter festival.

Or there's the Morris Minor. To a Britisher 'an old lady who drives a Morris Minor' – and there's still a few of both around – is instantly recognizable as a 'type'. You could probably even have a stab at how many cats she has. What's the Finnish equivalent? The German equivalent?

Translators in the science fiction and fantasy field have an extra problem. Sf in particular is dominated by the English – or at least the American – language. Fans in mainland European and Scandinavian countries *must* read in English if they're to keep up with the field. This means that a foreign translator is working under the eyes of readers who're often buying the book to see how it compares with the English version they already have.

Ruurd Groot has the daunting task of translating not only the plot but also the jokes in the Discworld series into Dutch. Translating a pun is difficult but not impossible, he says, as long as it is a pun in the strict 'linguistic' sense: making fun by crossing the semantic and formal wires of words or expressions. And even when it proves impossible to invent an equivalent pun for the destination language, a deft translator may solve the problem by 'compensating' – introducing a pun for another word somewhere else in the sentence in such a way that the value of the original pun is restored.

Strangely, the similarity of the English and Dutch languages is not always helpful. Many Dutch words and expressions have been borrowed from English and, of course, the same thing has happened in reverse, especially in the sixteenth and seventeenth centuries; the English word 'forlorn', for example, comes from the Dutch *verloren* = 'lost'. The side effect of this circumstance is that many Dutch readers of Terry's original English text do not always catch what he really wrote; words may *look* familiar, but meanings have changed with time.

In *The Colour of Magic*, Terry refers to the '*Big Bang* hypothesis'. Sadly for Ruurd, the erotic Bang-pun proved untranslatable. In Dutch, the theory translates as *oerknal*, which provides no hand-holds. However, they do refer to *het uitdijend heelal* – 'the expanding universe'. Ruurd altered this slightly to the *het Uitvrijend* Model – sounding much the same – and which could be taken to mean 'the Making Love Outwards Model'. When the author heard this he apparently sat there grinning and saying it's the best-ever title for a scientific theory.

Much more difficult is the translation of jokes on local traditions or institutions well known to English readers. And there are special considerations here. Dutch readers of some sophistication (as readers of TP tend to be, it goes without saying) would never accept substituting a reference to a Dutch television series for a similar reference to a BBC serial.

Brits may blithely assume that everyone knows about morris dancing or 'A' levels, but it is the experience of the Dutch that most foreigners' knowledge of their country tends to run out somewhere south of the cheese, clogs and windmills department. Strangely enough, to a Dutch reader a reference to strictly Dutch ephemera would be jarring; they couldn't imagine someone in Britain, let alone on the Discworld, being aware of them. Sad but true.

Translators for 'large' nationalities – German, French, and so on – can maintain the fiction that everyone else is German or French and just localize the jokes in question. 'Small' nationalities have to replace little items of English/British arcana by references to globally known international, or more famous English, items. On the Discworld, that most international, or rather interstellar, of locations, strictly English or British references are allowed in a Dutch translation only if they are globally known – like the works of Shakespeare in *Wyrd Sisters*.

Ruurd could rely on the fact that many Dutch people know Shakespeare, if only from television – played by British actors and subtitled in Dutch. But in *Moving Pictures*, problems for the translator exceeded all reasonable proportions. The films referred to in the book are well enough known, but the average Dutch reader might not recognize many of the translated quotations from the dialogues.

In that case, he says, a translator can rely on a harmless version of snob appeal. If someone doesn't know or recognize something, the translator can write in a tone as if anyone reading it of course will know all and . . . it turns out that they do . . .

'IK WEET NIET WAT JIJ ERVAN VINDT, MAAR EEN BORD ROTTI ZOU ER WEL INGAAN.'

This is the closest that Ruurd could get to Death's line from *Mort*: 'I DON'T KNOW ABOUT YOU, BUT I COULD MURDER A CURRY.' A line for line translation here is impossible: a different colonial past means that 'curry' is not a household word in Holland. Also '. . . I could murder a . . .' in the sense of 'I could really enjoy a . . .' makes no sense in Dutch.

Casting aside the avoidance of 'localized' Dutch expressions on this occasion, Ruurd opted for 'rotti'. It is a near-funny word in itself, having the same echo of 'rotten' as it would in English. It belongs to the Surinam culinary tradition – Surinam having been a small Dutch colony in South America. 'Rotti', like curry, is very hot stuff. Its mention in the context, with the vague implication that Surinam is cosmically more famous than the Netherlands, helps to replace for the Dutch reader some of the fun lost during translation.

Granny Weatherwax, on the other hand, presents no problems (at least, not yet: as Ruurd says, translators of a series have to try to avoid painting themselves into a corner). Her name translates more literally into Opoe Esmee Wedersmeer, although Weerwas would be more direct. *Weder* is ye olde form of the word *weer*, meaning 'weather'. The *smeer* part is a word used for greasy substances as applied to shoes or cart axles, but also for the stuff secreted in our ear passages (earwax = *oorsmeer*). There is an etymological link with the English word 'smear'. Ruurd felt that the ordinary word in Dutch for 'wax' – *was* – seemed less suitable, as being too ordinary.

'Esmee' is, as in English, short for Esmerelda, and *Opoe* is an obsolete endearing way of addressing grandmothers in Dutch. The term is still used to refer to certain old-fashioned ladies' bikes – *opoefietsen* = 'granny bikes'.

This has overtones of the 'Morris Minor' . . . you see? They have one after all . . .

TERRY PRATCHETT:
THE DEFINITIVE INTERVIEW

Terry Pratchett is deceptively easy to interview. He is also skilled at deflecting personal enquiries, keeping Terry Pratchett the ebullient author carefully separated from Terry Pratchett the rather private person.

It is known that he was born in Beaconsfield, Bucks. He is forty-six. His parents are David and Eileen Pratchett, to whom he offers grateful thanks for 'pointing me in the right direction and just letting me get on with it. They took the view that if I was reading, that was all right.'

He worked in regional journalism for many years, and spent eight years as a press officer for what was then the Central Electricity Generating Board. He left when the income from his books made a day job ridiculous.

He is married to Lyn and has one daughter, Rhianna. And that is about it. Everything else to do with his life is referred to lightly in the hope that the interviewer won't detect, in the stream of words, that there are no actual biographical facts.

But about Discworld, he will talk at length:

*I know you get asked this all the time, but we still have to ask it here . . .
in your own words, where did Discworld come from?*

I used to say that the basic myth that the world is flat and goes through space on the back of a turtle is found on all continents – some school kids recently sent me a version of it I hadn't run across before. And once you get into Indo-European mythology you get the elephants, too. But I got asked so many times, and no one listens anyway, so now I just say I made it up.

Do you think of what you write as fantasy?

I suppose so. My views about this have gone all over the place in the last few years, but I think I've settled down now.

The trouble is that many people think the boundaries of fantasy lie some-where north of Camelot and south of Conan the Barbarian, which is like saying that *Star Trek* represents most of science fiction. And a lot of people who said they didn't like fantasy said they *did* like the books, so I got a bit confused for a while. But if it isn't fantasy, I don't know what it is.

You don't know what fantasy is?

Hang on . . . I'm thinking . . . yep. I could have a stab at it.

Go ahead . . .

Earlier this year I did a tour of Australia. We even took in Alice Springs. So I hired a car and we drove out to Ayers Rock, because I thought: this is my third time in Australia, and I've been to too many places where I haven't seen much beyond the road to the airport, so I'm going to do the Rock or die. Only you have to call it Uluru now because Australia has remembered it had an existence prior to 1770, or even 1642, and good for them . . . people have a name for some local feature for thousands of years and then a guy rides by on a camel and, because *his* people know about Geography with a capital G, it's been 'discovered' and 'named' . . .

Anyway . . . actually climbing the Rock is all part of the experience, so I got up really early and started out in the dark. And *then* I thought: I've never seen the southern sky at night. I remembered all those years when I wanted to be an astronomer and half the constellations in the star charts were science fiction to me . . .

I stopped the car and let my eyes get accustomed to the night and looked up and there they were. And this is desert sky I'm talking about; no smog, no city glare, stars clearer than I've ever seen them before. And there it was: a sky I didn't know . . .

That's fantasy?

Oh, no. That's just something new. This is the point . . . I looked down towards the horizon and there was Orion. It was the first constellation I ever learned to identify, when I was about eight or nine. I know Orion off by heart. But I was seeing Orion upside down.

The other constellations weren't unfamiliar. They were just ones I hadn't seen before . . . you know, 'Oh, that's the Sextant, is it? Oh. How interest-ing.' But Orion was *un*familiar – something old and commonplace presented in a new way so that you're almost seeing it for the first time. That's what fantasy should be.

I know you don't like the books being called parody—

—only because people use it as a convenient word; I get the impression that they think I'm parodying something but they're not quite sure what it is.

All right, but how would you describe them? I know that fans take great pleasure in identifying bits of dialogue that echo scenes in famous films, for example. And then you put an echo of Shakespeare and a parody of Aliens *into the same sentence—*

I think Shakespeare would have quite enjoyed *Aliens*. But he'd have put in some sub-plots. Hmm. If you can derive the film *Forbidden Planet* from *The Tempest*, then maybe you can work the process the other way around. [At which point the interview was put on hold briefly for some specimen speeches from Shakespeare's forgotten masterpiece, *Xenomorph*.]

And next there will be a reference to some genuine but obscure fact, like Wow-Wow Sauce or the phenomenon of the drone assembly—

People have written to me about both of them, you know.

Even drone assemblies?

It's part of the lore of beekeeping. The description in *Lords and Ladies* is pretty accurate.

I do bury, er, *resonances* and obscure references in the text, but I hope I do it in such a way that it won't spoil the narrative for readers who don't recognize them. And I don't use puns half as often as people think. Or invent too many weird ideas. I just pillage history.

For example, there's the 'Your Finger You Fool' gag in *The Light Fantastic*. I've had a lot of mail about that over the years. But I didn't come up with the idea! It's based on real historical fact – or at least on what's popularly believed to be real historical fact. In the great days of European exploration, the traditional way of finding out what a new animal or landmark was called was to point at it and ask some bewildered native what it was called, in a very loud English or Spanish voice. As a result, I believe, we call an animal a kangaroo when that really means something like 'What is this white idiot saying?' Although I came across a reference the other day that said no, this isn't true . . . I'd better follow that up . . . we're in Uluru country again . . .

I saw a book on the origin of place names recently which referred to 'Terry Pratchett's Surly Native' theory of place naming.

Hah. But I didn't make it up. And it'd be very hard to make up something as strange as the Dutch tulipomania in the seventeenth century, for example. Or the mysterious case of Thomas Crapper. Or the entire civic history of Seattle, Washington.

Can we just pause for a moment on the case of Thomas Crapper?

Well, if he invented the flush lavatory in Victorian times, how come the word was in use in the same scatological sense in the sixteenth century? I thought maybe he was bullied in the playground and grew up determined to make sure that being a Crapper was something to be proud of.

Do you deliberately go hunting for this sort of thing?

No. Research is what happens when you think you're doing something else. I collect Victorian commonplace books, which I suppose were the forerunners of books like *Notes and Queries* here or the *Straight Dope* series in the States. And I also keep a look-out for old and slightly skewed reference books, of which *Brewer's Dictionary of Phrase and Fable* is merely the best known. And if you put enough bits and pieces together in one place, you start making connections. I don't know. We're getting pretty close to the old 'Where do you get your ideas from?' question.

As a matter of interest, where do—

Look, 'ideas' is a misleading word. And probably meaningless. When people ask the question, they probably really mean 'What thing triggered the book?' They come from everywhere. The only one I can remember right now relates to *Small Gods*. I was watching the news one day and some alleged holy man in Iran or Iraq or somewhere was pictured standing in front of a fountain flowing with fake blood and telling people how truly holy it was to die for God. And I thought: no, even I can see through that one. The backbone of the *Small Gods* plot was created right there.

I'd be interested to know what kind of reaction you've had to Small Gods. *It's not a typical Discworld book.*

I get a different kind of mail. More . . . thoughtful, I suppose.

Really? It would be easy to imagine you got some mail suggesting you'd be burned in Hell.

You know, that's odd. I haven't had a single overheated letter about that book; they've all been positive. Whereas I've had one or two letters from the Celtic fringe complaining about the treatment of elves in *Lords and Ladies*. They said I was slandering the Tuatha de Danaan, which were probably the models for Tolkien's elves, by deliberately mixing them up with the Sidhe, who were more your basic faerie baby-snatchers. Which was all a bit bewildering. It's *all story*.

I want to stay in this area. What is your personal religious position? It's a valid question, given the way Death and the afterlife and the occult in general tend to figure in the books.

It's there in the pages. End of answer. Incidentally, the dead aren't occult. They're ancestors.

Elsewhere in this book the Discworld is referred to as 'a place of escape'. I get the impression you don't like the term.

It depends on how it's used. Back in the sixties and seventies 'escapism' was frowned on – 'escapist literature' was definitely a derogatory term. I think people have come round a bit now and know that escaping is fine provided you're escaping *to* rather than *from*. My writing career developed because I read science fiction, the ultimate escapist literature, but it gave me a love of reading in general and *that* gave me an education.

Did you expect the series to take off in the way it did?

Hah! It would probably have scared me if I had known. I recently had to clear nearly two months' accumulated mail because I'd been away on tour, and you look at the stack of envelopes and think: they never told me about this when I joined. It's a bit frightening . . .

What is your readership?

Well, according to the mail it's all ages and all sexes but with some bunching up in the 9–14 age range – partly because of a crossover with the alleged juvenile books like *Truckers* and *Only You Can Save Mankind* – another thickening of the curve in the 18–25 range and *another* one between 35–45. There's a significant number of parents who get introduced to the books by their children. People tend to assume that most of my readers are aged fourteen. The evidence of the mail suggests that this is because, if a fourteen-year-old boy likes a book, he says things like 'Brilliant!' But if his mum likes a book, she quietly writes a note to the author. Teachers and librarians say things like 'Your books are *really popular* among children who don't read.' I think I know what they mean, I just wish they'd put it a different way.

I notice that you seem to get a lot of mail from women.

About half of it. I suppose the easy explanation is that it's because of the witch books, but I don't really know. I never thought anything much about this and then someone said that most readers of fantasy are males under twenty-five.

I've got the impression, though, that the Josh Kirby covers put older people off.

I've had letters like that. So have the publishers. On the other hand, I get a lot from people who *like* the covers. I like the covers. The good ones are superb and the – ones I don't like so much are still pretty OK. And I know some of the horrendous experiences that authors can have with covers. Corgi tried an experimental reprint of *The Colour of Magic* with a non-Kirby cover a few years ago, just to see what happened. I don't think it made a lot of difference one way or the other, to be frank.

Do you see yourself still writing Discworld books in ten years' time?

No. Not even in five years' time. Certainly not on a regular basis, anyway.

There's only so much I can do with it. It's fairly flexible, but it has its limits. There are other things I'd like to do, especially after the success of the children's books. But if I have something to say that could be best said on Discworld, I'll use it.

So you find it restricting?

No. But it's filling up!

You've gone on record many times as saying that Discworld will never be mapped. But you've let that happen. There's the Ankh-Morpork Street Map and now you're saying that maybe the whole Discworld could be mapped.

Well, I used to say that the Discworld could only be mapped when I'd finished it. The practical fact is that I do have a rough idea in my head – not finely detailed, but enough to make sure that it doesn't take people in one book three weeks to do a journey that takes someone else a day in another book – and therefore it's probably possible to pull a map together from these clues.

It was fascinating to work on *The Streets of Ankh-Morpork*, though. It made me realize something very important about fantasy. I guess I'd shied away from being too definite about the city because, well, I thought it would restrict future invention; in fact, the mere act of mapping the city *encouraged* new ideas. Once you have shape and form, you introduce restrictions – and that generates ideas.

I suppose I now see the point that, *once the world has been established*, it can be mapped. I mean, that's how it's supposed to happen, isn't it? You don't start out by drawing the Jaggedy Mountains and the Wiggly River – you create a world, flesh it out over a dozen books, and then someone comes along and earns a wad of cash by mapping it. The Discworld certainly *is* mappable – occasionally people send me their ideas and they all look pretty similar.

But it seems to me that the Discworld society at least has changed a lot over the series. It seemed initially to be a fairly straight sub-Tolkien fantasy landscape. Ankh-Morpork was just another fantasy city. Then by degrees it became more like an Italian city state—

Ah. Lord Vetinari, the Patrician. I worked that one out. Ankh-Morpork was starting to look to you a bit like Renaissance Florence, ruled by the Medici. So it's a short mental bridge between the Medici and the Vetinari.

Right. Probably there're noble families called the Dentistri and the Physiotherapi . . .

But in more recent books we're almost in early Victorian times. Sometimes we're in modern *times.*

I can explain all this. Firstly, the Discworld *is not a real place*. It's scenery for the novels. Anyway, there's no reason why worlds should all develop in the same way. The Greeks had all the necessary theoretical knowledge and technical ability to invent the wind-up gramophone. The steam-powered gramophone, come to that. They just never did it. Whereas the Discworld is clearly waiting for steam and electricity and no one's got around to utilizing either of them, so all that ingenuity is being channelled in other ways.

In one of the books you call Discworld 'a world, and mirror of worlds'.

Yes. I get amused when people say – usually about Granny Weatherwax and co. – that they're just like people they know. I mean, they're supposed to be. That's one of the things a writer is supposed to achieve. But people seem surprised, as if a witch isn't traditionally meant to be like someone you know.

Tell me about Death . . . I think you've said you get more mail about him than anyone else?

Hmm . . . yes. Of course, there's *Mort* and *Reaper Man*, and he's the only character that appears in all the books—

And in Good Omens *and also* Johnny and the Dead, *I think.*

Well, you know how it is when a studio has a big star under contract – they try to put him in all their films . . .

He's really the generic medieval personification, right out of *The Seventh Seal*, but with a few adjustments. I *think* people like him because he's got this pathetic lack of any sense of humour and is powerful and innocent and vulnerable all at the same time. It's true that he was a lot nastier in the first few books. By *Reaper Man* he's clearly going through some sort of mid-life crisis. Or mid-Death crisis.

You've said that you get rather more serious letters from old people, and, er, the relatives of the recently deceased.

Yes, but that comes under the heading of private correspondence, I think.

I've seen some of the fan letters. What do you think of them?

The mail is fairly huge, and just about every letter wants me to *do* something, even if it's only write a reply. I *think* I manage to answer everything, sooner or later. It's the requests for signed photos that always throw me. Who cares what an author looks like?

It was a breakthrough for me when I suddenly realized, one day, that I could say 'no' to things, that if the diary was really full up I could turn something down politely and needn't feel guilty. I still *do* feel guilty.

The Discworld must be terribly difficult to translate. Do you have much to do with the translators?

I know the Spanish translator won a prize for *The Colour of Magic*! And someone attempting to translate *The Colour of Magic* into Polish read the first page and said he didn't believe it was possible to think like that in Polish. I get on very well with the Dutch translator, who takes a kind of skewed delight in tracking down the 'right' words, and the German translator also contacts me quite regularly – someone recently told me they thought *Reaper Man* was *better* in German, which is some kind of triumph for the translator. I do get some occasional enquiries from the others, but mostly the translators do their own thing. I don't envy them. A lot of foreign fans are bilingual, and it's hard to please everyone.

Someone said I should ask you where you get your shirts . . .

Look, all that happened is that when I was on tour in Australia in 1990 I found a shop in Melbourne that sold really good cotton shirts, of a kind I've never been able to find anywhere else. So I bought some. And when I went through again in 1992 I bought some more. And when I went through again in 1993 I bought some *more*. But I don't buy *all* my shirts in Australia. Just some of them.

Fans and Fanmail

A survey of the cardboard boxes in which Terry Pratchett stores his fan mail, if that's the proper word for it, turns up one or two constants.

1) A statistically significant number of readers meet other Discworld fans while on holiday on otherwise unspoilt Greek islands; one went so far as to claim to have met *him*, which shows pretty good eyesight since his diary reveals that at the time he was in Australia.

2) A large number of GCSE students do projects on him.

Terry: Oh, yes. The less inventive letters go like this: 'Dear Mr Pratchett, I am one of your greatest fans, I have read all your books, I am doing a project on you for GCSE, can you please send me everything, can I please have it by Friday because it's due in on Monday . . .'

A browse in his correspondence files suggests that he tries to oblige rather more than he lets on, even when the letters contain twenty numbered questions on the lines of 'Is writing a puffish thing to do?' and 'I'd like to be a writer when I leave school. Are you on Flexitime?'

The lengthy ones get the Update, an A4 page in really tiny print which contains answers to most of the frequently asked questions.

3) A large number of letters from people under sixteen are full of numbered sentences.

Terry: I don't know why. Maybe that's how they're taught to do it: 'Dear Mr Pratchett, Can I ask you some questions. 1) Where do you get your ideas from?' . . .

All letters are answered, except for those he refers to as the terminally weird or unreadable. He lives in constant low-key guilt that he might have missed some.

Terry: You're on tour, and a kid in the queue comes up with his mum and says, 'I sent you a letter' and you think, oh lor', did I answer it? I've got away with it so far.

I try to reply to everything because I once wrote to J.R.R. Tolkien praising one of his books, and I got a reply. It wasn't a long one, but it was polite and he'd signed it and I've always thought, if he could do it with the kind of postbag *he* got, I should too.

4) The Baconians. There *are* obscure references sometimes buried deep in the text, but some of the keener fans search beyond that and write letters demonstrating that the initials of 'Bloody Stupid' Johnson, who built the Mighty Organ of Unseen University, are BSJ – which is JSB backwards, as in Johann Sebastian Bach, as in organ music, see?

5) Fans send in photos of themselves in 'Discworld' places. Apparently there's a pub called the Shades in or near Skegness. There's certainly a town in France called Oouks. So far no one has found Power Cable, Nebraska, but it is surely only a matter of time. And home-made badges turn up (many versions of 'Librarians Rule Ook'). And suggestions for Discworld games and recipe books. And cakes (these sometimes turn up in signing queues).

And always, there are more letters.

Letters from teachers and parents follow an almost standard line.

Observation of a Discworld signing queue at an ordinary, city-centre bookshop (as opposed to one near a university, where the leather jackets creak like a tea clipper beating around Cape Horn) bears out claims that probably half of Terry Pratchett's readers are female. The general age of queuers appears to be in the mid-twenties (which may prove nothing; they may just be more likely to have an hour or two to spend in a queue). But there's a lot of evidence that he has a big following among young teenage boys – particularly those who, as we saw in one librarian's happy phrase, 'don't read'. Regular letters talk about reluctant readers and dyslexic boys who, after a dose of Discworld, are sprinting if not to university then at least to reading as a hobby. One letter put 12 GCSEs down to a massive course of Discworld books at the right time (there is no guarantee that this works for everybody).

Reviewers occasionally point out the lack of the basic sex act in the books (this will probably stop now that Corporal Carrot, in *Men At Arms*, has felt the Disc move for him). In fact there *is* sex in the Discworld books, but it usually takes place two pages after the ending. There is often, too, a lot of sexual atmosphere and, when Nanny Ogg is around, some fairly explicit coded references. It's a winning formula – if you know what she's getting at, well, you know, and if you don't then you probably won't notice. (Letter from an American reader: 'I asked my mom what "priapic" meant. She said she thought it meant curly-headed. So we looked it up in the dictionary and found out 1) that it didn't mean curly-headed and 2) wow, what it really meant.') An adult might feel that full enjoyment comes from spotting genuine historical references and hidden jokes, and might wonder whether anyone under eighteen could really understand the wound-up psyche of Granny Weatherwax or the middle-aged gloominess of Captain Vimes of the City Watch. But they seem to.

What some of the young readers like (according to Anne Marley of Hampshire County Library) is that the Discworld is a place to which they can escape but, at the same time, find familiar characters to whom they can relate – even if, *superficially*, that character is a witch, a 7-foot skeleton or an orang-utan. They like the way that everyday things, everyday situations and everyday attitudes are transposed on to the Discworld and given that special spin.

Terry's popularity is spread, as it often is with the older fans, by peer-group word of mouth. A mutual knowledge of the Discworld is something that young people can share; it's a world to which they belong and which belongs to them.

Although the books are literate and, perhaps, complex, the good use of dialogue to advance the plot and the descriptive passages carefully constructed in 'bite-size' chunks keep them lively enough to capture the reader's attention.

The humour is an important factor, says Anne. Younger readers frequently dub it 'anarchic' – and they welcome this. The contrasts, too, are appreciated: Death is the traditional tall, black-robed skeleton riding a flying white charger . . . but the horse's name is Binky; the Discworld is charged with raw magic, but a lot of the time it doesn't work properly and much of the real magic is down to 'headology'.

Finally, she said, young readers like the subtle way the novels deal with concerns such as equal opportunities and racial/religious discrimination. They are woven into the structure with no attempt to force them down the reader's throat as Big Issues . . . Mainly, however, the mail suggests they like them because they are 'brilliant' – a code word meaning enjoyable.

What writers traditionally have not had to face is electronic fan mail.

There is as yet no *formal* Discworld fan club. The mail on the subject suggests that Terry Pratchett backs away hurriedly from the suggestion. He doesn't give very coherent reasons. The general impression is that he finds it embarrassing.

But 'fan activity' is available to anyone with a computer and a modem. There is the 'pratchett' forum on CIX, the UK electronic conferencing system, and a rather larger one known as alt.fan.pratchett on the Internet (the huge worldwide computer network which shifts megabytes of information around the planet as effortlessly as Shakespeare sharpened his quill pen).

It is almost impossible to give a flavour of these things in print without sounding strange. It is a little like written CB, and something like being at a party. Or several parties, all in one go. Blindfolded.

In theory they are forums for those who appreciate the books, but exchanges segue into something completely different with extreme rapidity. On alt.fan.pratchett they generally head in the direction of the topics of food, traffic roundabouts, drink and, for some reason, pubic wigs. At the drop of a hat its members will argue about the origin of phrases like 'at the drop of a hat'. It is certainly international, with recurrent themes like Explaining Morris Dancing References To Americans, and it is somehow comforting to think that the big humming invisible network is carrying animated exchanges about the best actor to play Death if ever a film of *Mort* gets made.

Terry Pratchett started writing occasional messages to it late in 1991, but he generally reads the messages every day if only to stop them from piling up. Many of the personal mailings, at least around the start of the university terms, tend to be demands that he should state whether he is, or is not, him.

He said: 'When I first went on line I left myself open to about a thousand mailings on the lines of "Are you the Terry Pratchett or what?" It didn't matter what I replied. If I played it straight and said "yes" some of them would reply, "oh, go on, you're not, are you?" and I was damned if I was going to say "no".

'That's settled down a bit now. Anyway, there are at least two other Terry Pratchetts in the world – one's a kid and the other, last I heard, was an airline pilot in America. I was slightly embarrassed about saying, "Yes, I am the Terry Pratchett" in case they came back with "What? It was *you* who foiled that hijacking over Chicago?"'